Charity, self-interest and welfare
in the English past

The Neale Colloquium in British History

Charity, self-interest and welfare in the English past
Martin Daunton (editor)

Charity, self-interest and welfare in the English past

Edited by
Martin Daunton
University College London

UCL
PRESS

First published in 1996 by UCL Press

UCL Press Limited
University College London
Gower Street
London WC1E 6BT

The name of University College London (UCL) is a registered
trade mark used by UCL Press with the consent of the owner.

British Library Cataloguing-in-Publication Data
A CIP catalogue record for this book is available from the British Library.

ISBN: 1-85728-536-0

Typeset in Bembo.
Printed and bound by
Biddles Ltd, Guildford and King's Lynn, England.

Contents

CONTENTS

The Neale Colloquium in British History

Sir John Neale, the Astor Professor of English History at University College London between 1927 and 1956, was the distinguished biographer of Elizabeth I who produced a pioneering and influential study of her parliaments. In 1970, his publishers, Jonathan Cape, generously supported an annual lecture to mark his eightieth birthday, which was inaugurated by Dame Veronica Wedgwood. She was followed by many other distinguished historians, but there was no opportunity for discussion at a formal lecture. The Neale Lecture Committee decided to embark on a new venture in 1994–5: to make the public lecture the opportunity for a colloquium, where a number of related papers could be presented to complement and extend the lecture. The theme of the first colloquium was "And who is my neighbour? Charity, self-interest and welfare". We are grateful to Jonathan Cape for its continued support of the lecture, and to The Astor of Hever Trust, the Graduate School of University College London, and the Royal Historical Society for financial assistance. We were fortunate that Dr Richard Smith, FBA, the Director of the Cambridge Group for the History of Population and Social Structure, and himself a former student of University College London, agreed to give the first Neale Lecture in the new form which generated a lively and constructive debate. The colloquium will be an annual event and will be published by UCL Press.

Martin Daunton
Astor Professor of British History and *Chair, Neale Lecture Committee*

Notes on contributors

Olive Anderson is Emeritus Professor of History at Queen Mary and Westfield College, University of London. Her books and many articles on English history from the late seventeenth to the early twentieth century include *Suicide in Victorian and Edwardian England* (1987). She is currently writing on mid-Victorian developments in matrimonial law.

Lynn Botelho has recently completed her doctoral thesis at the University of Cambridge on "Provisions for the elderly in two early modern Suffolk communities". She is Assistant Professor of History at Indiana University of Pennsylvania, and is editing *The Cratfield churchwardens' accounts, 1640–60* for the Suffolk Records Society.

Martin Daunton is Astor Professor of British History at University College London. His most recent work is *Progress and poverty: an economic and social history of Britain, 1700–1850* (1995), and he is now completing a second volume on the period between 1850 and 1939. He is also writing a book on the politics of taxation in Britain since 1842, and is working on the changing limits of the British state and its relations with the market and voluntarism.

Joanna Innes is a Fellow of Somerville College, Oxford, and editor of *Past and Present*. She is currently completing a book on eighteenth-century English social policy.

Paul Johnson is Reader in Economic History at the London School of Economics. His current research interests include the economics of old age, the history of the welfare state, and the impact of law on market activity in Victorian England. He is co-author, with Jane Falkingham, of *Ageing and economic welfare* (1992) and editor of *Twentieth-century Britain: economic, social and cultural change* (1994).

Colin Jones is Professor of European History at the University of Warwick. His books include *Charity and bienfaisance: the treatment of poverty in the Montpellier region, 1740–1815* (1982); *The charitable imperative: hospitals and nursing in ancien régime and revolutionary France* (1989); (co-edited with Jonathan Barry) *Medicine and charity before the welfare state* (1991); *The Cambridge illustrated history of France* (1994); and, with Laurence Brockliss, *The medical world of early modern France* (forthcoming).

Jane Lewis is a Fellow of All Souls College, Oxford and Director of the Wellcome Unit for the History of Medicine. Her most recent works on the history of women and social policy are *Women and social action in Victorian and Edwardian Britain* (1991) and *The voluntary sector, the state and social work in Britain* (1995).

Brian Pullan is Professor of Modern History at the University of Manchester. He is a leading expert on the history of Venice and of charity in the early modern period. His most recent publications are (edited and translated with David Chambers) *Venice: a documentary history, 1450–1630* (1992) and *Poverty and charity: Europe, Italy, Venice, 1400–1700* (1994). He is currently working on a general history of poverty, charity and poor relief in Italy from the late fourteenth to the late eighteenth century.

Richard Smith is Director of the Cambridge Group for the History of Population and Social Structure and a Fellow of Downing College, Cambridge. He has written extensively on demographic history and its relationship with welfare systems, and on the land market in medieval and early modern England.

Pat Thane is Professor of Contemporary History at the University of Sussex. Her publications include (co-edited with Gisela Bock) *Women and maternity policies: women and the rise of the European welfare states* (1991). She is currently completing a book on the history of old age in England.

Keir Waddington recently completed his doctoral thesis on "Finance, philanthropy and the hospital: metropolitan hospitals, 1850–98" at University College London, and is now a Research Fellow at the Wellcome Institute for the History of Medicine working on the history of the Bethlem Hospital in the twentieth century.

1

Introduction

Martin Daunton

Recent developments in social policy, in both Britain and other countries, have forced historians to move from Whiggish accounts based on a linear progression towards a welfare state, which dominated the historiography in the 1950s, 1960s and 1970s. Titles such as *The Victorian origins of the British welfare state* or *The evolution of National Insurance in Great Britain: the origins of the welfare state*,[1] with their assumption that history was marching to a pre-ordained end, which seemed unproblematic in the 1960s, are now jejune. One benefit of the political developments of the 1980s and 1990s to historians – regardless of their views as citizens – is that the challenge to the welfare state has led to the death of teleological interpretations and produced a much greater sensitivity to the wide range of possibilities in coping with risks in society.

Precisely at the moment when historians were viewing the past through the distorting lens of the contemporary welfare state, it was being called into question by politicians who doubted whether Britain could raise sufficient tax revenue. Since 1985, these doubts have been translated into policy, with a much greater emphasis upon personal provision through private pensions, contributions to the costs of long-term care in old age, and an increasing reliance upon non-governmental agencies.[2] The simplicity of a linear trend from a harsh, punitive poor law to a benign welfare state, or from charity to state provision, with a gradual extension of citizenship from legal rights to political enfranchisement and social entitlement,[3] has given way to a greater awareness of complexities and ambiguities. The collapse of the old grand narrative poses a challenge to historians: how is it to be replaced without simply creating a mass of case studies and a stress upon exceptions and confusions?

One answer is provided by Richard Smith in his Neale Lecture: an understanding of the systematic relationship between social policy and demography, which is seen as an independent casual factor. His interpretation makes an important point for contemporary debates on policy, for it is often claimed by the New Right that, for example, income support for single mothers has unfortunate demographic consequences; and much the same point was made at the turn of the eighteenth and nineteenth centuries in relation to poor relief in support of wages. By contrast, Smith argues that the welfare system did not determine the pattern of household formation, but was an integral part of it: they should be considered together as part of a single system. In his approach, different social policies are to be understood as so many means of adjusting resources to needs in any demographic and social structure. At the heart of Smith's interpretation is the "nuclear hardship" thesis: in a society where marriage entailed the formation of a new household of a couple and their children, difficulties emerged when the nuclear family was disrupted. Who would care for the elderly, for widows and widowers with dependent children, or for orphans? These problems would be particularly intense in two demographic circumstances. First, the timing of marriage and births could mean that the costs of child-rearing were particularly burdensome precisely at the point when parents were entering old age; available resources might therefore be directed down the generations to the young rather than up the generations to the elderly. Such a tension might not arise so acutely where the age of marriage was lower, and births were concentrated in the first years of marriage.[4] There was also a variation over time in the ratio of children to elderly within the dependent population, which could influence the flow of resources between generations.[5] Secondly, the shifting age structure of the population could reduce the availability of kin to provide support. In the seventeenth century, there were fewer "carers" available to look after the elderly than in the late eighteenth and early nineteenth centuries when population growth was more rapid and kin were more available to provide for the elderly. These demographic factors therefore led to variations in the extent of "nuclear hardship", but problems nevertheless remained which made it essential for the collectivity – the parish in the case of England – to provide supplementary support where the nuclear family could not cope. The provision of welfare to others might, indeed, be an act of self-interest which provided security for couples to form independent households on marriage, confident in the knowledge that provision would be made for their spouse and children: relief was not directed to a separate underclass but was an established part of the social system to which a large number of people might have recourse. Such a view of the old poor law as a resource open to all was to be a theme in radical politics in the nineteenth century, when the new poor law was denounced as an attempt to destroy a property right granted to the people in compensation for the theft of monastic property and common land.[6]

Demographic change is certainly an important influence on social welfare, as is shown by recent concern about the cost of providing pensions and long-term healthcare for the elderly. The politics of social policy is as much a matter of generational as class conflict, and interests might coalesce around different categories of risk as well as around different categories of employment or class.[7] Richard Smith's analysis of the underlying structural, demographic features of welfare provision is therefore indispensable, but is it an adequate substitute for the discarded grand narrative? As Colin Jones remarks, another feature of the recent past has been a shift from social structural to cultural approaches, which has led to increased scepticism about the emphasis of the Cambridge Group for the History of Population and Social Structure on the mechanisms for balancing population and resources. The cultural approach is more concerned with meanings, which has the danger of losing sight of material reality in a conflicting babble of messages and signs. It should, however, be possible to combine the concern for meanings with the socio-structural patterns stressed by the work of the Cambridge Group.

Smith refers to the availability of "kin carers", which he measures by computer simulations of the population. But how did people at the time define kin, and how did this change over time and vary between areas? Studies of aristocratic families have shown that kin may be "fictive", drawing upon a wide network of often tenuous family connections in order to secure the appearance of continuity, which often involved a change in name. Although this issue was most significant in the inheritance of large landed estates, it might also arise in the case of small agricultural holdings and trades, where there might be a system of informal or formal adoption.[8] Kin may be an imagined grouping, as in the case of the Scottish clans were there was a "pretense of blude", a willingness to act *as if* people were kin.[9] Another way in which kin would be imagined was through godparents, by which more or less distant members of the kin and non-family members were given responsibility for the spiritual wellbeing of a child. Although godparents might neglect even their spiritual duty, the relationship could equally be extended into material care when the child was orphaned, or needed some assistance. Here was a way of "stretching" kinship. Concern for kin could also involve the dead as well as the living, for Brian Pullan reminds us that charity in Catholic countries was directed to prayers for souls in Purgatory, with many bequests to pay for masses and chantry chapels. Kin is, therefore, a much more slippery concept than the simple definitions of computer simulations. Thus one theme in Pat Thane's chapter is the precise meaning given to the "liable relatives" clause in the poor-law statutes, which was contested and fitted into different interpretations of intergenerational support. Although some historians conclude that care for parents was somehow "unEnglish", Thane argues that there was "intimacy at a distance". Clearly, there is a need to move from the social and demographic structures to a more nuanced account of sentiment and feeling, without losing sight of the considerable shifts in demographic realities.[10]

Much the same process of imagined identity applies to the collectivity. The importance of the parish in England, with its ability to raise finance through compulsory taxation, emerges very clearly from Smith's chapter and is confirmed by Pullan's comparative work on Italy. The parish was the basic unit of religious organization throughout Europe, but it was only in England that it also became the basic unit of civil government, with no role for the priest and with the power of compulsory taxation for poor relief. But perhaps a word of warning should be entered against making a watertight distinction between the religious and the civil roles of the parish, which may rest upon anachronistic twentieth-century assumptions. Puritan clerics wished to move beyond routinized services to all members of the parish, and might subdivide inhabitants into different categories of salvation or damnation, and enter into closer relations with a religious elite. Dissenters might entirely secede from the parish structure and form their own, self-selecting communities. These tussles over the nature of the parish as a religious unit cannot be entirely separated from the parish as a civil unit, and complicated its assumed solidarity as a means of providing welfare. The nature of the parish as a religious organization is an important theme in the Neale Colloquium for 1996 on the "long reformation", and is apparent from Dr Botelho's contribution here. Nevertheless, the distinctive civil role of the English parish does stand out, and contrasts with the situation in Scotland, where it did not develop the same civil functions or acquire the same powers of taxation.[11] The difference in the institutional pattern needs to be explained, and one possible reason for the unusual nature of the parish in England is the precise way in which the so-called "domain state" (the exploitation of physical resources to sustain the ruler) gave way to a "tax state". The date of the change varied between parts of Europe, and so did the means by which the taxes were extracted. The tussle over resources was more complex than the demographic balance stressed by the Cambridge Group for the History of Social Structure and Population, for it also involved competing claims on the agricultural surplus by the crown for taxes and lords for rent.[12] One episode in the tussle, as Smith points out, was the imposition by the English Crown of a tax quota on each community in 1334. The need to allocate the Crown's claim for money between members of the parish led to the emergence of administrative procedures which could be utilized by the parish for its own needs, and were available to cope with "nuclear hardship" when other welfare institutions, such as confraternities, were destroyed or weakened by the Reformation. Thus the parish did not simply emerge in response to the destruction of the confraternities, for it had a prior existence as part of a wider and active world of charity and hospitality. A simple polarity between the parish and charity is therefore misleading before the Reformation, and should also be avoided after the Reformation when the parish often provided trustees for the plethora of endowed charities which ran almshouses or handed out various doles, at least until the early nineteenth century when administrative reform started to weaken the secular functions of the parish.[13] The emergence of a parish-based poor law was, therefore, not a simple response to a crisis created by the destruction of existing patterns of relief by the Reformation, for there were continuities in the role of the parish in England. By contrast, the parish in Scotland failed to respond in the same way. One explanation is the nature of the central government, for a parish-based system would entail chaotic particularities unless there was some co-ordinating central body which could ensure that each parish formed part of a single national system. In England, the Privy Council and subsequently parliament laid down the basic framework which was co-ordinated by the local Justices of the Peace to secure a degree of uniformity; in Scotland, the Privy Council was weak until the 1660s and the attempt to create local Justices on the English model was not successful. Further, there were considerable differences in the structure of agrarian society. In Scotland, local landowners obtained greater power in the administration of parish funds collected by voluntary contributions, and compulsory assessments could only be introduced with their consent. Although the result was a less generous system of poor relief than in England, it probably caused few problems in most rural areas, for many families held small plots of land as sub-tenants and cottars which gave them some means of subsistence.[14]

Despite the broad contrast in the significance of the parish between England and other parts of Europe, differences should not be exaggerated. The parish was not uniformly important even within England, in part because the tussle between the Crown for taxes and the lord for rent did not have a uniform outcome. The aim of the manorial lord was often to convert his rights to labour services or money payment into absolute ownership, removing any property rights held by the peasants and demanding a rack or market rent. Success in achieving this ambition was by no means constant across the country, for in many cases the tenants were able to sustain at least a partial property right through copyholds, customary tenure or life-leaseholds, and even in some cases to secure the freehold. Where property rights were sustained in whole or part, the smallholder would secure a larger part of the surplus, and might well have a greater reliance on the assets of the farm.[15] Such a pattern applied to the West Riding of Yorkshire, where smallholdings survived and sustained a land and kin-based pattern of support. The outcome was, therefore, akin to the so-called "European" pattern of relief.[16] There might be a similar outcome in, say, Cumbria where customary tenure survived into the eighteenth and early nineteenth centuries; or in parishes in the forest areas where there were considerable communal resources which might make access to the poor law unnecessary.[17]

The pattern of welfare was therefore shaped both by the nature of taxation, and by the transformation of property rights. Perhaps the significant feature explaining the emergence of rate-supported parish relief within England was the demise of a peasantry and the loss of property rights in land, which created the need to deal with a population of landless labourers. Such an interpretation is both more political and conflictual than the functional explanation favoured by Richard Smith, who sees nuclear families and parish-based welfare as complementary rather than a compensation for dispossession.

The significance of the parish as a collectivity varied between parts of England, and there were other possible identities or collectivities. In some areas, the parish and manor were coterminous, but elsewhere a manor was spread across several parishes and discrepancies between the two units might make it difficult for the manorial lord to impose his wishes. The manorial court played an important role in registering copyholds, and it could continue to form part of the system of government into the

eighteenth and early nineteenth centuries, even in large urban centres such
as Manchester.[18] Again, in forest areas the community might be defined by
the authority of the rangers or forest regulations, and access to the communal resources could be more or less controlled. At one extreme, the
interests of the large landowners were asserted and the claims of residents
to resources were severely restricted; at the other extreme, regulations
collapsed so that incomers could participate; and in intermediate cases,
established residents were able to protect their interests against both the ter-
ritorial ambitions of large landowners and the desperation of migrants.[19]
Such concern for the exploitation of common resources was not restricted
to forest areas, for Norma Landau has show that it equally applied to the
rural parishes and small towns of Kent, where parish officers used the settlement laws to protect resources available to all residents from appropria-
tion by poor immigrants. The settlement laws laid down rules about which
parish would provide poor relief, and gave permission to parish officers to
remove to their parish of settlement anyone renting property below £10 a
year or to grant a right to residence on condition that the parish of settlement issued a certificate agreeing to pay the costs of poor relief. Parishes in
many parts of the country used settlement laws to regulate immigration
until the end of the eighteenth century, making a distinction between
desirable and undesirable incomers. There were two concerns: the need to
limit migrants who would, as residents, gain access to common resources
whether or not they had a settlement in the parish; and the responsibility
for paying poor relief which depended on the parish of settlement. Control
over migrants became less important as enclosure reduced the significance
of wastes and commons which were open to all residents, but settlement
remained crucial as a means of limiting the costs of relief. An individual's
settlement might be in a parish where apprenticeship had been served
many years previously, or where parents or grandparents held a settlement.
In principle, all English men and women had a settlement in some parish
in the country, and parishes could be charged with manslaughter if they
refused relief to people without a settlement who died as a result; in practice, many people fell out of the system, not least the Irish and Scots.[20] In
Bristol, the Prudent Man's Friend Society was formed in 1812, and offered
rewards for the conviction and removal of vagrants to their parish of settlement; 289 were removed in 1813. Other non-statutory agencies catered
for those who were excluded, filling the gaps in the public provision of
welfare. The Strangers' Friend Society, for example, offered assistance to
"the friendless and afflicted stranger – the widow and fatherless child who

are destitute of parochial aid"; and the Asylum for Poor Orphan Girls was particularly concerned to assist children whose parents had resided in Bristol without a settlement.[21] Bodies such as the voluntary hospitals were simply not concerned with patients' settlement status.

The poor law therefore entailed many exclusions from the collectivity, and should not be too readily portrayed as a solidaristic pooling of risk by the total population. As Lynn Botelho's comparison of two parishes indicates, there were considerable discrepancies within a small area, depending both on the balance between the demand for relief and available local resources, and on the social assumptions of those controlling relief. Not only was eligibility policed by the parishes, but the narrow, local, fiscal base limited the scope for spreading risks between rich and poor areas. Only in 1865 did the union become the fiscal unit rather than the individual parish, and only in 1870 were costs of indoor relief spread between parishes in the metropolis. Until these changes were implemented, the costs of the poor of St George in the East, one of the most straitened parishes in the East End of London, fell on the ratepayers of the area without any contribution from the rich inhabitants of St George's, Hanover Square. Similarly, large landowners in the country could limit the population in "close" parishes, and pass the cost of poor relief of their seasonal agricultural labour onto the "open" parishes. What stands out are the limits to the coverage of the parish-based poor law, rather than its inclusiveness.[22]

The settlement laws meant that social insecurity could only be tackled in part through the state system, and England appears less divergent from the rest of Europe when other forms of provision are added. Certainly, it is necessary to prevent the reappearance of teleological approaches by assuming that continental Europe was lagging behind England in the process of development towards a superior, "modern", publicly funded, collectivist social policy. It is more helpful to consider a range of approaches, each with its own strengths and weaknesses. In Germany, the town or *Gemeinde* with a Common Chest was used to relieve the poor rather than the parish, which might have the virtue of pooling risks more effectively between rich and poor within the town; in France, the *seigneurie* fulfilled a similar role. Pullan's chapter on early modern Italy indicates that welfare provision by the confraternities, conservatories and charity banks was more developed in the towns than the countryside, which led to migration from country to towns at times of particular hardship. It does not necessarily follow, however, that the Italian countryside was incapable of dealing with social risk at other times: much would depend upon the pattern of property rights, the nature of tenure, and the structure of the family. What is at issue in England is not only the emergence of the parish and compulsory poor rate, but also the disappearance of a range of institutions found in Italian cities. Although the Reformation had a role in destroying many of these bodies in England, the contrast was not simply between Protestant and Catholic countries, for the highly centralist monarchy in France was hostile to confraternities. The disappearance of urban confraternities and the survival of the parish in England meant that the English poor law was more suited to dealing with social insecurity in rural than in urban areas, so that the administrative structure of poor relief arguably contradicted the changing economic structure of England as it became the most urbanized society in Europe. It could be argued, however, that urbanization was encouraged by the existence of the poor law, which provided a safety-net for people to leave the land and take the risk of finding work in the towns, with at least some assurance that their parish of settlement would support them in times of hardship.[23] The poor law might therefore help to explain the early, and marked, release of population from the land, allowing English towns to obtain more labour, with an ability to shift the costs of maintenance in times of distress back to the rural parishes. By contrast, transfer payments in Italy were more likely to flow from the towns to the countryside.

Although the right to tax in support of the poor was more extensive in England than in Scotland or continental Europe, the rate-funded poor law has received disproportionate attention at the expense of other elements in the "mixed economy of welfare".[24] Historians should devote more attention to the changing proportions in the mixture. Joanna Innes provides an excellent account of the changing assumptions about the proper mix of agencies, indicating that contemporaries were both aware of the unusual scale of public relief in England, and at times doubtful whether the choice was correct. The debate did not stop with Malthus, but continued through the creation of the new poor law and the welfare state, and continues in the present with a renewed emphasis on private and charitable provision. One of the most intriguing and important tasks facing historians is to find an explanation of the changing proportions in the mixture over time and between countries, and the precise relationships between the parts.[25] The elements in the mixture may be crudely divided between four sectors according to their administrative or institutional form: the purchase of services such as pensions from the commercial, for-profit sector; the provision of services such as education or health care through central or local public bodies; the non-profit or community sector which consists of public-serving charities such as voluntary hospitals and member-serving self-help bodies such as friendly societies; and the household sector, where the role of unpaid and usually female work is crucial in the care of children and the sick or disabled.

The distinctions are crude, and the boundaries between sectors rather vague. Bodies may migrate between categories or have a dual identity, such as the endowed charities which often relied upon the parish as trustee. It is, indeed, possible to characterize welfare systems not only by the relative proportions of each method of delivery, but also by the nature of relationships or alliances between the sectors. In Australia, for example, there was no tax-funded public poor law in the nineteenth century and there was considerable reliance on charitable bodies. Less immediately apparent was the high proportion of revenue which came from government subventions, amounting to about two-thirds of the revenue of the largest charities in Victoria.[26] In the case of England, government grants were paid to some voluntary bodies, such as the Foundling Hospital in the eighteenth century, and to educational societies after 1833. In the interwar period, it was accepted that voluntary bodies should work with the state where a personal, individualized contact was more important than the rule-bound provision of benefits.[27] Similarly, the provision of social insurance in Britain in 1911 relied, at least in part, on existing "member serving" friendly societies and trade unions.[28]

The recent trend towards a greater reliance on voluntary bodies or non-government organizations for the delivery of welfare has led political scientists to analyze their contractual relations with both the state and recipients: how is service delivery monitored; what discretion should non-government bodies have in determining who should be assisted; how does the balance of interests within voluntary bodies change between "clients", voluntary workers, donors and the increased power of accountable bureaucrats; how far can recipients of services bargain and shape the system, by forcing the charities to respond to their needs or forming pressure groups such as the Child Poverty Action Group which campaign for the recognition of a new category of need?[29] As Colin Jones notes, a similar re-examination of charities in the past is moving away from crude "social control" theories of the imposition of hegemonic bourgeois values on the working class in order to preserve capitalism and the social order. One alternative has been to view philanthropy as the basis of consensus, bringing together members of both the middle and working class in the creation of the "peaceable kingdom" of the nineteenth century which was based on shared values of decency and independence, and animosity to the undeserving poor.[30] But both interpretations can miss the complexities and variations of charity. Their form could vary: there were endowed charities with trustees managing investments in land or securities; "subscribers' democracies" based on annual donations and an active involvement by the donor; or institutions which became more professional and bureaucratic, drawing on a variety of sources from fees, insurance schemes, and grants as well as donations. Charities could entail tussles within the elite in order to raise status or create new networks of patronage; they could involve attempts to bury differences or could be the site of deep political and religious divisions.[31] Recent work on the structure of income of contemporary charities indicates considerable divergence in the relative importance of personal giving, donations by businesses, and grants by foundations.[32] The charities themselves, as Waddington shows in the case of London's voluntary hospitals, actively manipulated responses from donors, creating a market for benevolent action which was linked with a tussle for authority within the hospital between subscribers, administrators and the medical profession.

The beneficiaries of charitable acts also varied, and was much more than a relationship of dominance of elite donors over poor recipients. As Pullan shows, the concept of the "shame-faced poor" with the need to show sensitivity to their dignity was important in Italy. The concept was less significant in England, although there were bodies such as the Sons of the Clergy to ensure that orphaned or destitute sons were placed in respectable trades; and the livery companies of the City played a similar role for the genteel poor. There were differences in the extent to which charity was directed to the living as acts of corporal mercy or to the dead as spiritual mercy, a motivation which declined in England after the Reformation. Paupers might be treated as the undeserving authors of their own misfortune, or as objects of mercy who would help donors to their salvation. Charities were in the market for recipients of their bounty, and the poor could – within severe restraints – drawn upon the range of services on offer and present their claims in the way best fitted to the expectations of the donors. The relationship between donor and recipient was, in any case, often mediated by middlemen or, in many cases, middlewomen. In Italy, priests were vital to a system which did not rest on the fiscal power of the parish, acting as the representatives of applicants and evoking a response from charitable bodies. Similarly, the Daughters of Charity who served the poor in early modern France were themselves drawn from the poor, playing a dual role in both receiving support for their own maintenance and passing it on to others. In late Victorian England, the intermediaries were often women, drawn from the prosperous middle class. These women, as Jane Lewis argues, might have more influence in shaping welfare provision in a philanthropic, local system than in a state-directed system which gave more power to male policy-makers and marginalized women. It could be that women used participation in charity in the nineteenth century in order to enhance their own freedom of manoeuvre, at the expense of restricting the lives of those they set out to help, and that they operated within the existing discourse on philanthropy; it has even been suggested that they were extending the ordered relationship of mistress and servant from the household to the city.[33] Such approaches and debates suggest that philanthropy should be viewed as a social relationship which was open to diverse cultural meanings, in which charity workers and their "clients" were active in constructing the discourse which constrained them.

Voluntary societies did not only consist of charities operated by the better-off to cater for the poor or disadvantaged; they also included a large number of mutual organizations such as the friendly societies which were run by their members to provide "contingency" insurance against illness. Although these bodies had a membership which was considerably larger than trade unions, they have only recently been the subject of serious analysis. They have suffered from a dual historiographic neglect, from historians of social policy who have seen them as withering away with the rise of the welfare state, and from historians of the working class who have seen them as ideologically suspect bearers of bourgeois values. Their significance is now more readily accepted, and has indeed become the subject of debate. To some historians, they were associated with the "labour aristocracy" which separated itself from the rest of the working class. To others, they were the means by which a wider identity could be formed, moving beyond the highly particular artisan identity to a wider social grouping, and developing an ideology of collective assistance which was distinct from the individualistic self-help of the middle class. Others have argued that the values of the friendly societies should not be found in the process of class formation in the nineteenth century; rather, the societies should be seen as a continuous tradition based on gilds, with their active cultural life, participation in civic ritual, and sense of group solidarity. On this account, participation and sociability were more important than simple economic advantage, at least until the second half of the nineteenth century with the growth of national, affiliated societies and the development of tension between conviviality and economic rationality. Paul Johnson has, indeed, argued that members of the friendly societies should be seen as essentially individualistic and self-interested. The means were collective, for a working man did not have sufficient income to accumulate savings to deal with social risks, but could hope to insure against the contingency of ill health; the choice was therefore economically rational, and the end was essentially individualistic. Not everyone will be convinced by his reduction of decisions to economic rationality, with its simplifying assumptions about behaviour; and he might be describing a change in the nature of membership in the later nineteenth century which obscures the customary survivals in the eighteenth and early nineteenth centuries.[34] The nature of friendly societies needs more attention, and so does their gradual demise. There was nothing pre-ordained about their replacement by public bodies, for the Liberal insurance scheme of 1911 enlisted them as "approved societies", and similar mutual bodies continued to play an active role in the welfare systems of other European countries. Their demise cannot be taken for granted, but needs to be explained in terms of their own internal financial difficulties, their manipulation by the state to constrain welfare, the willingness of working-class bodies to rely on tax-funded provision as more equitable, and an acceptance of the state as neutral between classes.[35]

Voluntarism and the market may be seen as alternatives to taxation, and public choice theory assumes that individual citizens make a rational choice between methods of funding welfare according to their assessment of self-interest. Economists usually assume that individuals are driven by a desire to maximize their utility, and they seek to explain support for philanthropy or redistributive social policy, which seems to contradict self-interest, in terms of a personal cost–benefit analysis. Individuals are aware of the interdependence of society, and therefore make a decision to maximize their own utility by improving the wellbeing of others. It might be worth paying the costs of welfare – in the form of charitable gifts or taxes – in order to secure property against the threat of the disaffected, or because an individual made a rational calculation of the risks of personally suffering "nuclear hardship".[36] Such an approach is obviously open to attack for its simplifying assumptions about behavioural motivations, and it is difficult to move from individuals making rational calculations of their personal economic benefit to wider political conflicts over social policy, with its different forms and redistributive implications.[37] Perhaps most serious for a historian, the rational choice approach makes it difficult to explain change. At one point, philanthropy appears as a sensible choice to purchase deference and social stability, and at another taxation. What is not clear is why there should be a shift from one approach to another, and why the choice of risks to be insured varied over time and between societies. One way of proceeding may be to develop the economic argument, by suggesting that the individual's choice was shaped by a changing balance between demand and the technical possibilities for the supply of welfare services: a modest income level and a narrow range of welfare provision would lead to a uniform good which could be most effectively supplied by a public body; a higher level of income and the possibility of more differentiated provision of, say, medical care or cover against old age would lead to reliance on the market in order to construct a personal packet of services.[38] Although such factors are clearly relevant, they do not go far in explaining the wide variety of social policies adopted by different societies at broadly similar levels of income and welfare provision. It is necessary to move beyond the simplifying assumptions of economics, and to pay more attention to patterns of state formation.

There has obviously been a broadly inverse relationship between taxation and private benevolence in Britain, for the level of charitable donations was considerably higher in the eighteenth and nineteenth centuries, when the tax rate was low, than in the twentieth century, when tax rates rose. There have also been clear signs of tax resistance in many countries since the 1970s, which has led to greater reliance on private, market provision of social services. Voters have, it is true, made self-interested choices about their gains and losses from tax-funded welfare, which may be understood through a careful analysis of "fiscal sociology". When public expenditure was a low proportion of the gross national product, it was easier for working- and lower middle-class voters to impose increased burdens on a minority in receipt of large incomes; but at some point, increased expenditure exceeded the revenue available from large incomes, and the impact of high marginal tax rates moved down the pyramid of income, so changing the pattern of voting and making it more difficult to increase public expenditure.[39] Such an approach provides a general context for changes which have occurred in many countries since the 1970s, but it should not be assumed that the outcome was preordained. Political parties may seek to define the self-interest of voters by giving tax breaks to particular groups such as families, the elderly, or savers; and tax policy may be used to construct electoral alliances around ideological constructs which may shape voting behaviour. Edwardian Liberals, for example, argued that taxation should be used to benefit producers at the expense of parasitical landowners, which Labour extended into an attack on all "unearned" income; in the 1930s, Conservatives tried to draw a distinction between a respectable "public" and self-interested labour. Social categories were not fixed but interpreted, with contested meanings.[40] It is also necessary to analyze the role of institutions such as the Treasury or the City, and pressure groups such as the Trades Unions Congress or Federation of British Industries, which may constrain or release government spending.[41] Much more attention should be paid to the formation of the state than is apparent in most economic analyses.

One important consideration is how far the tax system achieves a high level of consent, which makes individuals willing to accept the state as trustworthy. In Britain, there was a wide acceptance that central government taxation was equitable, and that the state was neutral between classes; the result was a greater willingness to rely on tax-funded welfare schemes.[42] In Germany, central government taxation was more problematical as a result of competition between the Reich and the state in a federal system, and trade unions were sceptical (with reason) about the even-handedness of the state and were consequently more inclined to maintain separate institutions than their British counterparts. The role of employers also varied between countries. In France, a much larger share of total funding of social services came from employers' contributions than in Britain. French employers created *caisses de compensation* to pay family allowances, either as a means to stabilize the workforce or to restrain wages; such a strategy was not feasible in Britain, because stronger unions were hostile to such a manipulation of the wage bargain, and because the feminist case for the endowment of motherhood made family allowances appear as an attack upon the male breadwinner. The existence of the *caisses* provided the basis for the French state to provide support for family allowances after 1932. In other cases, the state could impose welfare costs directly on employers, as in Australia where they were required to pay a full wage to sick workers and a high minimum wage was enforced through a government arbitration system which removed the worst problems of poverty. Employers were compensated by a high level of protective duties, which helped to create a consensus in favour of a "'wage earners' welfare state"; and government preferred a system which minimized public expenditure on welfare, for a high level of foreign public indebtedness led to fiscal weakness. What is

needed, therefore, is a more ambitious analysis of patterns of state formation and not simply an abstract or highly generalized assessment of the
rational choice of individual voters in pursuit of self-interest.[43]

Attempts to understand the process of state formation and debates over
social policy often start from the interests of particular classes and economic interests, but Peter Baldwin argues that classes defined in relation
to the means of production are less important than the actuarial categories
of risk defined in relation to the means of security. The welfare state is,
after all, not necessarily a means of redistributing resources from the rich
to the poor, for it also redistributes resources over an individual's own life-
cycle or between categories of risk such as age or health which are only
partly related to social class. Baldwin argues that these abstract categories of class and risk intersect in different ways, and take on specific content, according to historical circumstances.[44] His approach therefore rests
upon an analysis of the emergence of a "solidaristic" welfare state in terms
of the actuarial interests of different risk categories, and this categorization
of interest groups by risk rather than occupation or income is taken a stage
further by Johnson.

Johnson's approach casts doubt on the division of welfare into the four
sectors of market, government, charity and the family, and he also questions the extent to which the welfare state is indeed "solidaristic". His
contention is that welfare should be categorized not in terms of its provision by private or public bodies, but by three other features. The first was
the type of risk pool, which could cover the entire group at risk or be
restricted to certain elements; the second was the type of redistribution,
whether between people or merely over an individual's own life; and the
third was the nature of entitlement, which could be a contractual right
determined by actuarial principles or a solidaristic right to relief by need,
according to norms of social justice. By applying these categories to the
new poor law, Liberal welfare reforms and welfare state, Johnson undermines any simple notions of linearity, for different elements of social provision moved in different directions without any obvious progression from
an individualistic to a solidaristic approach, and the nature of redistribution was not determined by private or public provision. What he does not
provide is any explanation of the conflicting trends which he lucidly
describes, which leaves historians of social policy with a still more difficult
task. How is the actuarial outcome of different methods of delivering
welfare to be explained, and how is it to be integrated with Baldwin's
analysis of risk categories?

The conclusion of Johnson's chapter may be taken as a general theme of this volume: most social risks, most of the time, have been met in a variety of ways which are obscured by simple dichotomies between private and public, individualistic and collectivist approaches. The task of the historian is to establish the precise mixture at any time, paying due attention to variations between parts of a country as well as between countries; to describe the interrelationship between the different elements rather than to treat them as distinct; and to explain why the boundaries between the different parts of the system changed over time. It should not be assumed that the provision of a social service by a public body was necessarily more solidaristic than provision by the market or a voluntary body, for much depended upon the nature of the risk pool and the pattern of entitlement. The explanation for the differing and changing mixtures will not be found in simple economic models of utility-maximizing individuals, or through a class-based analysis. What is needed is an appreciation of the complexities of risk categories, which may be shaped by demographic factors such as shifts in the age distribution, or by changes in the economic structure with the rise of landless labourers or the onset of mass unemployment. The outcome is shaped by the formation of the state: were confraternities accepted, did the parish acquire civil functions, did central government taxation secure consent, were services delegated to employers or voluntary organizations? Cultural meaning must also be inserted into the discussion, for the definitions of kin collectivity, interest group or risk category were all interpreted and contested. This volume is a contribution to a massive task with which historians will continue to grapple as politicians pursue their own labour of restructuring the welfare state. Perhaps historians and politicians are in a similar plight: a realization that problems need to be solved, and a lack of confidence that a simple answer is to be found.

Notes

1. The books are by D. Roberts, published in 1960, and B. B. Gilbert, published in 1966. Such an interpretation continued in the standard surveys by D. Fraser, *The evolution of the British welfare state* (London, 1973) and U. Henriques, *Before the welfare state* (London, 1988). Similarly, the medical services of the new poor law were portrayed by R. G. Hodgkinson in the light of one of the key elements of the post-1945 welfare state in *The origins of the National Health Service: the medical services of the New Poor Law, 1834–1871* (London, 1967), and the history of philanthropy was viewed by both W. K. Jordan and D. Owen as part of a linear trend towards

state provision of welfare: see respectively *Philanthropy in England, 1480–1660* (London, 1959) and *English philanthropy, 1660–1960* (London, 1964).

2. On the debates on the finance and viability of the welfare state, see R. Lowe, "Resignation at the treasury: the Social Services Committee and the failure to reform the welfare state 1955–7", *Journal of Social Policy*, **18**, 1989, pp. 506–26.

3. T. H. Marshall, *Citizenship and social class* (Cambridge, 1950).

4. See the changes in the life-cycle and the relationship between generations outlined in M. Anderson, "The emergence of the modern life-cycle in Britain", *Social History* **10**, 1985, pp. 69–87.

5. See R. M. Smith, "Transfer incomes, risk and security: the roles of the family and the collectivity in recent theories of fertility change", in *The state of population theory*, D. A. Coleman & R. S. Schofield (eds) (Oxford, 1986), pp. 201–2.

6. J. Harris, *Private lives, public spirit: a social history of Britain, 1870–1914* (Oxford, 1993), pp. 111–2.

7. See P. Baldwin, *The politics of social solidarity: class bases of the European welfare state, 1875–1975* (Cambridge, 1990).

8. See for example L. Stone & J. F. Stone, *An open elite? England, 1540–1880* (Oxford, 1984) and L. Bonfield, "Marriage settlements and the 'rise of great estates': the demographic aspect", *Economic History Review* 2nd series **32**, 1979, pp. 483–93.

9. R. A. Dodgshon, "'Pretense of blude' and 'place of thair duelling': the nature of highland clans, 1400–1745", in *Scottish society, 1500–1800*, R. A. Houston & I. D. Whyte (eds) (Cambridge, 1989), pp. 168–98.

10. Similar points have been made about the mechanistic account of population growth in E. A. Wrigley & R. S. Schofield, *The population history of England, 1541–1871: a reconstruction* (London, 1981) which argues that the age of marriage moved in response to wage rates in order to control the balance between population and resources.

11. R. Mitchison, "The making of the old Scottish poor law", *Past and Present* **63**, 1974, pp. 58–93 and "The poor law", in *People and society in Scotland (1)*, T. Devine & R. Mitchison (eds) (Edinburgh, 1988), pp. 252–67.

12. See R. Bonney (ed.), *Economic systems and state finance* (Oxford, 1995).

13. There is now a large literature on pre-Reformation charity and on the links with the parish: see F. Heal, *Hospitality in early modern England* (Oxford, 1990) and "The idea of hospitality in early modern England", *Past and Present* **102**, 1984, pp. 66–93; M. Rubin, *Charity and community in medieval Cambridge* (Cambridge, 1987); J. Bennett, "Conviviality and charity in medieval and early modern England", *Past and Present* **134**, 1992, pp. 19–41; B. R. McRee, "Charity and gild solidarity in late medieval England", *Journal of British Studies* **32**, 1993, pp. 195–255; M. K. McIntosh, "Local responses to the poor in late medieval and Tudor England", *Continuity and Change* **3**, 1988, pp. 209–45. On the parish and endowed charities, see M. Gorsky, *Charity, mutuality and philanthropy: voluntary provision in Bristol, 1800–70.* (PhD thesis, University of Bristol, 1996), especially ch. 5.

14. J. Innes, "Parliament and the shaping of eighteenth-century English social

policy", *Transactions of the Royal Historical Society,* 5th series **40**, 1990, pp. 90–91; Mitchison, "The making of the old Scottish poor law" and "The poor law"; T. M. Devine, "Social responses in agrarian 'improvement': the highland and lowland clearances in Scotland", in *Scottish society*, Houston & Whyte (eds), pp. 148–68.

15. The literature on the demise of the peasantry is as vast as it is controversial: see, for example, H. J. Habakkuk, "La disparition du paysan anglais", *Annales* **20**, 1965, pp. 649–63; M. Spufford, *Contrasting communities: English villagers in the sixteenth and seventeenth centuries* (Cambridge, 1974); R. W. Hoyle, "Tenure and the land market in early modern England: or a late contribution to the Brenner debate", *Economic History Review* 2nd series **43**, 1990, pp. 1–20; C. G. A. Clay, "Lifelease-hold in the western counties of England, 1650–1750", *Agricultural History Review* **29**, 1981, pp. 83–96.

16. See Thane later in this volume, citing S. King's thesis; this pattern of land owner-ship was also linked to rural industrialization, with land used to provide security for loans and to sustain artisanal production: see P. Hudson, *The genesis of industrial capital: a study of the West Riding wool textile industry, c.1750–1850* (Cambridge, 1986).

17. C. E. Searle, "The Cumbrian customary economy in the eighteenth century", *Past and Present* **110**, 1986, pp. 106–33; N. Gregson, "Tawney revisited: custom and the emergence of capitalist class relations in north-east Cumbria, 1600–1830", *Economic History Review* 2nd series **42**, 1989, pp. 18–42; for a brief discussion of forests, see J. Thirsk, *England's agricultural regions and agrarian history, 1500–1750* (London, 1987), pp. 48–51.

18. For example, F. Vigier, *Change and apathy: Liverpool and Manchester during the indus-trial revolution* (Cambridge, Mass., 1970).

19. For an example of the exploitation of resources by all-comers, see the comments on Charnwood Forest by D. Levine, *Family formation in the age of nascent capitalism* (New York, 1977); see also V. Skipp, *Crisis and development: an ecological case study of the Forest of Arden, 1570–1674* (Cambridge, 1978) and P. A. J. Pettit, *The Royal Forest of Northamptonshire* (Northamptonshire Record Society **23**, 1958).

20. See the data cited by Innes in Ch. 7, n23; for the control of migration, see N. Landau, "The laws of settlement and the surveillance of immigration in eighteenth-century Kent", *Continuity and Change* **3**, 1988, pp. 391–420 and "The regulation of immigration, economic structures and definitions of the poor on eighteenth-century England", *Historical Journal* **33**, 1990, pp. 541–71. On the his-tory of settlement and its survival into the new poor law, see P. Styles, "The evolu-tion of the law of settlement" in his *Studies in seventeenth-century West Midland history* (London, 1978), pp. 175–204, and M. E. Rose, "Settlement, removal and the new poor law" in D. Fraser (ed.), *The new poor law in the nineteenth century* (London, 1976), pp. 25–43.

21. Gorsky, *Charity, mutuality and philanthropy*, pp. 204, 207, 289.

22. M. E. Rose, "The crisis of poor relief in England, 1850–90" in *The emergence of the welfare state in Britain and Germany, 1850–1950*, W. J. Mommsen (ed.) (London, 1981) and S. Banks, "Nineteenth-century scandal or twentieth-century model?

A new look at 'open' and 'closed' parishes", *Economic History Review* 2nd series **41**, 1988, pp. 51–73.

23. E. A. Wrigley, *People, cities and wealth* (Oxford, 1987), p. 13.

24. The phrase of G. Finlayson, who directed attention to the continuation of charity alongside the poor law and welfare state, rather than its simple disappearance: see "A moving frontier: voluntarism and the state in British social welfare, 1911–49", *Twentieth Century British History* **1**, 1990, pp. 183–206 and *Citizen, state and social welfare in Britain, 1830–1990* (Oxford, 1990); see also the work of F. Prochaska, who adopts a more assertive stance and almost implies that the emergence of state welfare should be regretted: *The voluntary impulse* (London, 1988).

25. For some brief comments, see M. Paci, "Long waves in the development of welfare systems", in *Changing boundaries of the political: essays on the evolving balance between state and society, public and private in Europe*, C. Maier (ed.) (Cambridge, 1987), pp. 179–99.

26. R. A. Cage, "The origins of poor relief in New South Wales: an account of the Benevolent Society, 1809–62", *Australian Economic History Review* **20**, 1980, pp. 153–69 and *Poverty abounding, charity aplenty: the charity network in colonial Victoria* (Sydney, 1991); B. Dickey, *No charity there: a short history of social welfare in Australia* (Sydney, 1987); R. Kennedy, "Charity and ideology in colonial Victoria", in *Australian welfare history*, R. Kennedy (ed.) (London, 1982), pp. 51–83 and *Charity warfare: the Charity Organisation Society in colonial Melbourne* (Melbourne, 1985).

27. Jane Lewis discusses the Guilds of Help in her chapter in this volume; see also E. Macadam, *The new philanthropy: a study of the relations between the statutory and voluntary social service* (London, 1934); C. Webster, "Health, welfare and unemployment during the depression", *Past and Present* **109**, 1985, pp. 204–30; M. Brasnett, *Voluntary social action: a history of the National Council of Social Service, 1919–69* (London, 1969); A. Olechnowicz, *The economic and social development of interwar out-county municipal housing estates, with special reference to the London County Council's Becontree and Dagenham estate*. (DPhil thesis, University of Oxford, 1991); B. Harris, "Voluntary action and unemployment: charity in the south Wales coalfield between the wars" in *Unemployment and underemployment in historical perspective*, E. Aerts & B. Eichengreen (eds) (Leuven, 1990), pp. 101–10 and "Government and charity in the distressed mining areas of England and Wales, 1928–30", in *Medicine and charity in western Europe before the welfare state*, J. Barry & C. Jones (eds) (London, 1991).

28. For the way in which the state could use these bodies to limit expansion of welfare provision, see N. Whiteside, "Private agencies for public purposes: some new perspectives on policy making in health insurance between the wars", *Journal of Social Policy* **12**, 1983, pp. 165–94.

29. For example, P. D. Hall, *Inventing the non-profit sector and other essays on philanthropy, voluntarism and non-profit organisations* (Baltimore, 1992); L. Salamon, *Partners in public service: Government nonprofit relations in the modern welfare state*, (Baltimore, 1995); S. R. Smith & M. Lipsky, *Nonprofits for hire: the welfare state in the age of contracting* (Cambridge, Mass., 1993).

30. For "social control" approaches, see G. Stedman Jones, *Outcast London: a study in*

the relationship between classes in Victorian society (Oxford, 1986); P. McCann, "Popular education, socialization and social control: Spitalfields, 1812–24", in *Popular education and socialization in the nineteenth century*, P. McCann (ed.) (London, 1977), pp. 1–40; J. Donzelot, *The policing of families* (New York, 1979); for a more subtle account of the role of voluntarism in forging a middle-class identity, containing divisions within the middle class and assisting in the control of the working class, see R. J. Morris, "Voluntary societies and British urban élites, 1780–1850: an analysis", *Historical Journal* **26**, 1983, pp. 95–118 and his *Class, sect and party: the making of the British middle class, Leeds 1820–50* (Manchester, 1990). The alternative view is associated with B. Harrison, *Peaceable kingdom: stability and change in modern Britain* (Oxford, 1983) and above all in the work of F. Prochaska, *The voluntary impulse*; "Philanthropy", in *Cambridge social history of Britain, 1750–1950, III, social agencies and institutions*, F. M. L. Thompson (ed.) (Cambridge, 1990), pp. 357–93; and *Royal bounty: the making of a welfare monarchy* (London, 1995).

31. See Jones's discussion of the work of Cavallo and Smith in this volume; also Gorsky, *Charity, mutuality and philanthropy* for Bristol, and Morris, *Class, sect and party* for Leeds, who provide contrasting accounts which stress respectively conflict and the creation of a unified middle class.

32. Data supplied to the conference on "Systems of benevolence" at the Australian National University, August 1994, by Mark Lyons.

33. See the chapters by Pullan, Jones, Waddington and Lewis in this volume. The paper by van Leeuwen discussed by Jones has wide implications for the modern period: see also S. Ostrander & P. Shervish, "Giving and getting: philanthropy as a social relation", in *Critical issues in American philanthropy: strengthening change and practice*, J. van Til et al. (eds) (San Francisco, 1990). The literature on the role of women in nineteenth-century philanthropy is extensive: see F. Prochaska, *Women and philanthropy in nineteenth-century England* (Oxford, 1980); R. McKibbin, "Class and poverty in Edwardian England", in his *The ideologies of class: social relations in Britain, 1880–1950* (Oxford, 1990), pp. 167–96; M. Vicinus, *Independent women: work and community for single women, 1850–1920* (London, 1985); A. Summers, "A home from home: women's philanthropic work in the nineteenth century", in *Fit work for women*, S. Burman (ed.) (London, 1979), pp. 33–63; S. Koven "Borderlands: women, voluntary action, and child welfare in Britain, 1840 to 1914", in *Mothers in a new world: maternalist politics and the origins of welfare states*, S. Koven & S. Michel (London, 1993), pp. 94–135; S. Koven & S. Michel, "Womanly duties: maternalist politics and the origins of welfare states in France, Great Britain and the United States, 1880–1920", *American Historical Review* **95**, 1990, pp. 1076–1108.

34. J. Foster, *Class struggle in the industrial revolution: early industrial capitalism in three English towns* (London, 1974); R. Gray, *The Labour aristocracy in Victorian Edinburgh* (Oxford, 1976); G. Crossick, *An artisan élite in Victorian society: Kentish London, 1840–1880* (London, 1978); Gorsky, *Charity, mutuality and philanthropy*, ch. 6; P. Johnson, *Saving and spending: the working-class economy in Britain, 1870–1939* (Oxford, 1985).

35. I have discussed these issues in "Payment and participation: welfare and state formation in Britain, 1900–51", *Past and Present*, **150**, 1996, pp. 169–216.

36. For example, A. Hirschman, *Shifting involvement: private interest and public action* (Princeton, 1981) views citizens as consumers of welfare services making rational choices according to cost and quality; K. J. Arrow, "Uncertainty and the welfare economics of medical care", in his *Essays in the theory of risk-bearing* (Amsterdam, 1971) argues that apparently redistributive measures are in fact insurance; see also K. E. Boulding, "Notes on a theory of philanthropy", in *Philanthropy and public policy*, F. G. Dickenson (ed.) (New York, 1962); and M. Hechter, *Principles of group solidarity* (Berkeley, 1987).

37. See the criticism from within economics by A. Sen, *On ethics and economics* (Oxford, 1987) and "Rational fools: a critique of the behavioural foundations of economics" in his *Choice, welfare and measurement* (Oxford, 1962). For comments on the difficulty of moving from the individual to society, see Baldwin, *The politics of social solidarity*, p. 22.

38. B. Weisbrod, *The voluntary non-profit sector* (Lexington, Mass., 1977).

39. R. A. Musgrave, *Fiscal systems* (New Haven, 1969), pp. 86–7; he develops the approach of K. Wicksell, "A new principle of just taxation", in *Classics in the theory of public finance*, R. A. Musgrave & A. T. Peacock (eds) (London, 1967).

40. A. Offer, *Property and politics, 1870–1914: landownership, law, ideology and urban development in England* (Cambridge, 1981); R. McKibbin, "Class and conventional wisdom: the Conservative party and the 'public' in inter-war Britain", in his *The ideologies of class: social relations in Britain, 1880–1950* (Oxford, 1990).

41. This is the theme of my forthcoming *Ransom of riches: the politics of taxation since 1842* (London, 1997); see also J. E. Cronin, *The politics of state expansion: war, state and society in twentieth-century Britain* (London, 1991).

42. See, for the general point on the exclusion of economics from politics, McKibbin, "Why was there no Marxism in Great Britain?", in *The ideologies of class*; the approach is developed in my "Payment and participation".

43. These comments are, of course, very general: see S. Pedersen, *Family, dependence, and the origins of the welfare state: Britain and France, 1914–45* (Cambridge, 1993); N. Ferguson, "Public finance and national security: the domestic origins of the First World War revisited", *Past and Present* **142**, 1994, pp. 141–68; J. von Kruedener, "The Frankenstein paradox in the intergovernmental fiscal relations of imperial Germany", in *Wealth and taxation in Central Europe: The history and sociology of public finance*, P.-C. Witt (ed.) (Leamington Spa, 1987), pp. 111–23; D. Blackbourn & G. Eley, *The peculiarities of German history: bourgeois society and politics in nineteenth-century Germany* (Oxford, 1984); F. G. Castles, *The working class and welfare* (Sydney, 1985) and *Australian public policy and economic vulnerability* (Sydney, 1988).

44. Baldwin, *The politics of social solidarity*, pp. 17–20. The lack of redistribution from rich to poor, after taking tax allowances into account, was noted by R. Titmuss in a lecture in 1955, reprinted as chapter 2 of his *Essays on the welfare state* (London, 1958); see also B. Abel-Smith, "Whose welfare state?" in *Conviction*, N. MacKenzie (ed.) (London, 1958), pp. 55–73 and J. Le Grand, *The strategy of equality* (London, 1982).

2

Charity, self-interest and welfare: reflections from demographic and family history[1]

Richard Smith

From a good deal that has been written in the fields of demographic and family history and from much of the discussion in the more polemical atmosphere of contemporary political debate, there would be little difficulty in detecting an interpretational preference for perceiving the way in which welfare relates to social behaviour. The most readily identifiable preference is that which treats demographic patterns and the familial configurations thereby generated as fundamentally induced in their relationship with social welfare, with regard either to its incidence or its organization. English historical research into the family and demographic change is reasonably well supplied with such preferred interpretations.

Two of the starkest positions concern the consequences thought to follow, on the one hand, from the introduction of the Tudor poor law at the end of the sixteenth century and the other, from the manner of that law's functioning in the very late eighteenth and early nineteenth centuries. In his characteristically spirited attempt to write an account of English family history that posited a distinct shift in both the form and function of kinship between the late medieval period and Tudor and early Stuart England, Lawrence Stone gave the poor law a particularly prominent role as causal agent.

> The principal area in which the function of peasant kinship can be shown to have been in decline in the seventeenth century is that of aid and welfare for the helpless, the sick and the indigent. In traditional societies these problems are handled by the conjugal family, the kin and the neighbours, with some minor help from the

23

church. . . . In about 1600 a nationwide system based on local compulsory taxation and expenditure was instituted and during the seventeenth century it became a fully functional organization run by the parish, which effectively relieved the kin, the conjugal family and the neighbours of their previous sense of obligation to provide relief to the sick and the indigent to save them from starvation.[2]

Lawrence Stone is not alone in viewing the poor law's implementation as responsible for a withering of kinship bonds and a shift towards a simpler family structure, a higher incidence of life-time celibacy and a later age of marriage when the family, as it were, was supposedly downgraded as a caring institution and replaced by the community in the guise of socially discriminating welfare-fund managers. So discriminating were these fund managers in the ways they assisted households and individuals that, in the opinion of some social historians allied to the "social control school", they were able to induce marital restraint in the seventeenth and early eighteenth centuries to such a degree that population growth was actually brought to a halt and noteworthy demographic decline facilitated.[3]

In a paradigmatically similar fashion, disciples of Malthus are, through his views, familiar with the debate about the supposed effect of indiscriminant assistance to young adult males, the so-called "able-bodied" poor, in the form of price-indexed wage payments or supplements – that is, the effect of these subsidies on the encouragement of recklessly early marriages. The fact that relief by scale increased in value upon marriage and with the addition of each child was held by Malthus to be "a direct, constant, and systematical encouragement to marriage by removing from each individual the heavy responsibility which he would incur by the laws of nature for bringing human beings into the world which he could not support".[4]

Similar views regarding the capacity of welfare to dissolve or undermine the *status quo* in family patterning are detectable in a dramatic statement of the Indian Famine Commission Report of 1880. Indeed these views reflect a climate of political economic opinion in which the arguments of Malthus continued to carry conviction.

> Even where the legal right does not exist, the moral obligation of mutual assistance is scarcely less distinctly recognised [in rural India]. . . Any form of relief calculated to bring these rights into

obscurity or desuetude, or to break down these habits by showing
them to be superfluous, would be an incalculable misfortune.[5]

The authors of this passage exemplify an interpretational preference for
perceiving the way in which welfare relates to demographic behaviour and
familial relationships which remains readily identifiable in the late twentieth century in the New Right's dedication to a policy of "self-reliance".
Such policies, if fully implemented as social practice, would, in effect,
oblige people to rely upon family and friends rather than the state as the
basic source of support. To do so is assumed to be a means of reinforcing
traditional ties and values, exemplified perhaps by Senator Chaney,
Minister for Social Security in an Australian government of the early
1980s, who stated:

> My personal preference would be to see a higher level of personal
> independence and family interdependence . . . with young people
> living at home and receiving support from their families, with hus-
> bands and wives recognizing their obligations of mutual support,
> with families committing themselves to the care of their aged
> members and parents accepting their primary responsibility for the
> care of their own children.[6]

Such thoughts are indeed vivid manifestations of the view which has great
currency – that welfare undermines the commitment of the family to stick
together and to assist its members.

The past decade has seen, at least within a small group of social and
demographic historians, a reaction against reductionist approaches couch-
ed in terms which tend to place demography so unequivocally downstream
of welfare. To some extent this recent tendency had a precursor in the work
of historians such as Mark Blaug who had been inclined to view the great
growth of poor-law expenditure in the late eighteenth century as more a
response to the changes in the material conditions of the poor consequent
upon the expansion in their numbers brought about by demographic
growth, especially in southern England after 1770 or 1780, and not a development inducing such behaviour. The roots of poverty in this interpretation lay in structural economic changes rather than any moral failure on the
part of the labouring classes. This stance is a good example of what some
have come to regard as a "demand side" approach to welfare in which
demography might be viewed as assuming the status of *independent* rather

than *dependent* variable.[7] Such thinking has recently been reiterated by Thomas Sokoll in his detailed, and in many respects exemplary, study of two Essex communities in the late eighteenth and early nineteenth centuries, to which further reference will be made later in this discussion.[8]

Confusion and contradiction continue to show through when demographers engage with welfare, whether the context is the past or the present. There is indeed irony in two themes that proceed concurrently and assume a prominent position in demographic thinking. One area of research has marshalled a good deal of evidence to suggest that an increase of welfare provision and social insurance by governments or politically-constituted agencies not organized around kin groups has effects that are both demographically and economically advantageous in Third World situations. Such state-directed wealth transfers are supposed to reduce both mortality and morbidity and are believed to be especially important in undermining the security value offered in old age by their children, and thereby leading to beneficial outcomes (to the collectivity) of lower fertility and diminished population growth rates. However, another focus of research, much of it policy oriented in developed economies, and influenced greatly by ideas that emanated initially from North America, tends to emphasize the drain upon economic growth and the increasing sense of "intergenerational injustice" that follow from recent and future age-structural changes. The ageing of the population in such economies is shown to have been caused demographically by increasing longevity and near or sub-replacement rate fertility. These improvements in life expectancy, especially at advanced ages, and the falls in family size norms, are in their turn viewed as partially attributable to an increasingly pervasive state welfare system which is, furthermore, believed to be largely responsible for the demographic developments which increase the numbers of those recipients from, but reduce the contributors to, the welfare funds.[9]

The most provocative and influential attempt to reverse the direction of the causal arrow linking welfare on the one hand and demography and family on the other hand, and consequently the most contentious, is the so-called "nuclear hardship" thesis which has been associated in particular with Peter Laslett who first used the term.[10] The assumption of this hypothesis is that the household system obtaining in early modern England was based upon the structural principles of nuclearity and neo-localism, that is to say, nuclear family households constituted the predominant household form and every marriage was, in theory, associated with the establishment of a new household. The aim of the hypothesis is to understand the functioning of that system by considering the cases which contradict its "logic". What happens under such a household regime when familial nuclei which form its basic constituents break up or fall apart? The vulnerability of such a household formation system implies a significant degree of assistance to "victims" from the collectivity or collectivities. As a consequence, the death of a spouse, unemployment or sickness of the principal breadwinner (or indeed of any major contributor to family income), and decrepitude, might undermine the viability of the rather tightly circumscribed group. Support therefore might come from a spectrum of resource possibilities that rest outside the co-resident domestic group. The wider kin group and altruistically inclined neighbours might fulfil a prominent role in such provision. In addition, there may be a place for a range of institutions extending from informal support such as that derived through access to gathering fuel in common lands, gleaning and begging, to formalized welfare from politically constituted agencies in the guise of the parish, the municipality and the state – elements of varying degrees of importance in what may be regarded as "the collectivity". We may regard the rate-based funds of the English old poor law as one manifestation of the collectivity – a collectivity that functions as an integral part of the household formation system rather than as an alternative to it. We need not suppose that the welfare system is prior to the household system in the causal or chronological sequencing, particularly if it can be shown that the poor laws were a continuation of a long-standing tradition of significant extra-familial support for dependents.

The conceptualization of "nuclear family hardship" has helped to provide a framework for assessing, and more effectively identifying, various categories of "deserving poor", e.g. orphans, married couples overburdened with children, widows and the elderly as well as enabling those living (in certain important respects) outside the socially and politically sanctioned household system – the "undeserving poor", such as vagrants, especially of the young adult male variety and unmarried mothers and their offspring. All the aforementioned may be regarded as "victims of nuclear hardship", but not all were equally worthy of support, in the eyes of their contemporaries, from the resources of the collectivity. Furthermore, their acceptability to welfare fund managers as eligible beneficiaries did not remain constant across time.[11]

There has to date been some rudimentary discussion of the possibility of this set of interrelationships to which I have just referred being less apparent, indeed less relevant, in joint household formation systems. Such systems are supposed to enable wider resort to assistance from both lineal and lateral kin within the household or outside, as in the case of patri-virilocal marriage systems where sons reside close to the father's hearth even though they may not actually reside under the same roof. Such systems have been found widely through Asiatic societies of both the past and the present as well as through significant tracts of historic southern and eastern Europe. Some particularly interesting work is now being done on the material circumstances of women in these situations, especially concerning the mortality penalty incurred by elderly females without living sons if they were so unfortunate as to find themselves widowed. In this respect some crude, broad-brush-stroked, geographical divisions have been drawn between areas of early modern Europe, with the north-western parts of the continent supposedly exhibiting "nuclear hardship" *par excellence*, and areas further to the east and some parts of the south displaying characteristics generally associated with joint household societies.[12]

In much of what follows in this discussion I provocatively take for granted the presence of "nuclear hardship" as a salient feature of the social structure over much of early modern Western Europe. Such "hardships" created problems which, of course, were greatly accentuated when high proportions of the population were dependent for their livelihood on the use of their own labour power as increasingly was the case in early modern England. It is also important to note that in addition to the vulnerability of those in a household formation system that depends on a high degree of economic and residential independence of married couples and their off-spring, there is a further hazard deriving from demographic processes that limit the availability of kin, even if such kin were regarded as the prime or sole providers of support for dependent persons. We now know much more about the availability of kin to an individual in past populations, thanks to the technique of micro-simulation and especially the outcomes created by the CAMSIM computer program or suite of programs developed by James Smith in collaboration with the Cambridge Group for the History of Population and Social Structure.[13] With such techniques we can now reconstruct past populations on the basis of the use of demographic parameters that have themselves been securely identified through increasingly sophisticated historical demographic research. We can, for example, estimate the extent to which secular demographic trends in early modern England implied secular trends in the number of living near-kin which people had over their life course. Such calculations reveal an interesting paradox. If at later ages (i.e. over 55 or 60) people showed a wish to live with mature, independent children, or with other relatives, and those children or relatives were willing to provide that facility, both children and other kin are considerably more likely to be available today than they were in the seventeenth century.[14]

However, such measures of kin availability are quite sensitive to shifts in the underlying demographic rates. The contrast between the seventeenth and late eighteenth or early nineteenth centuries is noteworthy. The apparent advantages of the present-day and the disadvantages of the late seventeenth-century elderly with regard to availability of "kin-carers" were significantly less when the conditions of very late Georgian and Victorian England are considered. Between the 1770s and the Poor Law Report of 1834 marriage ages were low and fertility was very high in comparison with preceding and subsequent periods. Under such buoyant demographic circumstances almost 80 per cent of the elderly would have had adult children alive and potentially available to support them.[15]

Notwithstanding the very large changes in, indeed volatility of, kin availability throughout the old poor law era, we should note the flawed capacity of the early modern demographic system to provide lineal-kin based assistance to one important category of progressively dependent persons: the elderly. Given that childlessness in old age was relatively common, if welfare obligations for fathers and mothers were assumed to fall primarily upon offspring, in many circumstances 40 to 50 per cent of elderly persons might have been without a son or a daughter and 30 to 40 per cent may have lacked both. Furthermore for those who did have children as they entered their sixties, intergenerational support may have been jeopardized by another feature of the household formation system. When marriage was late for both sexes (the late twenties, or even early thirties), neo-local in its residential consequences for bride and groom, and based upon assumed economic independence for the newly-formed household, as it was throughout much of northwest Europe, the parents of married couples would have begun to lose their children's earnings or labour power, and to lose each other in widowhood, and their own strength if earnings were derived from manual, wage-paid work, at the point in the life course when those children in their turn may have been severely pressed by the unfavourable balance of consumers to producers or earners in their own still youthful households.[16] This problem was summed up by a correspondent from Warwickshire reported in Booth's renowned survey of *The aged poor* (1894) who noted "that the children's own families are costing most just at the time of greatest parental need".[17] A similar recognition of an incompatibility of intergenerational interests emerges from a letter written in 1810 by an elderly pauper resident in Bethnal Green to the overseer of the parish of St John's in Colchester: "My children are all married and got familys which these dear times they have as much as they can do to support and therefore are not able to assist me."[18] These are relatively frequently encountered sentiments that surface in the Essex pauper correspondence of the early nineteenth century.[19]

It must be stressed that while the structural characteristics of the northwest European household formation system presuppose significant flows of support for victims of "nuclear family hardship" from the collectivity, it is not my intention to propose that family support for individuals was absent or indeed unimportant in the periods of dependency for an individual which were and indubitably remain significantly greatest in infancy, childhood and old age. Nor is there necessarily any relationship between the household formation system and the form assumed by the welfare provisions emanating from the collectivity. It was suggested earlier in this discussion that there is no reason to suppose that the household formation system is itself a product, in the English case, of the establishment of the old poor law, particularly if it can be shown that there had previously (i.e. pre-1601) been a significant role for the collectivity in dealing with welfare problems associated with identifiable types of "nuclear family hardship". None the less, the form assumed by the collectivity may well have influenced its effectiveness in dealing with those problems.[20]

Before a consideration is undertaken of the issue of the role of the "collectivity" prior to the formal establishment of the old poor law, it is necessary to consider certain of the more pronounced features of the English collectivity in its role as a welfare-provider in the early modern period. Three attributes, it may be suggested, distinguished the English welfare-providing collectivity in the early modern era. From the sixteenth century it came to be based for almost three hundred years thereafter on the parish, and at the level of the parish was funded by a statutorily-determined system that obliged parishes to raise a rate or local tax for the relief of their poor. It was also, from the mid- to late-seventeenth century, distinctive in being a means of welfare provision that was present throughout the country in a remarkably standardized form, notwithstanding the possibilities for considerable local or regional deviations from a "national norm". Furthermore, it was distinctive in providing cash benefits that were paid principally to persons in their own homes. To emphasize this latter characteristic is not to ignore the share of overall expenditure that was directed towards the provision of assistance to individuals as a consequence of their entry into such "indoor" institutions as houses of correction, workhouses or hospitals – the last mentioned institution dependent upon funds from the voluntary rather than public sector, to draw a somewhat anachronistic distinction. In addition, charitable activity was a sizeable part of the effort to provide assistance to the poor throughout the old poor law era. As Joanna Innes rightly notes: "The range of efforts directed towards the poor in England did not differ greatly from that to be found elsewhere in Europe. What was different was the balance between the parts."[21]

How a parish-based rating system came to loom so large is a subject that has not been ignored by historians and, notwithstanding the evidential shortcomings, some plausible explanations may be proffered. Before a system of compulsory rates was established, people unable effectively to support themselves without material assistance from others made use of various avenues of assistance. Some sought casual charity from their neighbours, in cash or kind. Those sufficiently well-placed within neighbourly networks might hope to benefit from various forms of contributory fund: one-off "help ales" at one extreme, the funds of long-established religious gilds or fraternities at the other – the latter particularly important from the late fourteenth century. Others might gain a share of the proceeds of collections taken at church or of incomes accruing to established charitable funds in the form of one-off benefits in cash or kind, or long-term care or subsidized housing, particularly from the late fifteenth century in an almshouse.[22]

The traditional medieval peasant "poor law" is conventionally seen as having been based upon family arrangements by which new tenants promised to the retired peasant shelter in the holding, food, clothing and fuel to the standard to which they had been accustomed.[23] Yet it is striking how large was the *public* dimension in these contracts or transactions. Many were not made between members of the family, but between departing and incoming tenants who were unrelated. They were registered in the rolls of the manorial court before a gathering of villagers who also policed the agreements to ensure that the retiring elder received his or her dues in accordance with the agreed terms.[24] The public involvement in welfare provision went beyond the curial monitoring of intra-familial and inter-personal maintenance agreements since what was to become a fundamental element in early modern poor law, the common box, is known to have existed and is frequently mentioned in the wills of testators of the fifteenth century who left money specifically for the poor or for the payment of the king's taxes on behalf of fellow disadvantaged villagers.[25]

Professor Christopher Dyer in the Neale Lecture of 1991, when discussing the nature of the medieval English village community, drew attention to a fourteenth-century development relating to a community's or vill's obligation to pay lay subsidies that, with considerable justification, he believes had important repercussions on later English developments. After 1334 tax quotas were assigned to each community and the villagers were expected to assess and to collect the money. For such a function to be fulfilled it was necessary for there to have been procedures for choosing individuals who were then required to make assessments of their neighbours and to cajole them into making their contributions.[26] Furthermore, there was much local experimentation at the level of the parish in the later fifteenth and early sixteenth centuries. English churchwardens' accounts from those decades survive in sufficient numbers to show how these officers gathered a rate primarily, although not exclusively, for expenditure on the church fabric, books and vestments. It is tempting to suggest that methods and personnel used in raising the state taxes were redeployed so as to service the needs of the parish. These accounts reveal parishes increasingly accumulating stocks of land and other gifts, used primarily to maintain the fabric of the parish church, but not infrequently to generate incomes that were directed towards charitable purposes. Dr Beat Kumin has shown that so substantial were the sums raised annually by the pre-Reformation churchwardens that they frequently exceeded the amounts secured by communities to meet the lay subsidies of the 1520s.[27] The concepts of compulsory parish rates and of obligatory payment based on money raised locally by parish officials which came to underpin the revenue-raising mechanisms of the Tudor poor law were therefore long-established before the dramatic events of the 1530s and 1540s dismantled so many of the institutions that had been responsible, in whole or in part, for welfare provisions in the later Middle Ages. The willingness to tolerate taxation in a local setting, which Paul Slack sees as so distinctive in explaining the pervasiveness of the rate-based system in the seventeenth century, may therefore have derived from long-standing habits that were not the creature of a major or threatening and unfamiliar revenue-raising principle that intruded into local practices after the 1540s and especially after the 1570s.[28] It has also been suggested that the sheer scale and near completeness of the destruction of many welfare-providing institutions as part of the English Reformation was so great that even the renewed volume of gifts and bequests by will-makers for the poor that is evident from the 1550s was insufficient to fill the shortfall that had arisen. Under such circumstances obligatory taxes, rather than voluntary provision, may have been viewed as a necessary means of securing the welfare funds required. Furthermore, as Paul Slack and Joanna Innes have both emphasized, a strong central government whose responsive representatives in the persons of the JPs in the localities succeeded in securing local responses that would have been unlikely in a less well-integrated polity.[29] In addition, this latter attribute was not a feature of English society that first became apparent under the Tudors but reflects a set of linkages between village and central government that are certainly detectable from the time of the Angevins, and some among the more optimistic school of Anglo-Saxon historians would regard them as of even greater age.[30]

The late sixteenth-century Elizabethan statutes which provided the legal foundations on which the system of parochial poor relief rested stressed four main functions:

1. To relieve in almshouses those unable to work – the old, sick and disabled who were to be supported in contexts which revealed a genuine preference for indoor relief on the part of those drafting the statute.

2. To provide work for those who were unable to work, but who were able-bodied. The stress was undoubtedly placed on putting the able-bodied to work, to such an exent that the parish officers were ordered to obtain stocks of materials ostensibly available for this purpose.

3. To apprentice children by redistributing them into households that were so constituted and situated that they would use their labour resources productively and profitably.

4. To assist those who found themselves in "family circumstances" that made them incapable of supporting themselves and their family by their own labours.[31]

By the second half of the seventeenth century, if not before, when we can begin to observe practice both because sources survive in sufficient numbers and because a majority of parishes were by then raising a rate to fund parish relief provisions, there appears to have been a significant discrepancy between the statutory theory and overseers' practice. Funds were continuing to be deployed disproportionately for the support of those whose own family circumstances were such as to make it difficult for them to support themselves and considerable resources were allocated to the sending out and payment of parish apprentices. These two areas of poor-law provision were dominant and swamped expenditure on indoor provision for the elderly sick and expenditure on materials that were to sustain the work of the unemployed or work-shy.[32]

In fact outdoor relief to persons in their own households assumed a pre-dominant place in the provision of relief. It should, however, be noted that in 1600 funds for parish relief were far from universal and the fact that they became available in almost all English parishes by the end of the seven-teenth century owed a great deal to the activity of the Privy Council before 1640 and to the influence and authority of county and municipal officers throughout the seventeenth century. The law officers of the Crown played a vital part in ensuring that parishes did their duty. What is perhaps of even greater significance, and John Walter and Roger Schofield regard as critical, was the degree to which the prevailing ideology of the social order "allowed or even required, the magistracy to intervene in the normal processes of social and economic life on behalf of the community at large".[33] Furthermore, the rate-based system by itself could not normally generate over long periods sufficient funds to deal with severe economic crises, but required under such conditions a community-wide response; in the English case this was secured by the parish subscription that entailed the parishioner contributing according to his or her means and more importantly inclination. Somehow it does seem that the propertied classes in early modern England solved the problem of collective action with regard to their dealings with the poor by their administration of a system of regular rate-based relief and irregular but very necessary voluntary redistributions that depended on the vast majority of benefactors trusting that their peers would do likewise. One suspects, in relation to a problem that preoccupies Abram de Swaan in his stimulating thoughts on this matter, the English welfare system in the early modern period was only minimally bedeviled by the "free-rider problem" in so far as it concerned the generation of reasonably adequate welfare funds.[34] With regard to one element in the title of the colloquium that gave rise to this book, de Swaan's preoccupations relate not only to the question of who is my neighbour, but also that of whether I can trust him or her to do what is necessary.

The discrepancy that we observe between initial statutory intent and subsequent practice in the form taken by relief may also have been matched by a failure of another much-quoted clause in the Poor Law Act of 1601 to be effectively implemented. That clause, which engages the attention of other authors in this volume, stated that:

> The father and grandfather, mother and grandmother, and chil-dren of every poor, old blind, lame and impotent person, or other

poor person not able to work being of sufficient ability, shall at
their own charges relieve and maintain every such poor person, in
that manner and according to that rate, as by the justices . . . in
their sessions shall be assessed.[35]

In this clause we appear to have a clear statement of certain highly specific obligations that were, or would be, heaped upon individuals to care
for their immediate relatives. If fully implemented such legislation would
reflect an early modern English society that was towards the familial pole
of the welfare continuum. Interpretation of the extent to which poor-law
officers in the 350 years after 1601 implemented that clause is far from
straightforward. The relative infrequency with which this clause was
enforced has inclined Dr David Thomson to conclude that family support
for the elderly was not a firmly established social norm.[36] But, as Professor
Thane argues in her contribution to this volume, the absence of case law
revealing implementation of the clause should not, unlike Dr Thomson, be
interpreted to mean that poor-law officials made no efforts to secure such
intra-familial support for potential or actual recipients of poor relief. It is
clear that they did make efforts, although the instances that survive in our
sources in the old poor law are infrequent. Such infrequency may in part
reflect the costly nature of the procedures in relation to the small savings
provided to the local ratepayers or, and more likely, a sympathetic understanding on the part of poor-law officers highly knowledgeable of their
local community and fully aware of the impossibility of familial care being
provided by many who were lacking in the resources required to service
the material needs of their close kin. It should not be forgotten that local
magistrates did take a hard line with men who abandoned their wives and
children, and in this area of familial responsibilities the evidence is relatively abundant.[37] We know too, from a growing body of detailed case
studies, many unfortunately as yet unpublished, that in seventeenth- and
early eighteenth-century communities many aged paupers, while they
were receiving relief, had adult children living in the parish. Further
more poor-law accounts frequently reveal instances of parishes paying for
nursing within families. Daughters and daughters-in-law were paid extra
allowances for nursing a parent, siblings were paid to care for one another,
and there were also payments to parents to care for their children.[38] Some
historians have interpreted such instances as the transformation of care
from an obligation into a commodity while others, I believe correctly,
prefer to see this as a means of inducing children to maximize the care

and attention they were willing *in toto* to give.[39] On these different interpretations hinges a fundamental debate about the determinants of familial
obligations on which it will be necessary to reflect further before this
chapter is concluded.

If, as it would seem, we currently find ourselves located in a minefield of
difficulties regarding our interpretation of legal codes as they relate to
actual practice in the matter of familial care, it might be supposed that
we have at our disposal much firmer evidence bearing upon the extent of
poor-law support for victims of "nuclear hardship". I will address this
matter with reference to the elderly upon whom some of my more recent
research has been focused. What proportion of the elderly were in receipt
of poor relief and what meaning should we attach to the wealth transfers
that they constituted? The debate on these matters has to date been most
actively pursued with regard to the nineteenth century and once again
involves Dr David Thomson as the principal object of our attention.
Dr Thomson was a pioneer researcher in this field in the early 1980s and
the bulk of his investigations were concerned with the years immediately
following the poor-law reforms of the 1830s when the values of self-
responsibility and familial duty were supposedly held with particular fer-
vour, at least by poor-law administrators and ratepayers. On what is still an
unfortunately small scattering of case studies from predominantly rural
areas in the southeast Midlands, Thomson argues that the majority of,
although far from all, elderly persons in England were maintained by the
poor law, receiving weekly pensions that bore a very close relationship to
the wages paid at that time to agricultural labourers. In addition, extra
payments were not infrequently granted for quite extensive periods of
need, for special diets, medicine, the employment of nurses or home-
helps, the purchase of alcoholic beverages, shoes and clothing. While
we need not accept Thomson's assessment of the generosity of poor-law
provision, we can note in the early 1840s in some rural areas that perhaps
two-thirds of women of the age of 70, and half of the men of that age, half
of the women aged 65–9, and a significant minority of women 55–60 and
of men in their sixties received a weekly pension.[40]

Charles Booth's survey of resource transfers within families in rural areas
in England and Wales, taken in 1892, provides evidence which shows what
proportion of the population over the age of 65 was receiving, either in
money or kind, income support from a variety of sources, including the
poor law, charity, their own earnings and means, and any financial aid
from relatives. Unfortunately Booth provides little solid evidence on the

specific quantities or monetary value of the help received. Notwithstanding this difficulty Booth considered that both the amounts transferred by relatives (principally children) and the numbers of elderly who benefited thereby surpassed the levels of aid from the poor law and from charity – the last mentioned source of income being of derisory importance. Altogether in this sample of marginally more than 9,000 persons aged 65 and over, one in four received some support from their relatives. This is more, as Booth himself had indicated, than were assisted by the poor law or by charity but considerably less than the numbers supporting themselves either from earnings or savings.[41] As Paul Johnson reminds us in his contribution to this volume, the most important conclusion is that "for most of the time most aged people were not dependent on public support at all". He is critical of Thomson's overdependence on poor-law evidence which he believes leads him to diminish the role of private provision and self-help. Of course, the 1890s are not the 1840s nor are the geographically wide-ranging investigations of Booth strictly comparable with the rather localized investigations of Thomson, focused as they have been to a disproportionate extent on one poor-law union in Bedfordshire. It is worth stressing, however, that in the context of poor-law history the late nineteenth century exhibited some distinctive, possibly unique qualities, when children were being pressed hard by the poor-law authorities to assume responsibility for their elderly parents, during a phase when out-door relief had become the victim of a severe cost-cutting campaign that had been centrally orchestrated.[42]

We cannot confidently form generalizations made on the basis of still somewhat patchy research of the extent of poor-law dependence among the elderly over the course of the nineteenth century. For the old poor law era we still lack a comprehensive body of research on this subject, although work on parish pensioners in a sample of 20 English communities in which links have been drawn between poor-law sources and parish registers that I have undertaken recently reveals some intriguing, although still somewhat provisional, patterns.[43] On the basis of more than 110,000 pension payments to persons of all ages made in these parishes between 1660 and 1740, it appears that those of all ages in receipt of weekly doles or pensions and their families made up about 5 per cent of local populations, although they constituted significantly higher proportions in towns where they rose to account for between 8 and 9 per cent of all residents. We can also confirm that there was significant growth in poor-law expenditure over the period, largely driven by pension payments and not to do with a swelling of outlays on casual benefits. This was only in part the product of a growth in the number of pensioners – indeed, it owed a great deal more to a significant increase in the size of the weekly pension from 4d to 9d or 1s in the north of England and from 6d to 1s 6d in southern communities. While there was a certain tendency for the north–south gap to narrow, the weekly pension remained higher in southern communities in this sample by a considerable margin. We can confirm that through this period pension expenditure on the elderly increased relative to other age groups. Prior to 1650, although it is difficult to be sure, given the small number of good pre-1650 account series, orphans assumed a more prominent place in the overall parish pensioner populations, especially in urban communities. Of those persons 60 years and over, whose ages can be established through information relating to their baptismal dates in the parish registers, 40 to 45 per cent were in receipt of a regular weekly pension, paid at a level in the south equivalent to a labourer's weekly wage. In this finding we observe patterns that are strongly reminiscent of Thomson's work on a rather restricted rural sample from the 1840s. A large minority received a weekly pension that would have met the bulk of their needs. None the less we should not lose sight of the key fact that the majority did not receive assistance from the parish. If we now consider the far easier calculation relating to overall expenditure on specific age groups we discover that over 50 per cent of all pension weeks in this sample were paid to persons 60 years of age or more. It would seem that this age group received a proportion of the pension funds that was between seven and eight times greater than their share of the total population. In these characteristics we can observe a very definite preference for prioritizing the elderly as a category of the "deserving poor". There was throughout this period for all pensioners, irrespective of age, a ratio of 2.5 to 3.0 women for every one male – a ratio that rises still higher for the pensioners who exceeded 60 years of age.

Given what we know of the English population at this period when it contained a proportion of elderly persons not to be exceeded again until the 1930s, and a deficiency of available kin that was exacerbated by low fertility, high infant and child mortality and high rates of migration away from many rural areas, these patterns are hardly surprising.[44] They would seem to be consistent with the notion of a demand-led response to welfare provision, although it would be judicious not to push this interpretation too far. Such caution would be justified since there was clearly a rising expectation of what the elderly came to regard as their entitlement to relief – a relief that was frequently given even when children were resident in the parish.[45] This period is of exceptional interest to the historical demographer in so far as it exhibits considerable *positive* rather than *negative* feedback in the relationship between mortality and fertility and real incomes.[46] A growth in parochial pension provisions to elderly persons may have begun as responses to age-structural changes themselves contingent on a fall in fertility and high rates of out-migration. But they were developments which may have proceeded to intensify that fall in fertility by reducing the propensity to marry, especially the enthusiasm of widows for remarriage, as well as making it easier for the young to depart in full expectation that parishes would carry a significant part of the costs of support for elderly dependents.[47]

By the mid-eighteenth century there are evident changes in the pattern of pension provision, although our analysis is restricted to a rather smaller sum of pension payments (45,000) made between 1750 and 1780. A noteworthy development concerns the value of pension payments which remained at their early-eighteenth-century levels with no detectable tendency to grow in nominal terms after 1750. This characteristic may in part have reflected the shift in the composition of the pensioner populations towards a larger share of beneficiaries who were increasingly likely to have been underemployed males and their wives and children, but it seems clear that the value of pensions given to elderly persons in the form of outdoor relief in their own homes did not rise in an era when living costs certainly inflated sharply. Furthermore we can observe a decline in the elderly component within the pensioner population which was considerably greater than would have arisen from the relative decline in the share of elderly persons in the total population which was then growing and acquiring an increasingly youthful age structure. These data reveal a particularly sharp drop in the proportion of pensioner weekly payments received by elderly females. In addition we observe a drop in the ratio of female to male pensioners of all ages so that by 1780 the sexual composition of the beneficiary population, although still more female than male, was very close to parity. It is also apparent in this sample of communities that where workhouses had been built during and after the 1720s there may have been a tendency for elderly females, in particular, to be admitted to them.[48] Such a development would have reduced the number of the more highly-paid pensioners who, had they continued as recipients of outdoor relief, would have been in receipt of the largest pensions which were always paid in the last year or months of life when their level of dependence had become particularly high. However, the removal of certain high-cost recipients of outdoor relief into workhouses was not a widespread development in this sample and is not likely to have been the principal determinant of this unambiguous masculinization of pensioner populations since it would appear to have applied to both those above and below 60 years of age.

If these findings can be shown to have had a wider applicability, we may have observed a development that is fully compatible with the investigations of Thomas Sokoll who, in his research upon the highly detailed and informative listing of Ardleigh (Essex) in 1796, concluded that there was an almost complete absence of elderly pauper solitaries and that half of all poor women aged 50 and over lived in lineally extended households with married daughters. In this Essex community the painful economic difficulties brought on by the high prices, harvest failure and severe weather placed great pressures on parish rates in the late 1790s. Here we must seriously entertain the possibility that we are observing the consequences of practices that involved the elderly female pensioners being excluded from contexts in which they were allowed to manage their own households or were refused support in their own homes with assistance from parish funds.[49] Malthus in his own writings in the 1790s protested at another reduction in the civic rights of the elderly – the growing tendency to place elderly persons in workhouses. Malthus's concern seems to have been fully justified from a preliminary observation of the strangely neglected listings of workhouse inmates collected by Sir Frederic Eden.[50] Evidence is certainly accumulating to suggest that the late eighteenth century witnessed a substantial decline, especially in southern and eastern agrarian counties, in the wellbeing of the elderly female. In Amartya Sen's terms their "capabilities" were severely trimmed – a fate they shared with the majority of women at other ages in this period, it would seem.[51]

Apart from the intrinsic interest of the surprisingly clearly defined chronological changes in the patterns of poor relief and the changes in the demographic attributes of beneficiaries, there are other features that stand out that enable us to gain a clearer sense of the most salient features of the system as a whole. From the incidence of pension provision within local communities we can conclude that the pension was by no means a strictly age-related benefit, nor was it provided as a right. In terms of definitional issues raised by Paul Johnson in his chapter in this volume we are observing, at least from the mid-seventeenth century, a *solidaristic* entitlement procedure in which benefits were related to some socially defined concept of desert, and in which discretionary judgements about the level of needs and eligibility were being made which were certainly subject to change as well as reflecting differences between town and country and northern and southern regions.

There is frequently a sense in which we can observe the pension being given as a supplement to earnings, and the steady increase in its value as the beneficiary ages reflects an increasing incapacity to work for reasons of deteriorating health and growing decrepitude. At least until the late eighteenth century and probably throughout the whole period of the old poor law, women predominated among the elderly collectioners and began to receive rate-funded support at an earlier age than men, so that by age 70 a sizeable majority of women would have been in receipt of a regular pension, some for many years. This pattern is clearly present by 1700 and in this respect mirrors those characteristics that have been recovered by David Thomson, through his superior, more accurate, census-based research from 1841 onwards. Males, however, were less readily apparent among those receiving assistance over the age of 65 than would appear to be the case in Thomson's earlier nineteenth-century samples. This contrast may, however, reflect the fact that many of Thomson's samples came from areas of especially low agricultural wages and high rural unemployment in the southeast of England, with the result that his data may possibly have been distorted or biased by the presence of large numbers of elderly males receiving income supplements or unemployment benefit through the poor rates rather than retirement or disability pensions. However, these may well have been characteristics that were also beginning to make their presence felt in the later eighteenth century.[52]

The persistent attempt to combine a poor-law pension with a modicum of self-help in the form of income-generating employment well into old age that is apparent in the late-nineteenth-century data collected by Booth also appears as a characteristic deeply etched into local practice in the old poor law era. Some examples may demonstrate this point. Dr Mary Barker-Read in her pioneering research has reconstructed the poor-law benefit history of Katherine Sheaf of Cranbrook, Kent, who as Katherine Miller married Richard Sheaf in 1648.[53] I regard her case as exemplary. A son was born to Katherine in 1649 when she was 25 and she was widowed in 1678 at the age of 55. From that moment in 1678 until 1682 she received occasional relief during fairly frequent periods of "sickness". From 1682 when Katherine was almost 60 she was given a pension of 2s 6d per month (less than 1s per week), but continued to receive supplements during her recurrent periods of "sickness". Her rent was paid, although her weekly allowance of 8d was almost certainly insufficient to maintain her frail condition. What other income might she have received? It is not until 1686 (when she was 63) when the poor-law accounts of Cranbrook reveal a payment made for "cards" for her, that we can establish that she derived some earnings from the carding of wool. More cards are supplied by the overseer in 1690 when, in her 67th year, she is referred to for the first time as "old widow Sheaf". In her 68th year her pension was raised to 3s per month when she was also provided with winter fuel – indicative of her failing capacity to sustain herself. That year in June she was given a rather large casual payment of 11s on account of her illness, after which she was removed from her home to be lodged with a young widow who was paid 6d per week by the overseer for her houseroom. By this time widow Sheaf was receiving a pension of 1s 6d per week, a sum adequate to meet most of her basic needs. Indeed the parish, it seems, was supporting her completely in her 68th year at the end of which she died. Throughout this period, her son was a resident of Cranbrook as we know from later poor-law accounts that he went on to be one of the first inmates of the Cranbrook workhouse at the age of 73 after it was built in 1722.

The widow Foster does not appear in the family reconstitution of Whitchurch (Oxfordshire) despite being a pensioner for 24 years. She went on the parish within a few years of her husband's death when she was in her mid-fifties. Although no family is traceable from the parish registers, it is apparent from a casual payment of 1686–7 that she had at least one child. She starts off with a modest pension of 1s, with occasional help with clothing and house repairs. By the time she reached her mid-70s she was receiving a weekly pension of 2s 6d and the payment of a surgeon's bill of £6 17s 6d in 1690 is noteworthy. Those entering the system at a more advanced age than the widow Foster tended to be given fairly small and rudimentary pensions which only grew as, and if, they approached extreme old age, and their dependency increased. With many in this category either death came suddenly without long illness or incapacity so allowing little time for the pension to increase, or the final illness provided the catalyst for an elderly man or woman to go onto the pension list in the first place, usually for a brief period in such instances. Widow Foster's is an unspectacular, but very good, example of the incremental withdrawal from economic productivity and self-support that represents something close to a modal experience.[54]

This evidence suggests that by the end of the seventeenth century there had emerged a detectable sentiment that the elderly were entitled to communal support, even if there were close kin available and able to help.

This is, of course, not to say that no help of any kind passed between elderly persons and their children resident in the parish, but that such help, where it existed, was usually supplementary and no complete substitute for parish assistance. To take a further example from Whitchurch: the widow Sadgrave was probably almost 70 when she became a pensioner in the late 1690s, almost a quarter century after her husband's death. She is an example of the commonest sort of widow in receipt of parish support: one of those without children living at home. Although the pension was small, it quickly escalated to proportions which probably provided her full support. One daughter had been baptized in the parish and an Edward Sadgrave makes appearances in the poor-law accounts from time to time; it seems from these sources that a son lived across the county border in Moulsford in Berkshire who was given money to buy her clothes, but appears not to have been obliged to provide her with support from his own purse. Indeed her funeral expenses were met entirely by the parish when she was buried in 1705.[55]

By focusing on formal provision of welfare under the old poor law and by singling out the elderly for privileged attention, I have looked at one apparently "formal" relationship which has led me to give only very limited attention to the subjects of voluntary care through charitable organizations and informal care through the family. As Anne Digby has noted, "Familial care has traditionally been care of both first and last resort."[56] It is especially significant in relation to the theme of this volume insofar as society has invariably imbued it with a moral worth to such an extent that it is viewed in some quarters as *the* form of self-help *par excellence*.

Historians whose work takes them into this area still have a long way to go in clarifying their approach to the issues underpinning the question of obligations and support in families. Janet Finch, the sociologist who, it can be argued, has thought as deeply about this subject as any one, notes that it is necessary to draw a distinction between actual assistance offered to a relative and the reasons why it is offered. All too frequently it is assumed that care provided within the family stems from a sense of duty or responsibility. Politicians are especially prone to draw such conclusions because they are easy to reach and pleasing when offered to the electorate.

As I bring this discussion to a conclusion I enter a sociologically contentious area which is probably strategically unwise. Earlier in this chapter, in reflecting on one clause from the 1601 Poor Law Act, I have mused over certain of the difficulties created by the existence of legal rules and sanctions for the drawing of conclusions about the extent of familial support and have not addressed the issue of why that support was forthcoming. How do we know whether people offered support to parents out of a sense of duty or because they were threatened with prosecution? As Professor Thane reflects in her chapter in this volume, people may have felt affection to parents but have lacked the means to help. Some may well have possessed the resource but regarded it as improper to assist in this way.

It is hard, I would hesitantly suggest, to find compelling evidence that people assumed automatic responsibility for their relatives – including parents – who were old, sick and in various ways unable to support themselves. Medieval arrangements between agricultural tenants reveal the conditional nature of much of the support provided by children for parents. A theme of mutual advantage rather than duty is consistent with the notion that support is part of a two-way relationship between adults rather than a form of uni-directional assistance. It does seem possible to argue with conviction that reciprocal exchange on the basis of mutual advantage is the essence of support between kin, making the family a group whose relationships are founded on material considerations and not solely glued together by what Janet Finch calls "moral imperatives and ties of affection".[57] The real problem that has yet to be confronted by historians of welfare and family is how far support was given when the element of mutuality was absent.

In introducing the above issue we jump from the old poor law era to the very late nineteenth and early twentieth centuries to a well-known case which is relevant to all of us working on the earlier periods. The late nineteenth century was a phase when the poor law was used by Boards of Guardians to impose a very strict ideology of support for elderly parents by children. As Michael Anderson and Janet Finch both conclude in reflecting on this era, we can conceive of the law as attempting to engineer familial asymmetry and imbalance in the flow of resources contrary to a key principle that the maintenance of viable and stable relationships with kin depended upon a *balance* of mutual support. The net effect of this policy and practice was to induce a tension in, and probable withdrawal from, kin contact that was only re-established with the introduction of old-age pensions after 1908. That reassertion of the collectivity's role in welfare provision had the effect of strengthening rather than weakening family ties.[58] This phase is in some senses a paradigm case and rests very uncomfortably with the notion that family affection alone gives rise to material support between kin and that attempts to enforce support through the law are capable of promoting "natural affection". This historical instance suggests that we might be better advised to see cases where the old poor law was providing care for an elderly parent notwithstanding the presence of a child or children in the same community, or cases in which children were "paid" by overseers to see to elderly kin, not as practices undermining mutuality of familial support but as buttressing or enhancing it. To portray aspects of the old poor law in such terms may appear to run counter to much contemporary comment and to the conclusions of historians who see state and/or collectivity and kin as in fundamental opposition to each other. However, to do so is consistent with a view of welfare that serves to promote self-sufficiency and self-interest, if at the same time it promotes familial sufficiency. In proposing such a link we highlight a theme at the core of this volume.

Notes

1. This chapter was originally given as the Sir John Neale Lecture, on 3 February 1995. The text is very close to the lecture as it was delivered.
2. L. Stone, *The family, sex and marriage in England 1500–1800* (London, 1977), pp. 148–49.
3. For an influential article advancing the importance of the role of social control in achieving demographic restraint through poor relief practices in early modern Western Europe, see R. Lesthaeghe, "On the social control of human reproduction", *Population and Development Review* 6, 1980, pp. 527–48. On the English case, see, for example, W. Hunt, *The Puritan moment: the coming of revolution in an English community* (London, 1983), pp. 75–76. Two key texts from the seventeenth century which perceive a prominent role for poor-law officials in hindering marriage are those of Carew Reynel and Sir William Coventry reproduced respectively in *Seventeenth-century economic documents*, J. Thirsk & J. P. Cooper (eds) (Oxford, 1972), pp. 80 and 759. For some cautious comments on the plausibility of these arguments regarding the social stabilizing impact of poor relief in seventeenth-century England see P. Slack, *Poverty and policy in Tudor and Stuart England* (London, 1988), pp. 207–8.
4. E. A. Wrigley & D. Souden (eds), *The works of Thomas Robert Malthus*, vol. III, (London, 1986), p. 309–10.
5. Quoted in J. Drèze, "Famine prevention in India", Discussion Paper No. 3, Development Economics Research Programme, London School of Economics, and subsequently published in *The political economy of hunger*, J. P. Drèze & A. K. Sen (eds) (Oxford, 1990). See too a discussion of this passage from the Commission Report with considerable relevance to the issues discussed in this paper, in A. B. Atkinson & J. Hills, "Social security in developed countries: are there lessons for developing countries?" in *Social security in developing countries*, E. Ahmad,

J. Drèze, J. Hills, A. Sen (eds) (Oxford, 1991).

6. "Opening Address" in *Social policy in the 1980s*, J. Dixon & D. L. Jayasuriya (eds) (Canberra, 1983), pp. 4–5.

7. M. Blaug, "The myth of the old poor law and the making of the new", *Journal of Economic History* **23**, 1963, pp. 151–84. See too the very valuable review of these issues in M. J. Daunton, *Progress and poverty: an economic and social history of Britain 1700–1850* (Oxford, 1995), pp. 447–63.

8. T. Sokoll, *Household and family among the poor: the case of two Essex communities in the late eighteenth and early nineteenth centuries* (Bochum, 1993), ch.5

9. R. M. Smith, "Welfare and the management of demographic uncertainty", in *The political economy of health and welfare*, M. Keynes, D. A. Coleman, N. H. Dimsdale (eds) (Basingstoke, 1988), pp. 108–35.

10. P. Laslett, "Family, kinship and collectivity as systems of support in preindustrial Europe: a consideration of the 'nuclear hardship hypothesis' ", *Continuity and Change* **3**, 1988, pp. 153–75.

11. R. M. Smith, "The structured dependence of the elderly as a recent development: some sceptical historical thoughts", *Ageing and Society* **4**, 1984, pp. 409–28; R. M. Smith, "Transfer incomes, risk and security: the roles of the family and the collectivity in recent theories of fertility change", in *The state of population theory: forward from Malthus*, D. Coleman & R. Schofield (eds) (Oxford, 1986), pp. 188–211.

12. J. Hajnal, "Two kinds of pre-industrial household formation system", *Population and Development Review* **8**, 1982, pp. 448–94; M. Cain, "Welfare institutions in comparative perspective: the fate of the elderly in contemporary South Asia and pre-industrial Western Europe" in *Life, death and the elderly: historical perspectives*, M. Pelling & R. M. Smith (eds) (London, 1991), pp. 222–43.

13. J. Smith, "The computer simulation of kin sets and kin counts", in *Family demography: methods and their applications*, J. Bongaarts, T. Burch, K. Wachter (eds) (Oxford, 1987), pp. 261–5.

14. P. Laslett, *A fresh map of life: the emergence of the Third Age* (London, 1989), pp. 115–17.

15. *Ibid.*, p. 117.

16. Smith, "The structured dependence of the elderly", pp. 42–5.

17. Reported in M. Anderson, "The impact on the family relationships of the elderly of changes since Victorian times in governmental income maintenance provisions", in *Family, bureaucracy and the elderly*, E. Shanas & M. B. Sussman (eds) (Durham, 1977), p. 56.

18. T. Sokoll, "Pauper correspondence and the poor law in Essex c.1800–1834", in *Poverty and poor relief in England from the sixteenth to the twentieth centuries*, A. Digby, J. Innes, R. M. Smith (eds) (Cambridge: forthcoming).

19. Dr Sokoll is preparing a full edition of the Essex pauper correspondence to appear in the British Academy's *Records in Economic and Social History* series.

20. The effectiveness of rate-based system of welfare funding in which the overwhelming bulk of provision is in the form of outdoor relief, amply available in

rural areas, is contrasted with a voluntaristic system of charitable aid in which resources were heavily focused on towns in the form of indoor provision is discussed in R. M. Smith, "'Indoors' and 'Out of doors': contrasting epidemiological consequences of welfare provision in France and England c. 1650–1800" in *Poverty and poor relief in England*, A. Digby, J. Innes, R. M. Smith (eds) (Cambridge: forthcoming).

21. J. Innes, "The state and the poor: eighteenth-century England in European perspective" in *Rethinking Leviathan*, J. Brewer & E. Hellmuth (eds.) (forthcoming).

22. M. MacIntosh, "Local responses to the poor in Medieval and Tudor England", *Continuity and Change* **3**, 1988, pp. 209–45; J. Bennett, "Conviviality and charity in medieval and early modern England", *Past and Present* **134**, 1992, pp. 19–41; B. Harvey, *Living and dying in England 1100–1540* (Oxford, 1993).

23. F. M. Page, "The customary Poor-Law of three Cambridgeshire manors", *Cambridge Historical Journal* **3**, 1930, pp. 125–33.

24. R. M. Smith, "The manorial court and the elderly tenant in late medieval England", in *Life, death and the elderly*, M. Pelling & R. M. Smith (eds) (London, 1991), pp. 39–61; E. Clark, "Some aspects of social security in medieval England", *Journal of Family History* **7**, 1982, pp. 307–20.

25. C. C. Dyer, "The English medieval village community and its decline", *Journal of British Studies* **33**, 1994, pp. 407–29

26. *Ibid.*, p. 416.

27. B. Kumin, *The shaping of community. The rise and reformation of the English parish, 1400–1560* (London, 1996).

28. P. Slack, *Poverty and policy in Tudor and Stuart England* (London, 1988), p. 11.

29. *Ibid.*, pp. 12–13 ; Innes, "The state and the poor".

30. R. M. Smith, "'Modernization' and the corporate medieval village community in England: some sceptical reflections" in *Explorations in historical geography*, A. R. H. Baker & D. Gregory (eds) (Cambridge, 1984), pp. 140–79.

31. P. Slack, *The English poor law 1531–1782* (London, 1990).

32. P. Slack, *Poverty and policy in Tudor and Stuart England*, pp. 162–87. See too, W. Newman-Brown, "The receipt of poor relief and family situation, Aldenham, Hertfordshire 1630–90", in *Land, kinship and life-cycle*, R. M. Smith (ed.) (Cambridge, 1984), pp. 123–43; T. Wales, "Poverty, poor relief and the life-cycle: some evidence from seventeenth-century Norfolk", *ibid.*, pp. 351–404.

33. J. Walter & R. Schofield, "Famine, disease and crisis mortality in early modern society", in *Famine, disease and the social order in early modern society*, J. Walter & R. Schofield (eds) (Cambridge, 1989), pp. 68–9.

34. A. De Swaan, *In care of the state: heatlh care, education and welfare in Europe and the USA in the modern era.* (Oxford, 1988), pp. 13–51.

35. E. M. Leonard, *The early history of English poor relief* (Cambridge, 1900), pp. 133–4.

36. D. Thomson, "'I am not my father's keeper': families and the elderly in nineteenth-century England", *Law and History Review* **2**, 1984, pp. 265–6.

37. The best, and highly original, study is M. Barker-Read, *The treatment of the aged poor in five selected West Kent parishes from Settlement to Speenhamland (1662–1797).*

(PhD thesis, Open University, 1988).

38. *Ibid.*; S. Williams, *Medical care and demographic context in East Bedfordshire in the late eighteenth century.* (MSc thesis, University of Oxford, 1994); S. R. Ottaway "Age and want in eighteenth-century Essex", unpublished paper (Friends of Historic Essex Annual General Meeting, 22 July 1995).

39. A. Wear, "Caring for the sick poor in St Bartholomew's Exchange, 1580–1676", *Medical History*, Supplement No. 11, 1991, pp. 41–60.

40. For an article which conveniently summarizes his key findings and arguments, see D. Thomson, "The welfare of the elderly in the past: a family or community responsibility?", in *Life, death and the elderly*, Pelling & Smith (eds), pp. 194–221. For criticisms of Thomson's views see E. H. Hunt, "Paupers and pensioners. Past and present", *Ageing and Society* **9**, 1989, pp. 407–30.

41. For a useful discussion of Booth's survey see R. Wall, "Relations between the generations in British families past and present", in *Families and households: divisions and change*, C. Marsh & S. Arber (eds) (Basingstoke, 1992), pp. 79–83.

42. Thomson, " 'I am not my father's keeper' "; J. Quadagno, *Aging in early industrial society. Work, family and social policy in nineteenth-century England* (New York, 1982).

43. The following discussion is a greatly abbreviated version of a fuller report of this research in "Ageing and well-being in early modern England: pension trends and gender preferences under the English old poor law *c.*1650–1800", paper prepared for the session on "Old Age and Ageing" at the 18th International Congress of Historical Sciences, Montreal, 28 August 1995.

44. The relevant evidence is to be found in E. A. Wrigley & R. S. Schofield, *The population history of England 1541–1871: a reconstruction* (London, 1981), pp. 215–19.

45. Slack, *Poverty and policy in Tudor and Stuart England*, pp. 190–92.

46. R. M. Smith, "Les influences exogènes sur le 'frein préventif' en Angleterre 1600–1750", in *Modèles de démographie historique*, A. Blum, N. Bonneuil, D. Blanchet (eds) (Paris, 1992), pp. 173–91

47. See Slack, *The English poor law 1531–1782*, pp. 53–6.

48. Sir F. M. Eden, *The state of the poor*, vol. 3 (London, 1797), pp. 693–6.

49. T. Sokoll, "The household position of elderly widows in poverty. Evidence from two Essex communities in the late eighteenth century", in *Poor women and children in the European past*, J. Henderson & R. Wall (eds) (London, 1994), pp. 207–24; T. Sokoll, "The pauper household. Small and simple? The evidence from listings of inhabitants and pauper lists of early modern England reassessed", *Ethnologia Europaea* **17**, 1987, pp. 25–42.

50. William Otter, "Memoir of Robert Malthus" (published with posthumous 2nd edn of Malthus's *Principles of political economy* (London, 1816), pp. xxi–xxii.

51. A. Sen, *Inequality reexamined* (Oxford, 1992), pp. 39–53.

52. Hunt, "Paupers and pensioners", pp. 421–3.

53. Barker-Read, *The treatment of the aged poor*, pp. 66–7.

54. Smith, "Ageing and well-being in early modern England".

55. *Ibid.*

56. A. Digby, *British welfare policy: workhouse to workfare* (London, 1989), p. 127.

57. J. Finch, *Family obligations and social change* (Oxford, 1989), p. 75.
58. For fuller discussions of these issues see Anderson, "The impact on the family relationships of the elderly" and Finch, *Family obligations*, especially pp. 75–85. See too, E. Roberts, *A woman's place: an oral history of working class women 1890–1940* (Oxford, 1984), pp.178–82.

3

Some recent trends in the history of charity

Colin Jones

An enormous volume of historical writing in recent decades has revitalized the study of the history of charity, a field for long dominated by dewy-eyed sentimentalism, Whiggish certitudes and time-worn antiquarianism. The consequence has been a thickening of the historiographical undergrowth in just about every aspect of the topic and every major period from antiquity to the present; a greater comparativist awareness of spatial difference as, for example, the history of English charity is rethought against Continental example, and indeed against the broader ethnological record; a greater sophistication in the thematics of the field, as charity is inserted within a web of related concepts and practices ranging from poor relief to social control; a greater diversity in frameworks of analysis, from the finely focused microstudy through to broad-brushed comparativist approaches; and a wider range of focus, from the poor and sick for example through to a range of charitable donors and/or "professionals".[1]

One of the consequences of this innovatory, revivifying literature – which is well represented in the present collection – has been the highlighting of the deficiencies of the established paradigms within which historians have tended to confine the history of charity. The frameworks of analysis most in use have generally been strongly bipolarized – a point fully in keeping with the tendency of the historiography to dichotomize the charitable encounter between charitable donor (whether a philanthropic individual or the state) and the recipient. Just as the latter has been conventionally placed in stark relief against his or her benefactor, so (usually private) charity has been opposed (normally public) social welfare, (usually

51

informal) voluntarism to (more formal) systems of obligation and compulsion; local to central (or core to periphery); individualist to collectivist, and so on. A further, striking feature of the existing literature has been the tendency to situate those polarities sequentially along a chronological axis: thus, for example, the formulae "from charity to welfare", "from kinship to poor laws", "from informality to formalism", or "from private giving to state provision". A perceptible advantage of this kind of trajectory has been its relatively snug fit with over-arching modernization theory. The assumption has tended to be that all societies on the road to modernity, although following somewhat diverse routes, have generally reached the same goal, the modern welfare system.[2]

All these bipolarities, and the teleological trajectory invariably underpinning them, have been subjected either to heavy nuancing or else to outright rejection by recent studies. Perhaps the most spectacular victim of revisionist scholarship in this domain has been the demise of the grand narrative which seemed to lead all "modernizing" societies out of a regime characterized by the dominance of private charity and in the direction of a welfare state. In the 1960s, it might have been possible to imagine the potential universality of that *telos*. By the late 1980s and early 1990s, after the experience of the Reagan and Thatcher years, it was no longer possible so to do. The attack on the politics of what came to be christened "welfarism" seemed designed to suggest that far from being a universal *telos* for developing societies, the welfare state was a historical aberration. While we may safely reject such politically- and ideologically-driven views, they did have the incidental merit of beckoning historians towards fashioning accounts of the welfare state in particular, and charity, welfare and poor relief in general, which are, in comparison with those of an earlier generation, deteleologized, and which view the emergence and history of welfare states as a compelling historical option rather than as a blank inevitability. A more historically cogent and convincing history of charity and welfare is emerging from these bleak times. In this respect, some might argue, western society's loss has been the historian's gain.[3]

One feature of this work of revision has been the re-examination – and, largely, the revalorization – of charity in all past societies, as well as in the present. The significance and extent of private philanthropy in the nineteenth and twentieth centuries have been abruptly and upwardly revised.[4] For earlier periods, it is recognized *a fortiori* that the volume of private, informal giving probably was exceeded by the sum transferred through poor-relief schemes only in the most exceptional circumstances.[5] This has helped to undermine one of the most enduring themes in the history of charity in the early modern period, namely, the contrast between a "backward" Catholicism which held on to allegedly indiscriminate private giving, as against a Protestantism devoted to "forward-looking" poor-relief schemes which restrained or canalized private giving towards the "deserving" poor. The scholarship of a generation of French historians, working within the framework of a retrospective religious sociology sketched out by Gabriel Le Bras and carried further by Jean Delumeau, has placed an enormous question-mark against this dichotomized reading of early modern religion, and the charity which flowed from it.[6] The element of moral and spiritual compulsion to giving in post-Tridentine Catholicism formed a kind of "charitable imperative" acting on the wealthy which proved far from undiscriminating and followed lines of force in regard to desert and entitlement recognizably similar to those of Protestant Europe.[7] Divergence between Protestant and Catholic is probably less important a factor of differentiation than the varying levels of provision in town and country.[8] The scale of state involvement in Catholic Europe in poor-relief organization has also been reassessed.[9]

As this example shows, if changes within the broader political canvas of the 1980s and 1990s have impelled historians towards more nuanced, deteleologized accounts of charity, local changes in fashion within the historical profession have also had an important effect on the general tenor on writing in this domain. A major impetus behind research on the history of charity from the 1960s onwards, to take a further example, was the boom in social history, and in particular the concern to provide accounts of historical change which were not simply seen from the "top-down" vantage point of the social or political elite. The mushrooming of studies in the history of poverty and marginality – in the heroic age of "history from below", historical demography and analyses of social structure – is testimony to this generous and highly illuminating impulse of historical scholarship.[10] A single, if compelling example here is the work of the Cambridge Group for the History of Population and Social Structure, most notably perhaps Peter Laslett's iconoclastic studies of household and family.[11] By prioritizing census listings over other forms of evidence adjudged "literary", "qualitative" or "anecdotal", Laslett was able to draw the conclusion that household size was far smaller than earlier studies had suggested. This seemingly gave the lie to hallowed assumptions that families had shifted from extended to nuclear form and that early modern Britain had passed through a process leading "from kinship to poor laws". Laslett's careful morphological analysis revised one of the main terms, the family, in which the history of charity and poor relief had been written. His, and his Cambridge colleagues' emphasis on the vagaries of the family life-cycle offered a new way of approaching questions relating to the scale and outcomes of poor relief programmes and patterns of charitable benefaction.[12]

Laslett's initial assumption has been subject to considerable revisions since it was originally formulated.[13] Perhaps more revealing than the substance of those revisions – which do not in any case damage the thesis that the size and character of family and kin play a major role in the economy of the poor and the demand for surplus resources – is the changing tenor of debate around such questions in the 1990s, and in particular the growing influence of cultural approaches in questioning social-structural modes of historical argument. A fine recent article by Marco van Leeuwen, on the "logic of charity", in which the author sketches out a model for the functioning of poor relief in pre-industrial Europe, provides a helpful reference point here.[14] Though, like earlier such accounts, it is concerned to factor in both the societal context and the general effects of poor relief, what is impressive about the model proposed is the way in which, drawing on recent scholarship, van Leeuwen goes beyond purely social-structural accounts, and sketches in what he calls an "interaction system of poor relief", setting the charitable encounter in terms of "actors with interests" and "alternative ways to act". The charitable gesture is viewed moreover as the interaction between two actors, each with a range of choices before them. The inclusion of the poor as historical makers of their own fate needs to be stressed, for a good deal of earlier analysis made them the either deferential and/or subversive, but invariably pretty faceless, objects of charitable activity. Social historians working in the "history from below" and family life-cycle vein have however accustomed us to seeing poverty in terms of a variety of responses, each of which constituted a different survival option. Olwen Hufton's work on eighteenth-century France has been important here too in stressing the "economy of makeshifts" of the poor. On a related tack, Ellen Ross's fine studies of late nineteenth-century London have been important in highlighting the strategic uses of charity by the poor.[15] Such work also exemplifies historians' greater awareness of the role of gender in shaping popular responses to charitable action.

If we now have "faces in the crowd" – female as well as male – among the recipients of charity and can better appreciate the range of factors in their situation and motivation, the same is starting to be true too of charitable donors. Van Leeuwen's account is helpful here again in highlighting the role of individuals within the elite as historical actors. Much analysis of charity and poor law in the past had been essentially conceived of as demand-driven in an extraordinarily behaviouristic fashion: rises in levels of poverty, it was implied, triggered charitable, welfare and/or repressive action from the – again rather faceless – social elite. As, however, Sandra Cavallo has shown, in a path-breaking article on charity and welfare in early modern Turin,[16] changes in charitable approach and rises in levels of poor-relief funding may well be determined as much by shifts within the elite as by increases in aggregate levels of poverty (assuming the latter can be effectively calibrated). Under this prism, the elite becomes more of a disaggregated grouping, rather than the somewhat homogeneous unit, equipped with social-control objectives, who inhabited many earlier accounts. For Cavallo, a change in the direction of charitable policy may flow not from a rise in the demand for relief, but rather from factors such as the symbolic raising of an elite grouping's social status, the creation of new patronage networks or the shaping of power to serve its own material, moral and political interests. Bonnie Smith's well-known work *Ladies of the leisure class* in late nineteenth-century France could be read as a gendered gloss on this important avenue of enquiry.[17]

Conceiving of the history of charity and welfare as "supply-" as much as "demand-"side topics rescues it from being the sole province of the "history from below" approach, with its perennial tendency to minimize division within the social elite. The approach makes it an arena in which involvement, agency and intersubjectivity can be mapped more convincingly. To put it in van Leeuwen's terms, elites – or, better, elite groupings – driven by a variety of motives (he lists stabilizing social order, regulating the labour market, civilizing the poor, the advancement of their own status, etc.), may choose from an array of alternative control strategies (dispensing poor relief, food subsidies, police action, increasing wages, etc.), which themselves may conflict or mesh with the survival strategies of the poor.[18] In these terms, charity becomes, first, contextualized within a much broader and more dynamic range of purposive social activity and, secondly, it constitutes very much a two-way street, involving advantages and disadvantages on both sides of the charitable equation.

Van Leeuwen is, I would argue, attuned to the times in offering a more pluralistic and dynamic reading of the charitable encounter than has been conventional in a domain long dominated by binary, dichotomized approaches. Yet other factors need also to be taken into account. A diffuse disenchantment with tightly focused social-structural explanations for historical change – initially logged by Lawrence Stone in his pioneering article "The revival of narrative" – has swollen, under the pressure of a postmodernist critique of the teleological assumptions about social development implicit in much post-1960s social history, into what some have diagnosed as "the end of social history".[19] The latter view will probably not be shared by a majority of the historical profession in Great Britain (who seem pretty resistant also to the idea of wallowing around in the ambient ooze of postmodernity),[20] and much of the most illuminating work on the subject has been, and continues to be, done by social historians. Yet the intellectual context in which they are now operating has changed – and shows it. The demise of grand narratives has been concomitant with the rise of a methodological pluralism which leaves open more room for cultural elements. Indeed, when we look at van Leeuwen's account, it is noticeable how much about the history of poor relief in early modern Europe now seems to be ascribed to the variety of choices available to both the poor and the elite. The history of charity, it would appear, opens less on to social than to a more broadly conceived cultural terrain. The target is less to map out tensions and conflicts than to investigate the diversity of cultural meanings for all protagonists involved in the charitable act.

In his study of household size, it will be recalled, Peter Laslett insisted on the clear distinction between "scientific", quantitative data such as census listings on one hand and putatively "anecdotal", "literary" evidence on the other. Illuminatingly, such a hard-and-fast dichotomy no longer commands respect: the field is now full of scholars, often generally lacking confidence in quantification and the arithmetical calibration of social phenomena, and mixing and matching across the binary Laslettian divide.[21] It is as though a move has taken place from hard-nosed analysis of social morphology towards a "neo-anecdotalism", invariably informed by the insights of cultural anthropology and occasionally decked out in the colours of literary theory. The abandonment of grand narratives has led to a quest for generalizable micronarratives based on the microstudy.[22]

One of the main frameworks for the microstudy in the field of charity and welfare has been the community. For early modern England, this had tended to mean, more specifically, the parish community, in which operated that "intimacy at a distance" discussed by Pat Thane.[23] Though utterly comprehensible and logical to most English historians, given the parishional cadre within which England's poor laws operated, the choice is based more on institutional fiat than on cultural meanings of community to which parishioners may have subscribed. The parish appears a less unproblematic unit of analysis, moreover, if we cross the Channel. In continental Europe a good deal of charitable and poor relief activity was framed within different sites which seemingly achieved a similar kind of "intimacy at a distance" – the township, for example, the *seigneurie* or (in Catholic Europe) the religious confraternity. Brian Pullan has, for example, highlighted the significance of the latter as a pre-eminent framework for charity in early modern Italy, and the model can safely be applied to much of Catholic Europe.[24] When put under the microscope, the confraternity reveals no determinate geo-specific location: parishional confraternities jostle alongside urban, and even regional or national examples.

It seems important, then, not to take the form of community as an institutional or social given, but to examine the manifold ways in which community identity – and identification – were secured. "Community" is in some senses an elective, even an "imagined" concept – although who, in respect to charity, was doing the electing and the imagining (the poor themselves, the rich, central government, etc.), by what processes and in what contexts, varies. As, of course, does who is excluded, how and why, and questions relating to the policing of the boundaries of community.[25] The cultural contextualization of the charitable act thus entails the extension of the field of enquiry into the broader field of patterns of inclusivity and reciprocity within a given community. As Brian Pullan suggests,[26] for example, the burial service at local level was one of the most valued charitable services afforded to the poorer members of confraternities, and the latter were frequently regarded as also containing the souls of the dead departed. The distance from this world to the next evidently did not exclude some form of intimacy. Catholic theology in the early modern (as medieval) period placed great store by the spiritual utility of the pauper who, by inciting the wealthy to charitable acts, helped work towards the latter's salvation. If the arrows of social obligation pointed one way, in other words, the direction of spiritual obligation pointed the other. Such examples highlight the importance of placing the material specificity of charitable giving in the broadest of frameworks: charity might be accorded the poor in cash or in kind, but it might too be in non-material forms of service – spiritual, emotional, educational or whatever – as well as in material guise. And there could be material or symbolic returns on charitable donation. It thus seems helpful to let charity loose from the economistic and geo-specific confines in which historians of parishional poor relief have sometimes been content to leave it.

Placing the history of charity within broader patterns of reciprocity also has the signal advantage of fruitfully complicating the donor/recipient dyad around which so much work on the history of charity has been constructed. The time-honoured assumption that donors are from within the elite and their recipients situated at the base of the social pyramid consigns the middling sort, who could be at once recipients and donors, to a charitable limbo. It also does not in fact bear scrutiny in the light of much recent work. As Frank Prochaska has pointed out, for example, the bulk of philanthropic giving in modern Britain has been by the working class for the working class, and sprang from a mixture of motives (humanitarian, religious, family, etc.), which transcended the wish for social control.[27] Similarly, the confraternity – pre-eminent organ of early modern Catholic charity, as we have seen – was a cross-class body, and the services it performed were as much about mutuality between spiritual equals as about an act of control between economic superiors and inferiors. This is not to deny of course that the rich gave to the poor – nor even that this was not infrequently as part of a wish for social control, as van Leeuwen points out.[28] Rather, it is merely to suggest that a good many other things could also be going on in the charitable act.

To binarize the charitable act as occurring between the rich and the poor is not only to dichotomize social structure so as effectively to exclude from consideration the middling classes. It is also to lose from view the middling groupings actually involved in the organization and conduct of charitable activity. The latter groupings are particularly important, for example, in any analysis of late twentieth-century charity, with its managers of welfare funds, hospital trustees, charitable marketing agencies, retail outlets and so on. Such "cultural intermediaries" were also, however, present in early modern Europe, and need to be factored in to any plausible model of charity.

Much of my own work on the history of charity in early modern France, for example, has focused on the female religious community, the Daughters of Charity (*Filles de la Charité*), which was founded in 1633 by St Vincent de Paul and St Louise de Marillac.[29] Like others of the new kind of religious community to evolve in the seventeenth century, the Daughters of Charity were committed to charitable, educational and spiritual services beyond the cloister and "in the world", and were organized within the framework – again – of a confraternity. The Daughter of Charity was both charitable donor and recipient – and in the spiritual as well as the material register. A wealthy seigneur or philanthropically-minded township which employed such women to care for local paupers could be seen as wishing to secure their own, and their class's, social and political status as well as, through this good work, their own salvation. Like a number of other similar communities, moreover, the Daughters of Charity were essentially recruited from the poor themselves – their founders conceptualized the community as being composed of sturdy young peasant women able to take with equanimity the sheer slog of aiding the sick poor. Belonging to such a highly patronized and largely autonomous organization could allow women from humble backgrounds a means of achieving some measure of power within the localities where they worked and within the organization itself. Yet the possibility of achieving sanctity and working towards their own salvation within a regulated community by performing an *imitatio Christi* in the service of the poor was not the least advantage they derived from confraternity membership. Recipients of spiritual as well as material benefits, the Daughters of Charity were also charitable donors – again of spiritual as well as material goods – to the poor in their care. Cultural hybrids, then, such women defy any simplistic dyadic or economistic reading of the charity which they both embodied and dispensed.

In these remarks, I have endeavoured to describe some of the ways in which the dichotomized manner in which the history of charity has been told in the past seems to be falling apart in the hands of social and cultural historians. I have also tried to subvert perhaps the last and most enduring bipolarity to hold the field in the history of charity and poor relief – that between the charitable donor and the recipient. It is, finally, worth registering the growing importance of a further influence working to undermine traditional certainties in this domain, namely, the work of sociologists of power, to which we can append the historical *oeuvre* of Michel Foucault.[30] The latter's history of insanity in the "classical age" (the seventeenth and eighteenth centuries) and his work on the origins of the prison have important ramifications for the history of social control and, thereby, for the history of charity.[31] If historians have tended to be on the whole rather resistant to Foucault's empirical research, he none the less poses important questions about the nature of power which in important respects overlap with current work on the sociology of power. *Discipline and punish* is often viewed as an exemplar of a kind of anti-Whig history, preaching that far from the chronicle of humanity's improvement, the last centuries have witnessed a steady deterioration at the hands of bourgeois society. This is singularly to misrepresent the complexity of Foucault's thought and the importance of his message for the way in which historians think about power. In particular, Foucault attempts to propose a "de-centred" (as well as deteleologized) account of the workings of power. For Foucault, the latter was not located with one social grouping, and therefore available for expropriation by another. Rather, power is located diffusely within society, and the apparent holders of power are themselves enmeshed in webs of power which largely transcend them. Even if historians resist the "Foucault effect", there seems no denying the importance of the issues he raises. Innovatory scholarship on the nature and operations of power can thus be expected to take further the undermining of the dichotomized categories in which the history of charity has been written in which historians have latterly been assiduously engaged.

Notes

1. Although in the present chapter I shall be drawing mostly on detailed examples from my own area of research expertise, early modern Europe (in particular France), the general points hold, I believe, more widely. For a survey of the early modern (and medieval) field which highlights forms of charity relating to ill-health, see my "Charity (before *c.*1850)" in *Companion encyclopaedia of the history of medicine*, W. F. Bynum & R. Porter (eds) [2 vols.], II (London, 1993), pp. 1469–79. For the more modern period, again with a medical slant, see *ibid.*: W. F. Bynum, "Medical philanthropy after 1850", pp. 1486–94.

2. The best such histories, stressing diversity in welfare experience, are P. Baldwin, *The politics of social solidarity: class bases of the European welfare states, 1875–1975* (London, 1990); and A. de Swaan, *In care of the state: health care, education and welfare in Europe and the USA in the modern era* (Oxford, 1988).

3. Cf. Jonathan Barry's sagacious comments on this in "Introduction" in *Medicine and charity before the welfare state*, J. Barry & C. Jones (eds) (London, 1991), pp. 1–13. For how this is affecting the analysis of contemporary welfare systems, see especially H. Glennister & J. Midgley, *The radical right and the welfare state: an international assessment* (London, 1991); P. Taylor-Gooby, *Social change, social welfare and social science* (London, 1991); and C. Jones (ed.), *New perspectives on the welfare state in Europe* (London, 1993).

4. For a well-documented historical account, see for example F. Prochaska, *The voluntary impulse: philanthropy in modern Britain* (London, 1988).

5. It is Paul Slack's view that this extraordinary circumstance was in fact attained under the English poor laws by 1700: P. Slack, *The English poor law, 1531–1782* (London, 1990), p. 172. R. Jütte, *Poverty and deviance in early modern Europe* (Cambridge, 1994) provides a brisk and helpful recent overview of the European field.

6. The most characteristic and comprehensive exemplar of this approach is J. Delumeau, *Catholicism from Luther to Voltaire* (New York, 1977), although see too

its untranslated companion volume, *Naissance et affirmation de la Réforme*, 2nd edn (Paris, 1973). B. S. Pullan, "Catholics and the poor in early modern Europe", *Transactions of the Royal Historical Society*, 5th series, **26**, 1976, pp. 15–34, provides an extremely compelling account of this shift in the historiography, as it relates to poor relief throughout Europe.

7. On this theme, see esp. C. Jones, *The charitable imperative: hospitals and nursing in early modern and revolutionary France* (London, 1989).

8. Cf. Slack, *The English poor law*, p. 11. On the urban-rural discontinuum, see D. Hickey, *Resistance to reforms: Crown attempts to close local hospitals in France, 1530–1789* (Montreal, forthcoming).

9. This has often been done in the context of the (in fact heavily criticized) theses of Michel Foucault on the so-called "great confinement of the poor": see his *Folie et déraison. Histoire de la folie à l'âge classique* (Paris, 1961). Cf. N. Finzsch & R. Jütte (eds), *The prerogative of confinement: social, cultural and administrative aspects of the history of hospitals and carceral institutions in Western Europe and North America, 1500–1900* (Cambridge, forthcoming).

10. See Jütte, *Poverty and deviance*, for an excellent overview, and, more broadly, J. Sharpe, "History from below", in *New perspectives on historical writing*, P. Burke (ed.) (London, 1991), pp. 24–41.

11. See e.g. P. Laslett, *The world we have lost – further explored* (London, 1971); P. Laslett (ed.), *Household and family in past time: comparative studies in the size and structure of the domestic group over the last three centuries* (Cambridge, 1972); R. Wall, J. Wall, P. Laslett (eds), *Family forms in historic Europe* (Cambridge, 1983); R. Smith (ed.), *Land, kinship and life-cycle* (Cambridge, 1984).

12. For links between poverty and family structures, the work of Stuart J. Woolf is especially helpful: see S. J. Woolf, *The poor in Western Europe in the eighteenth and nineteenth centuries* (London, 1986); and S. J. Woolf (ed.), *Domestic strategies: work and family in France and Italy (seventeenth and eighteenth centuries),* (Cambridge, 1991). See too the still helpful overview in M. Anderson, *Approaches to the history of the western family, 1500–1900* (London, 1980).

13. The revisions come from Laslett and his colleagues as well as from the outside. For a recent update on the state of the question, with an eastern European orientation, see C. Wetherell, A. Plakans & B. Wellman, "Social networks, kinship and community in Eastern Europe", *Journal of Interdisciplinary History* **24**, 1994, especially pp. 639–45.

14. Marco H. D. van Leeuwen, "Logic of charity: poor relief in preindustrial Europe", *Journal of Interdisciplinary History* **24**, 1994, pp. 589–613.

15. O. Hufton, *The poor of eighteenth-century France, 1750–89* (Oxford, 1974); E. Ross, "Survival networks: women's neighbourhood sharing in London before World War One", *History Workshop* **15**, 1983, pp. 4–27. This theme is also followed up in P. Mandler (ed.) *The uses of charity. The poor on relief in the nineteenth-century metropolis* (Philadelphia, 1990) – a collection to which Ross contributes.

16. S. Cavallo, "The motivations of benefactors: an overview of approaches to the study of charity", in *Medicine and charity* Barry & Jones (eds), pp. 46–62. See now

Cavallo, *Systems of charity in Turin, 1541–1789* (Cambridge, 1994).

17. B. S. Smith, *Ladies of the leisure class: the bourgeoises of northern France in the nineteenth century* (London, 1991).

18. See esp. van Leeuwen, "Logic of charity", p. 612, for a graphical representation of this model.

19. L. Stone, "The revival of narrative: reflections on a new old history", in L. Stone, *The past and the present revisited* (revised edn, London, 1987), of an article which appeared in the journal *Past and Present* in 1979. See too P. Joyce, "The end of social history?", *Social History* **20**, 1995, pp. 73–91. The views of J. C. D. Clark – like Patrick Joyce a true provocateur (though hardly a postmodernist one) – on the "Class of '68" are spasmodically illuminating in this regard too: see his *Revolution and rebellion: state and society in England in the seventeenth and eighteenth century* (London, 1986).

20. To judge, for example by some of the interventions on the future of social history to which Patrick Joyce's article (noted above) contributes. For references, see Joyce, "The end of social history?", p. 74nn).

21. Although I am using Laslett's influential work as symptomatic of more general trends, I am not attacking his positive contribution to social and cultural history, which is massive.

22. See for example the articles in L. Hunt (ed.), *The new cultural history* (Berkeley, California, 1988). Anthropological analysis on the gift is fruitfully utilized for the history of charity and poor relief in G. Stedman Jones, *Outcast London: a study in the relationship between classes in Victorian society* (Oxford, 1976); and R. Porter, "The gift relation: philanthropy and provincial hospitals in eighteenth-century England", in *The hospital in history*, L. Granshaw & R. Porter (eds) (London, 1989).

23. See Pullan in this volume.

24. See Pullan, "Catholics and the poor"; Pullan, "The old Catholicism, the new Catholicism and the poor", *Timore e carità: I Poveri nell'Italia moderna* (Cremona, 1982); and his contribution to this volume. On the confraternity more generally as a charitable form: G. Lebras, *Etudes d'histoire de droit canonique* [2 vols.] (Paris, 1973); L. Chatellier, *The Europe of the devout: the Catholic Reformation and the formation of a new society* (Cambridge, 1989); M. Agulhon, *Pénitents et franc-maçons dans l'ancienne Provence* (Paris, 1968). For the town as the arena of charitable activity, see for example K. Norberg, *Rich and poor in Grenoble, 1600–1814* (Berkeley, California, 1985); M. Dinges, *Stadtarmut in Bordeaux, 1525–1675: Alltag – Politik – Mentalitaten* (Bonn, 1988); J. Soubeyroux, *Paupérisme et rapports sociaux à Madrid au XVIIIe siècle* (Paris, 1978); and M. Lindemann, *Patriots and paupers: Hamburg, 1712–1830* (Oxford, 1990).

25. I am, of course, only suggesting for the parish community the same spirit of enquiry which Benedict Anderson brought to the nation-state in his *Imagined communities: reflections on the origin and the spread of nationalism* (London, 1983).

26. See Pullan in this volume.

27. Prochaska, *The voluntary impulse*.

28. Van Leeuwen, "Logic of charity", bases his model for understanding the rationale of charitable giving on the assumption that the poor were driven by the need for biological survival, the rich by the wish for social control. This limits the broader applicability of what remains, however, a very helpful essay.

29. Jones, *The charitable imperative*, especially chs 3–5.

30. C. Jones & R. Porter (eds), *Reassessing Foucault: power, medicine and the body* (London, 1993).

31. See M. Foucault, *Folie et déraison* (which was published in English translation in an abridged version as *Madness and civilization: a history of insanity in the age of reason* (New York, 1965); and M. Foucault, *Surveiller et punir* (Paris, 1973) – translated as *Discipline and punish: the birth of the prison* (London, 1979). It should be noted that a good deal of the flak which Foucault's work on insanity has attracted from historians has been based on a reading of only the English translation of *Folie et déraison*.

4

Charity and poor relief
in early modern Italy
Brian Pullan

In his excellent account of English poor relief, Paul Slack identified the three pillars of the developing system, about 1600, as the punishment of vagrancy, the provision of work and the introduction of poor rates levied by parishes employed by parliament as instruments of central government. Use of the parish as a unit of secular administration and a counterweight to an excessively centralized regime, made possible the operation of a remarkably uniform and effective system, which extended across a whole country.[1] "Only in England," writes Marjorie McIntosh, "were rates imposed in local communities of all sizes within a national system of poor relief backed by the central government."[2] Wilbur K. Jordan, in his eulogistic studies of private philanthropy in England, once attempted to displace the parish rates from their central position, and to argue that they were invoked only when the charity of individuals had failed.[3] Now, however, they seem firmly restored to their throne, with usurpers and pretenders put to flight; parish rates, it appears, were grossly underestimated in Jordan's flagship volume of 1959, and the contributions of testators greatly overvalued, their aspirations being confused with their achievements.[4] Some critics, John Walter among them, have warned trenchantly against a "teleological obsession with the development of administrative schemes" and premature suppositions that charity and informal poor relief had been replaced, as early as the 1590s, by parish rates.[5] Rates alone, it is conceded, could not cope with major crises. But seldom are attempts made to deny the importance, even the uniqueness, of a national system based on legally enforceable obligations as well as on moral imperatives to contribute to poor relief.

Students of most Continental countries, of both Protestant and Catholic Europe, will be familiar with Slack's first two items. Continental societies likewise threatened vagrants and unlicensed beggars with flogging and imprisonment. They too attempted to repel or expel these intruders and undesirables from the cities and return them forcibly to their places of origin, though usually without ensuring that their native towns or villages would do much to provide for them. They too, at least from the 1520s onwards, believed that the remedy for poverty and idleness lay in the provision of work – whether by apprenticing poor children and youths to craftsmen, sending them to sea, establishing public works and building programmes in times of crisis, or setting up workshops in beggars' hospitals and founding houses of correction for juveniles.[6] However, Continental arrangements for the poor were seldom based on the practice of regularly taxing local communities for the benefit of their poorer members, even where there appeared to be authority to do so. Luther's Leisnig Ordinance of 1523 had proposed levying a rate on all members of the community if the charitable endowments flowing into the Common Chest proved insufficient to support the local poor, but the suggestion was not widely taken up.[7] Bearing these points in mind, this chapter seeks to offer a broad account of poor relief in Italian states between the fifteenth and the eighteenth centuries and in doing so to address, albeit sketchily, three related questions. These are: whatever happened to the parish, whatever happened to the rates, and whatever happened outside the cities which contained the large charities characteristic of a highly urbanized society?

Discussion may be helped by making one or two points about the nature of poverty and charity as they were conceived in Italy. Here there was a hierarchy of poverty that reflected the ladder of status in the world at large. For the poor were not a social class or a uniform mass, but a pool formed partly by people descending from various social levels and retaining, when they did so, something of their previous social identity. There was a cleft between the public poor, who would openly seek alms or at least accept them at public distributions, and the "shamefaced" poor, who had to be sought out in their homes, treated with discretion, and even provided with separate wards in hospitals. This was reflected, for example, in the institutional structure of charity in eighteenth-century Bologna, which gave prominence to the two contrasting organizations of the Opera dei Mendicanti and the Opera dei Vergognosi.[8] The Mendicanti, the destitute poor who knew no shame, were threatened with starvation; the

Vergognosi, or shamefaced, poor were faced, not with loss of life, but rather with loss of honour or respect if their inability to live as their rank demanded became known. Definitions of the genteel or shamefaced poor varied with time and place; sometimes the name was confined to persons of noble birth or at least of civil condition, and sometimes it was extended to include respectable artisans who had fallen on hard times, the approximate equivalent of decayed householders in England or *Haussarme* in Germany.[9] There was, perhaps, always a tendency to apply disproportionately large sums to the relief of the shamefaced poor, if only out of a desire to preserve the existing social order, and hence to concentrate a large proportion of institutional and personal charity upon a relatively small group of supposedly deserving persons. The genteel poor are seldom conspicuous in accounts of English poor relief, but one can never fail to notice the efforts made on their behalf in Italy.

If this simple division into two categories seems unduly crude, it can be extended into four. First were the shamefaced poor, as above; secondly, the ordinary labouring folk who had no reserves or savings and lived from day to day by the work of their hands; thirdly, the "poor of Christ", who were either the patient victims of misfortune who had suffered disease, disability or accident, or persons who had in some sense chosen poverty and insecurity, by going on pilgrimages or vowing themselves to the religious life; fourthly and lastly, the outcast poor, the feckless, habitual sinners in need of redemption, such as vagrants and common prostitutes.[10] Voluntary poverty, the poverty of some of the "poor of Christ", was seldom if ever recognized as virtuous in Protestant Europe, where it savoured of attempts to earn salvation by good works. For Protestants the pilgrimage had become a spiritual journey rather than a physical expedition, undertaken alone or in company, to Rome or Loreto or Compostella or some more local shrine.

Poor relief in Italy, as in other parts of Europe, was powerfully influenced by the religious virtues of charity and mercy, although at least one humanist in the fifteenth century promoted the idea of something rather different – of a liberality or beneficence which would not be rewarded by God, but only by the gratitude of the recipient.[11] Charity was an all-permeating attitude, indeed a way of life with "two principal branches, that is, the love of God and one's neighbour, on which all the law and perfection of a Christian depend".[12] Vital to the cohesion of the social order, it was essential to rectifying, not only inequalities of material possessions, but also inequalities of talent or skill.[13] Works of mercy, springing from charity, could more easily be codified and enumerated. Fundamental were the six urgent works of corporal mercy to the living poor, including the visiting of prisoners, which were listed in the vision of the Last Judgement in St Matthew's Gospel.[14] Added to these, by the time of St Thomas Aquinas, was a seventh work of slightly smaller significance, the burial of the dead.[15] An eighth, the dowering of poor maids, was appended in the fourteenth century, although, popular as it became, this work was never recognized as part of the traditional canon. Perhaps seeking to create a memorial for themselves by changing the lives of their beneficiaries, rather than dispensing small sums of money that would be quickly consumed and leave no mark, testators and donors began to devote relatively large sums of money, measured in florins or ducats rather than in pence, to enabling poor girls of good reputation to marry or (more rarely) to enter convents.[16]

Beyond the works of corporal mercy, however, lay seven other works of spiritual mercy, which were also manifestations of charity, equally likely to be practised by devout individuals or organizations engaged in a search for religious merit. In a sense mercy towards the soul ranked higher than mercy towards the body, and that point was frequently made in the rules of sixteenth-century organizations concerned with the teaching of Christian doctrine or the reclamation of sinners. As listed in Cardinal Bellarmine's seventeenth-century catechism, much used by the schools of Christian doctrine for children and other ignorant persons, the seven works of spiritual mercy were

1. To give counsaile to the dout full.
2. To instruct the ignorant.
3. To admonish sinners.
4. To comfort the afflicted.
5. To pardon offences.
6. To patientllie support those that be troublesome.
7. To pray God for the quicke and dead.[17]

Few of these activities involved material or monetary transactions, but they were essential to many schemes of charity, especially those followed by religious brotherhoods, most of which moved easily – at least in theory – between the spiritual and the corporal forms of mercy. Much charity and mercy were directed towards the dead: not only towards providing a decent, well-attended funeral and a quiet grave, not only towards the counselling of *agonizzanti* on the point of death, but also towards easing the suffering of souls in purgatory. In the seventeenth and eighteenth centuries this form of charity was as popular as ever, and it was common for religious brotherhoods to establish Monti dei Morti or Death Funds. Premiums would be paid by subscribers, and mature in the form of a lump sum which would finance the recitation of masses – often several hundred – for the repose of their souls after death.[18] When Muratori argued, in a famous treatise on charity published in the 1720s, that charity should focus on the living poor rather than the dead, and that the dead could best be helped by giving alms on their behalf, his trenchant arguments incurred the wrath of more conventional churchmen.[19] One of the characteristics of charity and poor relief in Protestant countries was their greater tendency to concentrate upon the living poor.

Attempts have been made in other articles to describe the structure of institutional charity in major Italian cities, and so it will be treated very briefly here. Formal charity was generally dispensed, in any particular town, by a combination of at least four types of organization, administered for the most part by laymen who could expect some degree of priestly advice, co-operation, and (on occasion) interference. In any large city there were numerous religious brotherhoods or confraternities, varying enormously in wealth and status, attracting persons on all social levels from plutocrats to beggars, and capable of being adapted to almost any social or religious purpose. Some set out to perform every spiritual and corporal work of mercy, others to specialize in a single one such as the relief of prisoners or the burial of the dead; others still devoted themselves primarily to enacting ceremonies or maintaining churches, chapels or tombs. There were general hospitals, which dealt not only with sick and destitute persons within their own walls, but also dispensed alms to outsiders, and farmed out large numbers of abandoned children to foster parents in the surrounding countryside. There were plague hospitals, hospitals for incurables, and hospices for beggars. A third type of institution was the conservatory. Some conservatories accepted male orphans, but most of them were concerned with preserving or restoring female honour. Finally, the Monti di Pietà, or charity banks, initially set out to offer cheap credit by lending to poor persons on pledges at modest rates of interest, as an alternative to Jewish loan banks. Sometimes the apparatus of the city was further extended, during the sixteenth century, by establishing municipal granaries designed to supply food to the poor at less than the current market prices. In the larger cities, some kinds of supervisory or supplementary body, equipped with magisterial powers, were added during the fifteenth and sixteenth centuries. Among them were the Board of Public Health (Provveditori alla Sanità) in Venice, which was especially concerned with begging and prostitution, and the Office of the Poor, a general almonry established in Genoa about 1540.[20] These agencies seldom attempted to deprive existing establishments of their autonomy, save perhaps in Modena, where the formation of the Sacred Union of hospitals in 1541 provoked bitter resentment on the part of the deprived governors of the smaller institutions forcibly absorbed into it.[21] There were few or no Italian equivalents to the Common Chests of Germany and the southern Low Countries.

Hence, the most conspicuous feature of Italian urban systems was the presence of large institutions, maintained (though not exclusively) by voluntary contributions and endowments, serving the whole city and some of its rural hinterland, and seldom if ever linked to any parish. Although these bodies were in principle distinctive, their functions often overlapped, for it was common enough for confraternities to manage hospitals and conservatories, for hospitals to make personal loans, for conservatories to form part of general hospitals, and for Monti di Pietà to hold funds for, or make loans to, other charities. They were also knitted together by their governors, for prominent citizens, active in town councils, often held seats on the boards of several important institutions, these positions swelling their personal prestige and authority, and adding to the patronage at their disposal. Needless to say, there had never been any single central authority capable of imposing standardized arrangements on cities throughout the peninsula, and towns tended to make their own arrangements even within the same states: the organization of relief in, say, Brescia and Verona was not precisely the same as in the dominant city of Venice. But cities tended to imitate each other, and they were exposed to similar exhortations and proposals from visiting preachers, especially from the Franciscan Observants who did much to promulgate the Monti di Pietà and promote the formation of general hospitals during the fifteenth century.

One consequence of the clustering of well-endowed charities in cities was a kind of upheaval uncommon in England. In famine years, great numbers of starving peasants converged on the big cities in search of food and alms. Alarming, indeed terrifying, invasions occurred in the late 1520s, in the 1590s, in the late 1620s and the mid-1760s.[22] Dr Marc' Antonio Benaglio, a physician from Bergamo in the Venetian dominion, graphically described the influx of some 3,000 poor persons to the city during the famine of 1629, "most of them blackened, parched, emaciated, weakened, and in a poor state generally". Large contributions were made to their support by the Misericordia, the biggest confraternity in the town, which functioned as a general almonry; by individual citizens; and by the Cardinal Bishop of Bergamo. But, pondering the links between this terrible famine and the subsequent outbreak of plague, Benaglio reflected that the poor ought to have been assisted by sending alms to their own villages, and should have been sternly forbidden to approach the city. Such a procedure, he added, would have been just as meritorious in the sight of God.[23] Hence, it is worth asking what kinds of organized charity, if any, were available in the countryside: did one have to come to the town for alms, as he implied, and was there indeed a gross imbalance between the opportunities for obtaining relief open to townspeople and to countryfolk?

In fact the province of Bergamo as a whole, outside the regional capital, was extensively though patchily equipped with institutional charities.[24] "Misericordia" (literally "Mercy") was the commonest name for these small town or village foundations, and the term commonly referred to local almonries, the main functions of which were to support the poor and the clergy of the local community and contribute to the material needs of the church for wax, oil, or bricks and mortar. Sometimes described as confraternities, many had something in common with the French fraternities of the Holy Spirit – in that they were not exclusive brotherhoods uniting a section of the community in devotion or charity, but were roughly identical with the community as a whole, perhaps more influential than the parish in forming it, and governed by leading citizens of the community who served as syndics or presidents.[25] At Clusone (population 3,564 in 1596) in the Valle Seriana Superiore, the Misericordia first paid for masses in the principal local church and then dispensed its remaining revenues to the poor through six governors elected by the consortium of the Misericordia, an open assembly into which all residents could enter and cast a vote. Their accounts were subject to review by other officials chosen by "the community".[26] By contrast there were tiny foundations controlled by local families, presumably descendants of the original benefactor, such as the Cattanei at Santa Margarita on Monte Marentio, with a population of 107 entitled to enjoy three and a half *staia* or bushels of wheat.[27] Misericordie attracted legacies from well-to-do local personages or from local inhabitants who had made good abroad, and they were endowed with property, usually in the form of fields or meadows, and occasionally of water-mills. Rents for these were often paid, not in cash, but in produce, which was then converted into flour or bread, and distributed to the poor. Some Misericordie gave out salt. In years of subsistence crisis it was possible (as at Lovere) to sell land to raise sums of money to meet the immediate needs of poor persons threatened with starvation in the savage dearths of the 1590s.[28] Some Misericordie – and here again they resembled the fraternities of the Holy Spirit – did not discriminate between the richer and the poorer members of the community and distributed their revenues, or part of them, to everyone in "the neighbourhood [*vicinanza*]", as at Vil Longo in the Val Calepio, where the small Misericordia was controlled by the family of Bozi.[29] Some Venetian governors, particularly in the famine years, disapproved of the practice and said so.[30]

Most of the larger foundations, however, favoured both the clergy and the secular poor. One hundred and forty-three out of 249 localities surveyed in 1596 were equipped with charities of some sort: if not with institutions specifically described as Misericordie, then with other confraternities or with food or wine stores that sold to the poor at less than current market prices, as at Piazza or in the three parishes of the Val Fondra.[31] Communities endowed with charities had an average population of about 800, whereas those without averaged some 300, a large proportion of them lying in the areas known as the Quadra di Isola and the Quadra di Mezzo. These were close to Bergamo itself and therefore probably able to draw on the generosity of Bergamo's own opulent Misericordia; they may have accounted for many of the invading peasants described by Benaglio, but it is impossible to say so with confidence. Of 100 Misericordie listed in the survey, the functions of which are clearly described, 60 devoted their revenues to the poor alone, while 26 divided them between the poor and the church or clergy, and 14 adopted other policies.

Hence, it would be wrong to imagine that formal, organized charities were unknown to the countryside. The townships and villages of Tuscany, too, had been well-endowed with confraternities in the late Middle Ages, many of them embracing the greater part of the local community.[32] For some hospitals the natural setting was the countryside rather than the town, the village and the open road, close to the natural barriers created by rivers or streams, rather than the squares or streets of a city. To take in strangers, especially pilgrims making sacred journeys, was a traditional work of mercy. Many rural hospitals situated near the main roads to Rome were in effect cheap inns for travellers, which would also provide shelter for the local poor and sick.[33] Conflict could arise between a hospital's fundamental obligation to accept strangers and its duty to the local poor, as late as the eighteenth century, when suspicion of pilgrims was mounting.

Even in famine years, the priests of Altopascio, a village 14 kilometres to the south-east of Lucca which formed part of the estates of the Grand Dukes of Tuscany, were callously reminded by the Deputies of the Royal Possessions that their local charity was intended for visitors and travellers and not for local residents. But at least one priest informed the Deputies of a long tradition of using the hospital's resources to assist the inhabitants of Altopascio, and during the 1770s it was converted into rooms capable of housing poor tenant farmers who had been evicted from their holdings – an important concession to the grim realities of life in a village where most peasant farmers, and especially sharecroppers, were labouring under a massive burden of debt to their landlords.[34]

Monti di Pietà could likewise be adapted to rural needs, by taking the form of Monti Frumentari, which were often the brain-children of lay confraternities in townships or villages. Their principal function was to supply seed corn on very easy terms, in order to relieve peasants of the need to borrow from local moneylenders, and to spare them the terrible choice between consuming the seed-corn, to escape the immediate threat of starvation, and keeping it to sow the next harvest. Loans were generally made between January and June, on the strength not of pledges (as in the city) but of guarantees given by more prosperous neighbours. Interest, fixed at modest levels, was sometimes forgone.[35] However, these Monti had a somewhat unstable existence and were unevenly distributed between regions. In a northern province, the Bresciano, episcopal visitations between 1597 and 1606 revealed a situation full of promise, since more than a quarter of all parishes in the diocese were now equipped with Monti Frumentari. These were thicker on the ground in the plain, where 38.8 per cent of parishes possessed such institutions, than in the foothills or the mountains, where the proportion sank to less than 20 per cent. However, the Monti proved highly vulnerable to the most severe economic crises, and many were extinguished after 1630 by the inability of peasants to repay loans in the wake of repeated harvest failures. When Marco Dolfin visited his diocese between 1702 and 1704, he found that only 9.4 per cent of parishes were still running these institutions, and that some of the Monti had suffered grievously, not only from the marauding of French troops, but also from the depredations of corrupt local notables.[36] In the south, towards 1700, the Bishop of Benevento, Vincenzo Maria Orsini, established a lasting reputation as a founder of Monti Frumentari. After his elevation to the papacy he used his supreme office to reproduce the tried institutions of Benevento in the Papal States and in other parts of the southern kingdom. One-fifth of the religious confraternities in the diocese of Benevento (69 out of 344) established Monti Frumentari in Orsini's time, and the practice of doing so became almost universal in the province of Lucania. But in the regions of Cilento and the Valle di Diano, which formed the greater part of the southern province of Principato Citeriore, between 1750 and 1800, only 5 out of 66 known confraternities were administering Monti Frumentari.[37]

Two points will now be apparent. One is that although institutional charities were not peculiar to towns, and had counterparts in *borghi* and villages which were often realistically adapted to local conditions, the distribution of charities was lumpy and uneven, dependent upon local initiative and vulnerable to economic crisis and maladministration. A second point is that poor relief in Italy can be discussed at length without ever mentioning the parish: parishes are very much the Cinderella of the subject, and they tend to be invoked as afterthoughts, if at all. Even in the countryside it seems to be the confraternity or the Misericordia, rather than the parish as such, that establishes the more significant kinds of organized charity, of which the parish priest himself, as in parts of the Bergamasco, may be a beneficiary. It sometimes happened, however, that a parish priest had considerable control over local institutions even though they were not part of the parochial structure. Indeed, in Altopascio, the parish priest, together with the Grand Duke's estate bailiff, dispensed the tokens which entitled candidates, locals or strangers, to be admitted to the hospital.[38] And in the year of the French Revolution the parishioners of Bonefero in Capitanata, in northern Apulia, complained to the King that their priest was exercising the despotic authority of a factional chieftain over the local Monte Frumentario – indeed, that its administrators were elected at his pleasure or not at all, and that:

> the whole population are subjected to his wishes by means of the distribution of grain from the aforesaid Monte Frumentario, because he denies it to those who are not of his party and gives it to those who depend upon it, so that nothing can be done in this village except by his will.[39]

If the parishes are to be seriously discussed, three issues must be borne in mind:

(a) the role of parish priests, both within their own parishes and within wider organizations;

(b) the function of confraternities based on parish churches, which included some or all of their parishioners;

(c) the powers of the parish community itself, and its capacity for receiving and raising funds and endowments intended for the sole benefit of its own poorer members.

On the first point, it was a fifteenth-century country priest who inspired one of the most widely read and lastingly popular accounts of hard-headed practical charity. A famous joke-collection focused on the career and adventures of Piovano Arlotto, i.e. Arlotto Mainardi (1396–1484), priest of San Cresci a Macioli in the diocese of Fiesole near Florence, and sometime chaplain to the galleys which plied between Pisa and the northern ports of Bruges and Southampton.[40] Born to a Florentine tradesman who died bankrupt, Arlotto showed better business sense, and succeeded in increasing the income of his dilapidated parish from a mere 40 to approximately 150 gold florins per annum. But he kept very little for himself, and seldom had more than a few ducats in reserve. He consumed only four out of the twenty-one measures of grain which the parish yielded annually, and gave away the rest, mostly to his own parishioners, organizing generous weekly distributions of bread during the severe famines of 1475 and 1476. The Piovano lent grain freely, expecting no repayment; he guaranteed the debts incurred by his friends and parishioners with city tradesmen; and he gave lump sums as marriage portions to girls in the parish to save them from going to the bad. One of his greatest concerns was to keep people working and to save them from losing the tools of their trade; indeed, he sometimes encouraged poor men not to observe the festival days which threatened to deprive them of precious labouring time. When a woman lamented that because her husband, Bruogio, had failed to pay a debt of 16 lire, two working donkeys had been taken away from him, and explained that the impounded animals were vital to the support of the couple and their seven children, the Piovano, defying the December weather, removed his fur-lined cloak and told her to pawn it and redeem the donkeys. His charity was varied and imaginative, and would defy quantification and sorting into tidy categories, for it ranged from giving his breviary to a young priest who had lost his own, to paying the fees of an animal castrator who removed a diseased testicle from a tenant farmer's labourer. However open-handed (practical charity was for him the essence of Christianity), he was nobody's fool. Indeed, his replies to fraudulent beggars who tried to con the public by piously canting hard-luck stories were gleefully recorded by his anonymous biographer. "Don't you see," he said to one of them, "that I am a priest? I am in the same trade as you, and can do it better. Go and beg alms from someone in a different line of business!" [41]

No doubt some of these stories had gained in the telling, but they projected in a cheerful, unsanctimonious fashion the image of a good parish priest with no pretensions to sainthood, and they showed what could be done at the priest's discretion. No-one claimed, however, that the Piovano was a typical parish priest: even the officials of the Florentine commune recognized his uniqueness by imposing exceptionally low assessments, for they knew that to tax him would be to deprive the poor. He contrasted dramatically with the parish priest of Santa Maria Impruneta, who left a huge sum at his death and incurred the censure of the jurist Paolo dal Castro.[42] Indeed, the stereotype of the avaricious parish priest who keeps everything for himself was very much present in Italian *novelle*, the half-entertaining, half-moralizing light fiction which often had some foundations in fact. Told more than once was the grim cautionary tale of the parish priest who was forced, on the orders of Bernabò Visconti, lord of Milan, to dig his own grave and be buried in it alive for having refused a free funeral to a pauper or (in one version) a pilgrim.[43] Matteo Bandello, the Dominican storyteller of the mid-sixteenth century, observed in a discourse addressed to Filippo Saulo, Bishop of Brugnate, that:

> the priests who have benefices and pay special attention to their temporal possessions ought all to be burning with charity and to be the most generous and courteous folk in the world, for they have less need to think of their goods than any other kind of men, since they know that after their deaths the benefices they hold and enjoy can never be part of an inheritance, because they cannot bequeath them at will. But - shame upon this degenerate world! - when you want to speak of a miser you say a priest. This is certainly very wrong, for the misconduct of two or three ought not to slur the respectable lives of the others, and in our time there are many good priests who live in a most saintly fashion and freely give away their goods.

After making this judicious statement, and tactfully numbering the bishop among the charitable clergy, Bandello recounted the story of Don Pietro, the gourmandizing parish priest of Mazzenta near Milan who spent all his money on capons, quails, turtle-doves and other delicacies, kept no hospitality whatever, and was therefore – according to the rules of *novelle* – fair game himself for tricksters from the city.[44]

Much depended on personal choices made by the priest, and in subsequent centuries there were indeed complaints of meanness on the part of parish clergy, as in Vicenza province in the eighteenth century. Most priests here did little more than visit the sick, and the archpriest of Malo was repeatedly in dispute with parishioners who thought him a miser. Priests claimed, not unreasonably, that they had obligations to keep up appearances and live according to their rank – and, indeed, since the sixteenth century reforming bishops had tried to insist that parish priests should detach themselves from the people and cease to share in the lifestyle of their fellow villagers.[45] A good deal also turned on the priest's income. In some parishes of the diocese of Naples in the seventeenth and eighteenth centuries priests had to, or chose to, forgo some of the tithes legally due to them because their flock were too poor to pay and there was nothing to be gained, especially from households headed by widows. Therefore, some clerical charity lay, not in the kinds of initiative pursued by the business-like Arlotto, but in a decision not to exact tithes. In 1746 the parish priest of Mugnano declared that in strict law the tithes should have yielded 100 ducats per annum, but, to avoid burdening the poor, he contented himself with 50.[46]

Particularly in the late seventeenth and the eighteenth centuries, both in urban and in rural settings, there were examples of parish priests who combined enterprise and intellectual sophistication with personal austerity and generosity. They included Benedetto Giacobini (1650–1732), parish priest of Cressa and then of Varallo in the diocese of Novara, an inspiration to the young Ludovico Antonio Muratori, who subsequently became his biographer. Stricken by what appeared to be a fatal illness, Giacobini left half his goods to the Church and the other half to the poor, and on making an unexpected recovery he insisted that his will should be executed during his lifetime.[47] Another archetype was the energetic priest whose personal experience of the evils of poverty was gained in a poor urban parish, and who embarked on action both on behalf of his own parishioners and of the citizens as a whole, by founding confraternities or congregations of well-to-do persons who would promote spiritual and material charity across a much wider area. Giulio Cesare Canali (1690–1765) was parish priest of Sant'Isaia in Bologna, an area chiefly occupied by silk-workers. He dreamed, with Muratori, of a society in which abuses of power, extravagance, and glaring differences of wealth would be tempered by the practice of charity. Within his own parish he established a small conservatory for endangered girls and fallen women, and he collected poor, sick old women from the parish in a house placed at his disposal. In the city as a whole he established two Congregazioni di Carità to visit the poor, the sick, the dying and the imprisoned, and also to teach Christian doctrine; women, clerics and laymen were enlisted in the enterprise as "proctors for the poor", and were encouraged to apply their own superfluous income to their support.[48] Muratori himself, a prolific writer, a distinguished scholar and librarian to the Dukes of Modena, was for a time priest of the poor and insalubrious parish of Santa Maria della Pomposa in Modena, and likewise divided his attention between his own parish and a city-wide enterprise. His Compagnia della Carità, founded in 1720, rested on the principle that the urgent needs of the living poor should have priority over all other charitable uses, with burials, commemorative masses and even the provision of dowries being left to other organizations. Systematic atonement should be made for the inadequacies of existing charities and stress be laid (not for the first time) on teaching trades to the younger poor persons, girls included.[49] For these able priests the poor urban parish was their point of departure, but was never treated as their only field of action or their only source of funding. Indeed, Canali's hospital for old women was able to expand, not by virtue of the support it received from parishioners in general, but by the generous bequest of a local aristocrat, the Marchesa Elisabetta Bentivoglio Magnani.

However they used their own income, parish priests undoubtedly became, in some parts of Italy, intermediaries between their own parishioners and the great charitable institutions of the city. They could be expected to know the circumstances of the poorer members of their flock, to describe and certify the nature of their poverty, and if necessary to write letters of referral. Descriptions of destitute persons admitted to the beggars' hospital of Cremona in the late sixteenth century, of their physical disabilities and of their lack of friends and relations, were generally supplied by parish priests, many of them outside the city of Cremona itself.[50] When, in 1583, a Venetian wool-carder named Hieronimo improved his application for an almshouse from the great confraternity of San Rocco by parading four barefoot and ragged children who were not his own in addition to two who were, one of several charges against him was that "He deceived not only your worships, but also the reverend father Zuanne Sappo, sacristan of San Raffaello, by causing him to certify that he, Hieronimo, had six children".[51] Conspicuous, in this and later centuries, was the role of parish priests in negotiations between foundling hospitals and poor parents who wished to surrender their children at least temporarily to the hospital, or to obtain other benefits. Some children were abandoned anonymously at the hospitals, simply by leaving them at the gates or placing them on the famous revolving wheel at the hospital entrance. But on many occasions the parents and their circumstances were made known to the institutions concerned. Whether the parent or parents were too poor to keep the child, or whether it was illegitimate, the testimony of the parish priest was of great importance. It might fall to him to explain how scandal would arise, domestic conflict break out and the mother's kinsfolk be dishonoured if the child were kept at home. Or he might assure the hospital authorities that because of a father's illness and the need for a mother to enter domestic service it would be impossible for them to bring up the child.[52] In Milan, parish priests were among the persons called upon to sign certificates enabling a mother, milkless and too poor to employ a wet-nurse, to get a child nursed without charge by the foundling hospital.[53] Parishes might not be a major source of income for the poor, but parish priests could be vital to the administration of discriminating charity by institutional structures which did not rest on the parish. One hopes that most of them were less gullible than the Venetian sacristan.

Parishes and confraternities seemingly stood for different principles, the voluntary association contrasting with the community of residents within a bounded territory – although, as already noted, there were confraternities which had become territorialized and offered their benefits to all members of the community. From the fifteenth to the eighteenth century, in Italy as in France, critics of confraternities accused them of undermining parishes. Conversely, in sixteenth-century Rome, there were critics of parishes who preferred confraternities, and caused parish churches to be handed over to them.[54] Many of the more vigorous confraternities of the later Middle Ages had been promoted by religious orders, especially the Franciscans and Dominicans, who thought in city-wide rather than parochial terms.[55] In principle there was no reason why a confraternity should not be attached to a parish church, but that did not make it capable of serving the whole parish. In fourteenth-century Florence the confraternity of San Frediano was a modest organization which concentrated on burying the dead and relieving the poor only in the streets closest to its own headquarters, leaving parts of the parish to the attentions of the centrally organized confraternity of Or San Michele.[56] Prestigious urban confraternities generally had a wide geographical range, recruiting their members from and distributing their benefits to an area much larger than the parish. Even the more localized bodies would base themselves on units other than the parish, on wards or quarters or particular streets and districts such as the Neapolitan *ottine*.[57] From the sixteenth century onwards, despite the bishops' efforts to insist on the importance of parish churches, there were new religious orders such as the Jesuits who formed confraternities around status groupings rather than parochial units, establishing religious organizations (as in Naples in the late sixteenth century) for nobles, clerics, lawyers, master artisans, domestic servants, or apprentices and journeymen, that like might evangelize like and redeem them from the dire effects of ignorance and poverty.[58]

For all this, bonds between certain new forms of confraternity and the parish became tighter from the sixteenth century onwards, when bishops and some religious orders strove to ensure that all parishes should be endowed with confraternities of the Blessed Sacrament, the Rosary, and the Christian Doctrine. Those of the Sacrament were most intimately associated with a mixture of spiritual and material charity. Their social appeal was more plebeian than that of many late medieval eucharistic confraternities, and in cities their officers were frequently chosen from the ranks of minor professional men, newly arrived merchants, artisans, or shopkeepers.[59] Stated most clearly by the Company of the Holy Sacrament at Santa Minerva in Rome, their primary objective was to keep the consecrated host in the parish churches with becoming splendour, and to ensure that on journeys through the streets to visit the sick it was properly escorted, accompanied by candles and torches, and not left to a solitary clergyman.

Reverence for the sacrament, expressed through such ceremonial, was chiefly a weapon against "the insane pride of modern heretics, who in these days wickedly speak" against it.[60] But it led naturally into spiritual charity, into counselling the patient to make use of the sacrament and to prepare if need be to make a good death. It also prompted giving alms to the invalid, and inspired practical actions, such as bearing the sick to hospital upon a covered bier.[61] In some cities these confraternities seemed to foreshadow a new system of parochial relief. When, in 1529, the Venetian Senate attempted to introduce a new system of poor relief which would involve the parishes, they included instructions to the effect that the Corpus Domini brotherhoods should urge the faithful to give alms "until this arrangement concerning the parishes has been placed on a firmer footing".[62] In the Venetian province of Brescia the confraternities of the

Sacrament were responsible for establishing many of the rural Monti Frumentari.[63] By 1600 the Venetian brotherhoods may well have been mainly concerned with supplementing the inadequate incomes of parish churches. But in Rome they retained their interest in the poor, and in his vast celebration of the charities of Rome, the paradigm for Catholic Christendom, Carlo Bartolomeo Piazza later praised their power to promote neighbourly solidarity among parishioners, "for they know that by their friendly encounters they get to hear of the needs and wants of the poorest families, in order to give them assistance".[64] Some bishops, especially the redoubtable Carlo Borromeo of Milan, attempted to standardize the confraternities of the Sacrament by prescribing model regulations and endeavouring to insist that all priests should adopt them.[65] In the diocese of Fossano, parish priests were made responsible for the supervision of elections to office in the confraternities and for scrutinizing their accounts and administrative acts.[66] Not surprisingly, the distinction between the confraternity and the body of parishioners began to disappear, even in towns. In 1656 a report on the confraternity attached to the collegiate parish church of San Giorgio al Palazzo in Milan explained that

> It is governed by a prior, vice-prior, treasurer, clerk, and others of the parish, and there is no fixed number of members, but all parishioners may be present and vote in the chapter, which must never be held unless the provost and the *canonico curato*, or at least one of them, is present.[67]

Such alliances with the confraternity may have made the parish a more efficient organ for poor relief, though they did not eliminate the older confraternities which were not parochially grounded. But could the parish, left to itself, provide adequate financial foundations for relief, and had it the power to tax its prosperous inhabitants, rather than exhort them to give what they could afford? Rating of a kind was considered by the Venetian Senate in 1529, when attempting to introduce a scheme designed to suppress begging and systematically relieve the deserving poor in the city. By virtue of this legislation, parish priests, charged with raising alms by exhortation from the pulpit and personal approaches to the well-to-do, were flanked by lay deputies elected by an assembly of parishioners and representing, respectively, the nobles, citizens, and artisans of the parish. Parochial assemblies were also called upon to vote a "voluntary tax" for the support of the poor.[68] However, the power of legal coercion was missing.

Perhaps the profound Catholic conviction that acts of mercy were good works, to be undertaken by the free will of the giver (though often in response to intense moral pressure and threats of supernatural sanctions), inhibited legal compulsion, at least as a regular device. A scheme introduced in Mantua during the famines of the 1590s provided for "rooms [*camarate*]" to be opened in each parish for poor persons who could not be accommodated in the four major hospitals of the city; it is uncertain how these were to be financed.[69] Both the Venetian and the Mantuan schemes appeared to be using the parish to supplement existing arrangements based on hospitals and confraternities: the parish was not, as it came to be in England, a front-line unit under government control.

Given the uneven distribution of wealth and poverty between urban parishes, one wonders how well-equipped they generally were to carry the main burden of poor relief. Some students of early modern cities see rich and poor living cheek-by-jowl and stress the absence of the slums and *beaux-quartiers* of a later epoch; others point to poor parishes, inhabited by large numbers of low-paid and insecure industrial and agricultural workers, usually situated on the outer edge of the city. Evidence from Verona supports both parties. Here a fiscal survey of 1558 revealed that in the city as a whole about 58 per cent of the population could be called poor, either in being assigned to the two lowest tax brackets and hence exempted from paying direct taxes, or in being on poor relief, or both. There were large concentrations of these have-nots in the parishes "outside the walls", the proportion rising to 91.79 per cent of households in Quinzano and 82.55 per cent in Torresella Tomba. Nobody in Quinzano incurred more than a modest tax assessment. A system of parochial relief might well have been workable in central parishes such as the Pigna, San Pietro Incarnario or the Braida, where rich and poor were neighbours, and the poor were of a different sort – not poor textile workers or tillers of the soil, but booksellers, saddlers, coachmen, swordmakers and other types of craftsmen or servant.[70] But where high levels of poverty prevailed it must have been convenient to draw on the resources of larger, more centralized institutions which could transfer wealth across a wider area. A possible alternative was to introduce a system of cross-subsidies, to enable the richer parishes to assist the poorer. These were certainly tried out in Venice during the great plague epidemic of 1576, when the parish priests and lay deputies were required to spend half the money they collected in the parish which had raised it, and to send the other half to the Heads of the Sestieri, the six large administrative districts, each containing on average about 12 parishes, into which Venice was divided.[71] But there is as yet not much evidence that such sophisticated methods were widely or consistently used; the Venetian scheme was the product of a dire emergency.

Taxes imposed for the benefit of the poor were not unknown in Italy, but they were seldom the result of regular or systematic arrangements. Sometimes governments chose to assign revenues to institutions which were under their special protection, though mainly supported by voluntary contributions; the government subsidy might well take the form either of an allocation of certain judicial fines, or of an assignment of particular indirect taxes, such as those conferred by Pope Sixtus V in the 1580s upon the new and short-lived beggars' hospital in Rome.[72] In emergencies they resorted to direct taxation, basing their assessments on tax registers drawn up for other ends, or levying extra instalments of general purpose taxes and applying them specifically to poor relief. Parish officers could be called upon to collect these taxes, even though they had no role in assessing them. The Venetian government resorted to such measures at least twice during the sixteenth century in order to finance increasingly desperate measures against the plague, when the disruptive effects of disease and the quarantine regulations intended to contain it paralyzed the economy and threw thousands of families on to public relief.[73] In 1629 the city of Bergamo levied an instalment of the *sussidio* to help it cope with the invasion of starving peasants already described, and censuses of the poor were compiled by two gentlemen in each parish.[74] Taxation, however, was not a routine measure, and sums raised by taxes were liable to be surpassed by the offerings of large charities made in response to government appeals; in Bergamo, the 4,000 *scudi* raised through the *sussidio* fell short of the 6,000 *scudi* contributed by the Misericordia of the city.

George Orwell's Winston Smith, having received the forbidden work by Emmanuel Goldstein, reflects that the best books are those that tell you what you know already.[75] That is a source of consolation, because this chapter may only have served to confirm, with the aid of details and nuances, what people have long supposed to be the case. It is broadly true that the more formal kinds of organized charity in Italy depended heavily on large institutions located in cities and supported mainly by private funding. Hence the spread of opportunities to obtain relief was very uneven, and there were seasons of dearth in which the rural poor flocked to the cities and at least some of them had to be fed until the next harvest had been gathered. These disturbances reflected the pattern of urban growth in Italy, the large number of great cities dominating rural hinterlands, the concentration of wealth in cities. But it should be said that the countryside was not destitute of institutional charity, and that some of its organizations were adaptations of charities which had evolved in cities. Parishes, so important in England, were eclipsed by other institutions, especially by confraternities, although with time it proved possible to bring the two together. Many parishes seemed incapable of generating enough transferable income to support their own poor without external assistance, but the parish priest and his local knowledge were vital to the functioning of a system not based on the fiscal powers of the parish. In Italy, as elsewhere in Europe, parish priests were called upon to carry out a variety of bureaucratic tasks – to register births and deaths, to compile censuses, to report plague suspects. It was natural that their duties should come to include the certification of desperate poverty. Such responsibility could bestow power on the priest, since without his support entry to charitable institutions might well be barred. Some priests might use their right to supervise local charities as an opportunity for exercising patronage in a corrupt and partial fashion. Some drew generously on their own resources, and set magnificent examples of personal charity and organizational skill. Others displayed none of these qualities.

England and the Italian states shared many common objectives, including the aim of suppressing begging and eliminating wilful idleness. However, their institutional structures were very different (confraternities did not survive the Reformation and the great hospitals of Tudor London, broadly similar to those of some Continental cities, found few parallels elsewhere in England). To some extent their notions of both the scope of charity and the nature of poverty were different. More prominent in Italy was the concept of a spiritual charity which embraced the souls of the dead as well as of the living, and certain forms of voluntary poverty, practised by the more austere monks, friars, and other clergy, continued to be revered and to make claims on the purses of charitable donors. True, we should reject some simple contrasts. As Colin Jones has warned, let all beware of crude antitheses between the "voluntary" charity of Catholic countries and the compulsory poor rates of Protestant England.[76] Both Catholic and Protestant societies depended heavily on exhortation as well as on legal coercion. In France or Italy, the religious obligation to give to the poor, and the social expectation that one would do so, at least by drawing on resources superfluous to maintaining the lifestyle appropriate to one's status, were so powerful that giving to charity could never be described as the act of an entirely free will. But it was unusual for an Italian Catholic to be told by officers of the state, the town or the parish precisely how much he or she should give and at what time, and to be threatened with legal sanctions rather than eternal punishment for failure to comply with their commands.

Notes

1. P. Slack, *Poverty and policy in Tudor and Stuart England* (London, 1988), especially pp. 126–8; see also pp. 11, 113–14, 121–3.
2. M. K. McIntosh, "Local responses to the poor in late medieval and Tudor England", *Continuity and Change* 3, 1988, pp. 234–5.
3. W. K. Jordan, *Philanthropy in England, 1480–1660* (London, 1959).
4. See the criticisms summarized in Slack, *Poverty*, pp. 162–4, 169–72, with references.
5. J. Walter, "The social economy of dearth in early modern England", in *Famine, disease and the social order in early modern society*, J. Walter & R. Schofield (eds) (Cambridge, 1989), pp. 109, 111, 121.
6. Two recent general surveys of charity and poor relief in Europe are B. Geremek, *Poverty: a history* (Oxford, 1994) and R. Jütte, *Poverty and deviance in early modern Europe* (Cambridge, 1994). T. Riis (ed.), *Aspects of poverty in early modern Europe*, III. *La pauvreté dans les pays nordiques, 1500–1800* (Odense, 1990) deals with the Scandinavian countries.
7. See the English translation of "The ordinance of a common chest" in *Luther's works*, J. Pelikan & H. T. Lehmann (eds) [55 vols] (Philadelphia, 1955–86), XLV, p. 192; cf. also H. J. Grimm, "Luther's contribution to sixteenth-century poor relief", *Archiv für Reformationsgeschichte* **61**, 1970, pp. 222–34; C. Lindberg, "'There should be no beggars among Christians': Karlstadt, Luther, and the origins of Protestant poor relief", *Church History* **46**, 1977, pp. 313–34.
8. F. Giusberti, "La città assistenziale: riflessioni su un sistema piramidale", in *Forme e soggetti dell' intervento assistenziale in una città di antico regime* (Bologna, 1986), pp. 25–7; A. Giacomelli, "Conservazione e innovazione nell' assistenza bolognese del Settecento", *ibid.*, pp. 219–64.
9. On the shamefaced poor, R. C. Trexler, "Charity and the defense of urban élites in the Italian communes", in *The rich, the well born and the powerful. Elites and upper classes in history*, F. C. Jaher (ed.) (Urbana, Chicago & London, 1973), pp. 64–109; A. Spicciani, "The 'Poveri Vergognosi' in fifteenth-century Florence", in *Aspects of poverty*, T. Riis (ed.) (Florence, 1981), pp. 119–82; G. Ricci, "Povertà, vergogna e povertà vergognosa", *Società e Storia* **5**, 1979, pp. 305–38.
10. For a general account of poverty in Italy, B. Pullan, "Poveri, mendicanti e vagabondi (secoli XIV–XVII)", in *Storia d'Italia. Annali I. Dal feudalesimo al capitalismo*, C. Vivanti & R. Romano (eds) (Turin, 1978), pp. 981–1047 – now reproduced in B. Pullan, *Poverty and charity: Europe, Italy, Venice 1400–1700* (Aldershot, 1994).

11. See G. Pontano's treatises, "De liberalitate" and "De beneficentia", in his *I trattati delle virtú sociali*, F. Tateo (ed.) (Rome, 1965).

12. From the statutes (1590) of the Roman confraternity of Orazione e Morte, as quoted in L. Fiorani, "L'esperienza religiosa nelle confraternite romane tra Cinque e Seicento", in *Le confraternite romane: esperienza religiosa, società, committenza artistica*, L. Fiorani (ed.) (*Ricerche per la Storia Religiosa di Roma* 5) (Rome, 1984), p. 190.

13. See L. A. Muratori, *Trattato della carità cristiana e altri scritti sulla carità*, P. G. Nonis (ed.) (Rome, 1961), pp. 28–9.

14. Matthew XXV, 31–46.

15. Aquinas, *Summa theologiae*, R. J. Batten (ed.), II-II, qu. 32, 2 (London & New York, 1964–), vol. XXXIV, pp. 244–5.

16. S. K. Cohn, Jr., *Death and property in Siena, 1205–1800: strategies for the afterlife* (Baltimore & London, 1988), pp. 28–31, and his *The cult of remembrance and the black death: six Renaissance cities in central Italy* (Baltimore & London, 1992), pp. 65–71.

17. R. Bellarmine, *A shorte catechism* (1614) (facsimile, London, 1973), pp. 85–91.

18. See especially V. Paglia, *La morte confortata. Riti della paura e mentalità religiosa a Roma nell'età moderna* (Rome, 1982), pp. 46–56; S. Musella, "Dimensione sociale e prassi associativa di una confraternita napoletana nell'età della Controriforma", in *Per la storia sociale e religiosa del Mezzogiorno d'Italia*, G. Galasso & C. Russo (eds) [2 vols] (Naples, 1980), I, pp. 357–8, 370, 375–8.

19. Muratori, *Trattato*, Introduction, pp. 33–48; the *Trattato* itself, pp. 231–40, 254–5, 267, 271.

20. For descriptions of the organizational structure of charities in Italian cities, B. Pullan, " 'Support and redeem': charity and poor relief in Italian cities from the fourteenth to the seventeenth century", *Continuity and Change* 3, 1988, pp. 177–208; B. Pullan, "Povertà, carità e nuove forme d'assistenza nell' Europa moderna (sec. XV–XVII)", in *La città e i poveri. Milano e le terre lombarde dal Rinascimento all' età spagnola*, D. Zardin (ed.) (Milan, 1995), pp. 21–44. Studies of particular cities include B. Pullan, *Rich and poor in Renaissance Venice: the social institutions of a Catholic state, to 1620* (Oxford, 1971); J. Henderson, *Piety and charity in late medieval Florence* (Oxford, 1994); S. Cavallo, *Charity and power in early modern Italy: Benefactors and their motives in Turin, 1541–1789* (Cambridge, 1995). An important collection of conference papers is G. Politi, M. Rosa, F. Della Peruta (eds), *Timore e carità. I poveri nell' Italia moderna* (Cremona, 1982).

21. P. di Pietro, "Sulla Santa Unione degli ospedali e delle opere pie della città di Modena nel 1541", in *Atti del Primo Congresso Italiano di Storia Ospitaliera* (Reggio Emilia, 1957), pp. 217–27.

22. See Pullan, *Rich and poor*, pp. 243–4, 358; P. Clark (ed.), *The European crisis of the 1590s* (London, 1985); F. Venturi, "1764: Napoli nell' anno della fame", *Rivista Storica Italiana* 85, 1973, pp. 394–472; "1764–1767: Roma negli anni della fame", *ibid.*, pp. 514–43; "Quattro anni di carestia in Toscana (1764–1767)", *Rivista Storica Italiana* 88, 1976, pp. 649–707.

23. M. A. Benaglio, "Relazione della carestia e della peste di Bergamo e suo territorio negli anni 1629 e 1630", in *Miscellanea di Storia Italiana 6*, G. Finazzi (ed.) (Turin, 1865), pp. 419–20.

24. For much of what follows, see the survey of Bergamo and its province compiled by the Capitano Giovanni Da Lezze, a Venetian governor, in 1596: Archivio di Stato, Venice, Sindici Inquisitori in Terra Ferma, busta 63 (henceforth referred to as "Da Lezze Survey").

25. P. Duparc, "Les confréries du Saint-Esprit et communautés d'habitants au moyen-âge", *Revue Historique de Droit Français et Etranger*, 4th series, **36**, 1958, pp. 349–67, 555–85; J. P. Gutton, "Confraternities, curés and communities in rural areas of the diocese of Lyons under the ancien regime", in *Religion and society in Early Modern Europe, 1500–1800*, K. von Greyerz (ed.) (London, 1984), pp. 202–11; P. T. Hoffmann, *Church and community in the diocese of Lyons, 1500–1789* (New Haven & London, 1984), pp. 58–62, 105–8.

26. Da Lezze Survey, f. 211r.–213r.

27. *Ibid.*, f. 140.

28. *Ibid.*, f. 259r.–261v.

29. *Ibid.*, f. 282v.–283v.

30. Report of Cattarino Zen, Podestà of Bergamo, 15 June 1591, in *Relazioni dei Rettori Veneti in Terraferma*, XII, B. Polese (ed.) (Milan, 1978), p. 186.

31. Da Lezze Survey, f. 174v.–175r., 181r.–183v.

32. C. M. de la Roncière, "La place des confréries dans l'encadrement religieux du contado florentin: l'exemple de la Val d'Elsa", *Mélanges de l'Ecole Française de Rome: Moyen Age, Temps Modernes* **85**, 1973, pp. 31–77, 633–71, and his "Les confréries à Florence et dans son contado aux XIVe-XVe siècles", in *Le mouvement confraternel au Moyen Age: France, Italie, Suisse* (Rome: Collections de l'Ecole Française de Rome **97**, 1987), pp. 297–342.

33. For useful examples, N. Galassi, *Dieci secoli di storia ospitaliera a Imola* [2 vols], (Imola, 1966–70), I, pp. 30–31, 34, 111–23, 141, 153–7, 232–3.

34. F. McArdle, *Altopascio: a study in Tuscan rural society, 1587–1784* (Cambridge, 1978), pp. 1–7, 19–20, 107–8, 186–7.

35. D. Montanari, "I Monti di Pietà del territorio bresciano", in *Per il quinto centenario del Monte di Pietà di Brescia (1489–1989)*, D. Montanari & R. Navarrini (eds) [2 vols] (Brescia, 1989), I, pp. 231–70; also his *Disciplinamento in terra veneta. La diocesi di Brescia nella seconda metà del XVI secolo* (Bologna, 1987), pp. 228–32.

36. Montanari, "I Monti di Pietà", I, pp. 245–50.

37. A. di Spirito, "Stato delle confraternite della diocesi di Benevento nella prima metà del Settecento", in V. Paglia (ed.), *Sociabilità religiosa nel Mezzogiorno: le confraternite laicali* (special issue of *Ricerche di Storia Sociale e Religiosa*, new series, **19**, nos. 37–8, 1990), pp. 94–5; see also A. Cestaro, "Il fenomeno confraternale nel Mezzogiorno: aspetti e problemi", *ibid.*, p. 37, and F. Volpe, "Statuti di confraternite e vita socio-religiosa nel Settecento", *ibid.*, p. 80.

38. McArdle, *Altopascio*, pp. 182–4.

39. L. Allegra, "Il parroco: un mediatore fra alta e bassa cultura", in *Storia d'Italia.*

Annali 4. Intellettuali e potere, C.Vivanti (ed.) (Turin, 1981), pp. 930–31.

40. G. Folena (ed.), *Motti e facezie del Piovan Arlotto* (Milan & Naples, 1953), and F. W. Kent & A. Lillie, "The Piovano Arlotto: new documents", in *Florence and Italy. Renaissance studies in honour of Nicolai Rubinstein*, P. Denley & C. Elam (eds) (London, 1988), pp. 347–68.

41. Folena, *Motti*, pp. 3–4, 150–54, 159–61, 172, 201–2, 227–8, 283.

42. *Ibid.*, pp. 208–9, 211.

43. F. Sacchetti, *Il Trecentonovelle*, novella 59, A. Lanza (ed.) (Florence, 1984), pp. 115–17; cf. M. Bandello, *Le novelle*, Part III, novella 25, in *Tutte le opere*, F. Flora (ed.) [2 vols] (Milan, 1934), II, pp. 393–5.

44. Bandello, *Le Novelle*, Part III, novella 1, *ibid.*, I, pp. 661–8.

45. B. Dooley, "Aspetti dell' assistenza a poveri nel Vicentino settecentesco con particolare riferimento alla zona inferiore dell' antico vicariato di Thiene", in *Dueville – storia di una comunità*, C. Povolo (ed.) (Vicenza, 1986), p. 1244; Allegra, "Il parroco", pp. 922–4; Montanari, *Disciplinamento*, pp. 154–5.

46. C. Russo, "I redditi dei parroci nei casali di Napoli: struttura e dinamica (XVI–XVIII secolo)", in *Per la storia*, Galasso & Russo (eds), pp. 28–54.

47. Muratori, *Trattato*, pp. 751–2, 863–6.

48. Giacomelli, "Conservazione", pp. 172–6.

49. Muratori, *Trattato*, pp. 775, 777–88, 799–808 (for the statutes of the Compagnia della Carità), pp. 833–8 (for the first and second versions of Muratori's will).

50. M. Fantarelli, *L'istituzione dell' Ospedale di S.Alessio dei poveri mendicanti in Cremona (1569–1600)*, G. Politi (ed.) (Cremona, 1981), pp. 60–68.

51. Archivio della Scuola Grande di San Rocco,Venice, Registro delle Terminazioni 3, f. 71v.–72v., 74v., 21 August, 23 October 1583.

52. For examples, G. Cappelletto, "Infanzia abbandonata e ruoli di mediazione sociale nella Verona del Settecento", *Quaderni Storici* 18, 1983, pp. 423–9; F. Doriguzzi, "I messaggi dell' abbandono: bambini esposti a Torino nel '700'", *ibid.*, pp. 454–5, 463–4.

53. V. Hunecke, *I trovatelli di Milano. Bambini esposti e famiglie espositrici dal XVII al XIX secolo* (Bologna, 1989), pp. 90–91.

54. Pullan, "'Support and Redeem'", p. 186, with references; cf. Hoffmann, *Church and community*, pp. 38–9, 86, 103–8, 112–14.

55. R. F. E. Weissman, *Ritual brotherhood in renaissance Florence* (New York, 1982), pp. 44–6; B. Pullan, "The Scuole Grandi ofVenice: further thoughts", in *Christianity and the Renaissance: image and religious imagination in the quattrocento*, T.Verdon & J. Henderson (eds) (New York, 1990), pp. 291–2.

56. J. Henderson, "The parish and the poor in Florence at the time of the Black Death: the case of San Frediano", *Continuity and Change* 3, 1988, pp. 247–72.

57. G.Vitale, "Ricerche sulla vita religiosa e caritativa a Napoli tra Medioevo ed età moderna", *Archivio Storico per le Province Napoletane* 86–7, 1970, pp. 218–19, 237–8.

58. L. Chatellier, *The Europe of the devout. The Catholic reformation and the foundation of a new society* (Cambridge, 1989), pp. 18–20.

59. For examples, see D. Zardin, "Solidarietà di vicini. La confraternita del Corpo di Cristo e le compagnie devote di S. Giorgio al Palazzo tra Cinque e Settecento", *Archivio Storico Lombardo* **118**, 1992, pp. 366–7; Pullan, "Religious Brotherhoods in Venice", English version in his *Poverty and charity*, Item IX, pp. 10–11.

60. G. Barbiero, *Le confraternite del Santissimo Sacramento prima del 1539* (Treviso, 1941), pp. 269–70, 281–2.

61. C. B. Piazza, *Eusevologio romano; overo, Delle opere pie di Roma* [2 vols] (Rome, 1698), I, pp. 387–8.

62. D. Chambers & B. Pullan (eds), *Venice: a documentary history, 1450–1630* (Oxford, 1992), p. 305.

63. Montanari, "I Monti di Pietà", p. 246.

64. Piazza, *Eusevologio*, I, p. 517.

65. Zardin, "Solidarietà", pp. 364, 391–5.

66. Allegra, "Il parroco", pp. 925–6.

67. Zardin, "Solidarietà", pp. 364–5.

68. The text of the Senate's decree is translated in Chambers & Pullan, *Venice*, pp. 303–06; see also Pullan, *Rich and poor*, pp. 252–4.

69. R. Navarrini & C. M. Belfanti, "Il problema della povertà nel Ducato di Mantova: aspetti istituzionali e problemi sociali (secoli XIV-XVI)", in *Timore e carità*, Politi, Rosa, Della Peruta (eds), pp. 130–31.

70. P. L. Sartori, "Radiografia della soglia di povertà in una città della Terraferma Veneta: Verona alla metà del XVI secolo", *Studi Veneziani*, new series, **6**, 1982, pp. 55, 72–9. On the system of taxation in Verona: A. Tagliaferri, *L'economia veronese secondo gli estimi dal 1409 al 1635* (Milan, 1966).

71. Pullan, *Rich and poor*, p. 320.

72. *Ibid.*, pp. 417–18; P. Simoncelli, "Origini e primi anni di vita dell' ospedale romano dei poveri mendicanti", *Annuario dell' Istituto Storico Italiano per l'Età Moderna e Contemporanea* **25–26**, 1973–4, pp. 136–7, 139–40.

73. Pullan, *Rich and poor*, pp. 247, 251, 320.

74. Benaglio, "Relazione", pp. 419–20.

75. G. Orwell, *Nineteen eighty-four* (Harmondsworth, 1954), p. 161.

76. C. Jones, *The charitable imperative: hospitals and nursing in ancien regime and revolutionary France* (London & New York, 1989), p. 1.

5

Aged and impotent: parish relief of the aged poor in early modern Suffolk

Lynn Botelho

I

The elites of early modern England viewed their own approaching old age with horror, dread, and denial. Not surprisingly, Shakespeare would not allow the "glass" to "persuade me I am old", for it was common knowledge that old men seldom grew into their prescribed condition of oracles of truth and pinnacles of wisdom.[1] Instead, it was thought, old men chased after the young wives of others, argued unreasonably with their families, boasted long and often about past feats of youth[2], and, of course, indulged in their particular vice of drinking too much wine.[3] The older woman was just as bad, having "rent her face with painting" and "so bedeckte with gems all over, displaying her crop and bubbys" in foolish attempts to lure the favours of pretty young men, who, for their part, "cannot laugh need but think of an old woman that wears false locks".[4] That was, remember, the elite's view of their own old age. When commenting on the ageing process of others, especially the aged poor, literary men spared few details in describing the effects of "time's injurious hand" and "age's cruel knife".[5] Toothless and stinking, begging and grasping, the elderly poor were viewed as an open, draining sore on the otherwise healthy leg of society. Even the characteristically taciturn Statutes of the Realm vividly reflect this idea of the diseased and loathsome aged poor whose "comminge to gither and making a number do then fill the Stretes or high waies of divers Cities Towns markettes and fayres", sapping both the strength and the finances of many urban parishes.[6]

While it is all very well to discuss literary images of old age and popular

91

perceptions of the aged poor's financial drain upon the commonwealth, it is perhaps not the best means of discovering how most individuals in early modern England experienced old age and, in particular, survived during their final years. First, most people were not of the elite. Secondly, most people did not live in communities large enough to have had a sufficient number of old beggars to swell the King's highway or otherwise accost the delicate and privileged traveller. Instead, the majority of English people lived in villages, and most of these communities were small, seldom with more than a few hundred inhabitants. This chapter seeks to move past the world of image and stereotype, past the world of urban centres, past even the environment of the market town, to a world more typical of early modern England: the small rural village.

Local studies can be an extremely valuable tool for investigating specific historical questions. They can, in the words of Keith Wrightson, "make concrete and accessible the abstractions and generalizations of historical interpretation".[7] Most English local studies are based on the parish.[8] England is unique in early modern Europe in its adaptation of an ecclesiastical unit to serve a civic function. The parish, in fact, became the key component upon which English local government was organized. As a result, the legislative and governmentally directed response to poverty was based upon this geographically and spiritually defined area. As Brian Pullan points out elsewhere in this volume, parish-centred relief of poverty is perhaps unique to England. Many other countries expressed the same poor relief aims as England. The Netherlands and other northern European countries funnelled all their relief through a centralized Common Chest, however, and not through individual parishes. Other countries, like France and Italy, shared the Church of England's episcopal structure, ultimately resting upon a foundation of parish priests. Yet, poor relief in these countries operated along different lines, such as the confraternities of Pullan's early modern Italy. The English system was financed by a parochially allocated, yet secular, rate and distributed within the same boundaries. The role of the church in the relief of poverty was consequently different from that played elsewhere. Pullan writes persuasively of the strong and central role of the parish priest, not only broker of alms, but a conduit between charitable organizations and the poor. In contrast, the parish priest was all but removed from the distribution of relief in England, replaced and superseded by a civic officer, the Overseer of the Poor. The church's reduced role in poor relief was marked by its secular nature. Churchwardens, the lay leaders of the church, dispensed relief as they chose, accountable only to secular authorities and not to their priest.

This chapter focuses in depth upon two parishes in Suffolk, Cratfield and Poslingford, between the years 1500 and 1700, as a means of exploring a surprisingly neglected aspect of social history: parish provision for the indigent elderly. While some work does exist on the subject of old age in general, it is especially under-explored compared to the other stages of the life-cycle, such as childhood, youth, service, marriage, and even the final stage, death. Moreover, research has typically focused on the modern period, for example David Thomson's work on nineteenth-century England; or it approaches the subject in a theoretical manner, usually through an examination of household structures, as in the work of Peter Laslett and Richard Wall. Apart from a few individual articles, such as Margaret Pelling's work on Norwich, most early modern studies remain unpublished. It is, arguably, the early modern period that is the most neglected era of this generally neglected subject.[9]

This chapter takes as its focus the aged pensioner in the early modern English village. It seeks not only to explore the nature and frequency of parish pensions as an old age support, but it argues for the need to contextualize the study of poor relief by engaging with the complex interrelationship between structures of poverty and structures of community. In other words, this study considers the way in which economics determined the level of poverty, and suggests the manner in which the organization and collective attitudes of the village shaped its response to the elderly poor.

II

For this study, Cratfield and Poslingford were reconstituted from the parish registers for a two hundred year period.[10] Family reconstitution is essentially the "bringing together of scattered information about the members of a family", their baptisms, marriages, and burials, to illuminate its "chief demographic characteristics".[11] In this manner, the historian typically gains an understanding of a number of important demographic trends, such as family size and age at marriage.[12] My objective, however, was not to establish a wide range of demographic measures but simply to identify individuals over the age of 50. In order to include the maximum number of elderly, the reconstitution was carried forward until 1750, fifty years past the end of the study, thereby encompassing those who died after 1700.

Reconstitutions, however, have limitations. Because of the small size of both parishes, neither reconstitution can be considered statistically sound. Likewise, they cannot account for all the elderly inhabitants present in a community. Many would have entered village life as young adults, arriving at their new home through migration or marriage, and spending the rest of their lives within the parish. Lacking the full range of entries in the parish register, these individuals would not be recognized in a formal reconstitution. To include such people, it was possible to modify a technique employed by Mary Barker-Read to identify the elderly among these more mobile families. In cases where only the date of birth is missing, Barker-Read used the national average age of first marriage to calculate the age of an individual. Likewise, in instances where the marriage date is missing as well, she used a national average interval between marriage and first child to calculate an age at marriage, and then a rough age at death. Obviously, a framework built solely in this way can topple like a house of cards if too much is expected of it.[13]

However, there are ways of strengthening the structure. In this study I have calculated *parish*-specific ages of first marriage, and intervals between marriage and first child. In this way, I have supplied averages which directly reflect local custom and practice and therefore provide a better "fit" than the mass-produced national figures. Furthermore, this method has a tendency to produce conservative age estimates. Often a couple had their first children baptized elsewhere, or it may have been a second marriage for one or both of them. More importantly, I have not placed too much emphasis on the ages which this system generated. While not resulting in precise ages, this method does adequately identify those individuals who were somewhere in the final stage of life.

Having identified the people concerned, each village's extant records were explored, from wills to property deeds, from town books to overseers' accounts, and all information was collected and organized chronologically by individual. This produced 328 individual biographies, containing each person's recorded history from their earliest appearance in the documents – often baptism – through to their old age and finally to death. Each person's old age arrangements consequently came to light. I found that some received full support from the parish overseers, while others seemed to manage with only occasional charity in times of illness or distress. A few aged individuals neither paid the poor rate, nor received relief, surviving by unknown means. Still others, primarily the village elites and middling sorts, lived out their final years under schemes set forth

in their spouses' wills, often in security and comfort. In addition to identifying the source of an individual's support in old age, these biographies
allowed fundamental social divisions to be drawn among the old. They also
permitted a sensitive investigation to be made of the circumstances surrounding old age provisions, so gaining an understanding of the limitations placed upon the range of options. The provisions discussed below
represent only one band of old age arrangements discernible in these two
villages: those provided for the dependent elderly; and it draws upon the
biographies to place these aged pensioners in context.[14]

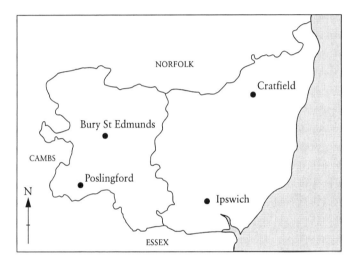

Figure 5.1 Map of Suffolk.

The two villages are located in different parts of Suffolk (see Figure 5.1).
Cratfield is in the northeastern corner of the county, not far from the market town of Beccles. It was small and rural, with a population which had
barely climbed past 300 by the end of the seventeenth century. It was quite
prosperous, however, with its wealth stemming directly from its involvement with Suffolk's famous dairy and infamous cheese industry.[15] In local
government it was fairly independent, with little manorial control, and
was administered instead by a loose group of eight to ten "chief inhabitants". Religiously, it conformed to the Church of England, weathering
the storms of both the Reformation and the Civil War without obvious
trauma.

The second village, Poslingford, is located in the cloth-producing Stour Valley, which runs from east to west, straddling the Suffolk/Essex border. Even including its nearby hamlet, Chipley, Poslingford's population was smaller than Cratfield's, peaking at just over 200 at the beginning of the seventeenth century and remaining fairly constant throughout the rest of our period. Economically, its fortunes were not completely tied to the area's cloth trade, being instead one of those "half agricultural, half industrial" villages which ringed the more cloth-centred communities, such as Poslingford's immediate neighbours, Cavendish and Clare.[16] The cloth industry did, none the less, leave its mark on Poslingford, producing a community whose wealth was visibly polarized. There were a few inhabitants clustered at the top; the same ones, not surprisingly, who formed the closed ruling oligarchy that characterized the village's administrative make-up. More inhabitants were found gathered at the lower end of the subsidy returns, plus many more who appeared on relief, too poor to be taxed. Poslingford's collective religious stance, like Cratfield's, was outwardly conforming, but the parish's chief inhabitants had a more "godly" bent to their religion, which, throughout the years of the seventeenth century, arguably influenced their decisions on behalf of the village.[17]

These are two communities that roughly resemble each other in population and geographical size, but are dissimilar in structure. Their outward similarities are critical, however, in that they allow us to compare them and explore the ways in which their different economic, social, and religious compositions affected each community's approach to, and provision for, their elderly members.

III

By collecting all such "short and simple annals of the poor", a fairly clear picture emerges of the type of aged person Cratfield chose to pension and how many.[18] Typically, the elderly, seldom more than three or four a year, would have first turned to their parish officers for occasional small handouts of cash, the annulment of their rate, or the payment of their rent. This state of *ad hoc* assistance would begin in their late forties and would continue for an average of fourteen years, slowly growing in size and frequency, until these aged individuals, now in their early sixties, were fully enrolled on the parish poor rate with an average 1s a week stipend.

Age preferencing did occur in Cratfield in the years prior to 1630, when all entry-level weekly pensions over 6d were given to those over 50 years of age. After 1630, the elderly entered the pension system at the same level as their younger counterparts, though the aged continued to receive the majority of the exceptionally large stipends, those of 2s a week or more. Initially, the large pensions were directed into the hands of old women; however, the decade of the 1630s seems to have witnessed a shift in priorities. Recipients of these stipends were henceforth drawn solely from the ranks of old, sick males. Thus, the early 1630s appear to be a significant turning point in the history of Cratfield's poor relief, though the reasons for this remain unknown. If only one apparent "shift" occurred during the 1630s, the phenomenon might well be explained as a problem associated with the manipulation of small numbers. However, two such changes, in age and gender, evolved during this decade, lending rather more weight towards the idea of a deliberate change in pensioning policy. Although there was neither a new vicar, nor new parish leaders, a change in the community's priorities probably occurred in the early seventeenth century.[19]

Poslingford tended to pension about the same proportion of its elderly population as Cratfield, though in actual numbers this only amounted to one or two aged people a year. Again, like Cratfield, the indigent elderly did not immediately receive a full parish pension and the security of a weekly sum. Instead, Poslingford's aged and needy inhabitants turned to the charity and goodwill of their neighbours, not to rate-based relief, and to a series of endowed charities established through the last will and testaments of the village's leading members and administered jointly by the parish officers. The amounts received were small, seldom more than a single shilling in a year, and those who qualified for such handouts, somewhere near their forty-fifth birthday, were carefully monitored so that very few individuals ever managed to collect from more than one fund in any given year. Those who did draw upon this charitable assistance did so for roughly a decade before moving into full relief at the parsimonious amount of 8d a week.

A distinctive feature of Poslingford's system was the rarity with which Poslingford's pensioners received their stipends directly. Typically, pensions were paid to the collectioner through a third party, who were often poor themselves. For example John Tyler, his widow, or Thomas Copping, were paid "for the relefe" or the "keeping" of particular individuals.[20] Of the 13 known third-party overseers all but one were marginally poor themselves, eight of whom received relief from the town's endowed charities, though never a pension. In addition, none were known to be close kin of their inmates. It seems quite probable that this arrangement included accommodation as part of one's "maintenance", as a housing allowance was never paid in addition to a third-party pension, though those few individuals receiving pensions directly did receive rent relief as well. Furthermore, only a fraction of all the poor received parish assistance either in the form of a pension or charitable relief, itself a strong sugges-tion that in this poverty-stricken parish only those deemed "worthy" were relieved and the old provided no exception.

Once pensioned, age mattered in determining the size of a Poslingford pension, though not in the way one might expect. Instead of age pref-erencing, the needy of this village experienced age discrimination. While the elderly had to make do with under a shilling a week, younger pension-ers were typically given 19d to support themselves. The injunction to "honour thy hoary head" did not extend to social welfare in this Suffolk village.[21]

IV

Did the elderly receive other types of assistance that would help offset the parish pension? While tracing individual acts of charity is at the best of times difficult, we must ask what other charitable sources were available to the indigent elderly. What, for example, was given by the church through the hands of appointed churchwardens? Furthermore, did the overseers supplement the weekly stipend with other forms of assistance and care?

It is at this point that many studies of poverty fall short of the mark. They typically look only to the weekly pension when pronouncing upon the effectiveness of poor relief.[22] A notable exception is John Walter's work on the social economy of dearth in which he stresses the importance of the "inter-relationship between formal and informal crisis relief" in the sur-vival of the poor.[23] None the less, many fail to integrate the other types of assistance necessary to produce a more comprehensive picture of an indi-vidual's poor relief career, potentially obscuring much higher levels of actual relief, as well as significant differences between parishes.[24]

Once pensioned in Poslingford, the aged poor could expect little else from their parish chest (see Table 5.1.). Wood for fuel, clothing for one's back and special care when sick were regularly provided for others, but seldom for the dependent elderly. Additional payments to the aged were

Table 5.1 Numbers and percentages of pensioners receiving miscellaneous relief.

		Cratfield (1625–1700)	Poslingford (1663–1700)
Fuel	No. of payments	80	93
	No. of times to aged pensioners	26	19
	% of total	**33%**	**20%**
Rent	No. of payments	47	47
	No. of times to aged pensioners	11	1
	% of total	**23%**	**2%**
Sickness	No. of payments	277	48
	No. of times to aged pensioners	66	8
	% of total	**24%**	**17%**
Nursing	No. of payments	52	9
	No. of times to aged pensioners	7	1
	% of total	**14%**	**11%**
Live-in assistance	No. of payments	0	3
	No. of times to aged pensioners	0	0
	% of total	**0%**	**0%**
Cash	No. of payments	689	13
	No. of times to aged pensioners	196	3
	% of total	**28%**	**23%**
Pauper burial	No. of payments	30	14
	No. of times to aged pensioners	9	2
	% of total	**30%**	**14%**
Food	No. of payments	15	1
	No. of times to aged pensioners	11	0
	% of total	**73%**	**0%**
Clothing	No. of payments	78	74
	No. of times to aged pensioners	4	14
	% of total	**5%**	**19%**

Source: Cratfield and Poslingford Churchwardens' and Overseers' Accounts.

strikingly disproportionate. In both villages, the elderly composed a minimum of 30 per cent of all annual pensioners, but typically received far less. For example, of the 74 different clothing payments 19 per cent went to those over age 50. Likewise, the Poslingford overseers made 48 entries recording payments in times of sickness, of which only eight went to elderly pensioners, only 17 per cent of the total. This is particularly telling as old age and illness are known to travel hand-in-hand and consequently it would not be surprising to find more payments to the elderly. Margaret

Pelling draws attention to the important function of "extra or temporary payments made to the poor in time of sickness". Yet, in Pelling's Norwich, there was a similar tendency to treat or cure the young, in preference to the old, which she rightly associates with a deliberate social policy, like that found in London. Poslingford's overseers may well have chosen to distribute their scant resources according to a similar philosophy.[25] These infrequent and low-level parish supplements confirm the nature of Poslingford's pensions; money was paid to a third-party overseer with the intention that they were then responsible for all necessities in all but the most extreme situations.

Poslingford's poor could, however, turn to the nearby clothiers in order to supplement their meagre pension by spinning wool for the cloth trade. Yet, even the healthy and young would have earned little from this source. Spinners were paid by the pound and the Suffolk Wage Rate of 1630 decreed that "every such servant being a single man and working by the pound to have by the pound 1d".[26] Even if the aged poor were as healthy, strong and vigorous as a "single man", and therefore able to spin as much wool, as quickly, there was no guarantee that they would have received the same pay for the same work. Elderly females, for example, seeking to supplement their income in this manner, were seldom paid on the same scale as males.[27] Even at the top price of 1d per pound, Suffolk spinners would not have earned a great deal. Work shortages and stoppages, competition for employment, and the general decay of the traditional cloth industry further decreased the potential earnings available to the aged poor from Suffolk cloth.

Cratfield, however, took a different tack with their old age collectioners (see Table 5.1). Odd jobs, rent, fuel, and care-givers were far from unknown additions to the parish stipend. Jobs such as running errands, "stowinge and brattlinge the woode for the poore", "mending the guildhall", tending the sick and washing the dead were dispensed by Cratfield's churchwardens to the community's poor, including the aged.[28] Employment of this type was directed towards either the good of the community generally or the needs of other poor specifically. As people aged, however, they were employed in this manner less and less often, though old men were still 2.5 times more likely to be employed than old women. As one became older, fuel and rent allowances were added to the relief package, perhaps replacing what had been derived from the proceeds of odd jobs. Nearly 60 per cent of aged pensioners received such gifts at various points during their old age, though never for extended periods of time.

The aged pauper of Cratfield could also expect additional relief when ill, or when nursing was needed. This was the case with Widow Eade for whom, when sick in December 1628, the churchwardens paid 14s "to John Alldus wife for lokeing to the Widow Eade & wachinge [watching] with hur in sikness".[29] Likewise, decrepitude and helplessness were softened by parish-provided keepers who often served for several years in this role. Even the poorest did not die alone. Often other poor people were paid to watch and comfort the dying, generally staying on after death to wash and properly lay out the body. Elisabeth Stannard is far from unique in receiving 2s 4d "for laying of him [Phinias Smith?] forth and watching with him that night he dyed".[30]

In Cratfield, there were a few things which the aged pensioner would not generally expect in addition to their pension, for example clothing and food. Only four old people received gifts of clothing, usually in the form of a complete suit, suggesting that their clothes were ragged through and through before they were replaced, at least at the parish's expense. An alternative supply was the active "second-hand clothing market", a source of cheap clothing for the poor, and one that bypassed the complexities of parish poor relief.[31] It is also clear that the pension was intended to meet one's ordinary food consumption. Illness could, however, sometimes result in gifts of protein, such as Widow Butcher's "rack of veall" in 1632 or Phinias Smith's "pint of butter" in 1680.[32]

Cratfield's pension was clearly intended to cover most of an aged person's daily needs most of the time. It is equally clear that the overseers' and churchwardens' joint poor relief scheme was extremely sensitive, humane and flexible, supplementing the pension as needed. It was so understanding, in fact, that it included a 1s payment for the do-nothing sexton Rubin Tallant on "the 5 of June [he] being Throwneout and lyeing abroad".[33] Seemingly, the welfare system was able to respond to and compensate for a variety of problems associated with poverty in general and old age in particular.[34] It could even, apparently, make allowances for Tallant's domestic strife.

V

The average old-age pension in Cratfield and Poslingford differed by only a few pence a week, yet the availability of additional forms of relief varied significantly between these two communities. The presence or absence of

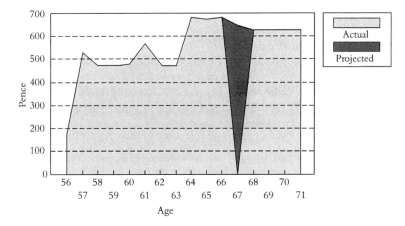

Figure 5.2 Mary Tallant.

non-stipendiary charity was the pivotal element in determining the relative levels of old age comfort available in either village. By looking in
detail at the lives of two representative aged collectioners, we can personal-
ize the statistical averages presented above, and also compare the relative
degree of support available to the elderly of both communities, assessing
the vital role played by non-stipendiary relief.

We can examine the course of a fairly typical old age pension in
Cratfield by looking briefly at the life and poor relief career of Mary
Tallant (see Figure 5.2.) Widow of the ne'er-do-well sexton, Rubin
Tallant, Mary received her first poor relief payment in her own right in
1654, the year Rubin died. She was about 56 years old. At the beginning
of her widowhood, Mary "took over" her husband's 12d a week stipend
for the remainder of that year.[35] Rubin's death was expensive for Mary,
not only in the loss of her husband's wages, but also in the cost of a decent
Christian burial, which in Cratfield ran to three or more shillings.[36] The
churchwardens appear to have responded to this expense by initially maintaining the level of her husband's pension, in spite of the smaller household. The following year her weekly sum dropped to 9d where it remained
until 1662 when it was increased again, at the age of 65, to 1s a week.
Mary Tallant had at least two, but probably three, grown children living in
the parish: Elizabeth, already 20 years old at the time of her father's death;
Robert, 29, and Thomas, 25 years old. By 1661 Robert was a ratepayer
and by 1655 Thomas was on parish relief. The presence of children,

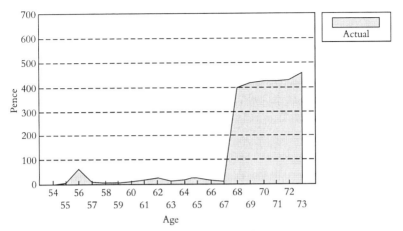

Figure 5.3 "Old" Thomas Plume.

including a rate-paying son, did not seem to alter the level of her relief. Her pension remained at 1s a week until her death at 71.[37]

Mary Tallant received additional assistance at times of acute illness. She was also awarded other sizeable cash payments periodically throughout 1663 and 1664, though their causes were not noted.[38] The parish helped her in other ways, including a house repair spree requiring 41 "nayles to use about the Widow Tallen's house" in 1658. The overseers' interest in Mary Tallant's dwelling might have been driven by more than simple charity. It is possible that she may have shared her house with the 64-year-old Rose Brown, for the accounts record 4d "given to Rose Brown & Widdow Tallowin for a key".[39] Whilst recognizing that this key might have been intended for things other than their front door, it does seem in character with what we know about the two women. Rose Brown had a long history of illness, including the "falling sicknes", and Mary Tallant had a history of caring for others.[40] Widow Tallant did not end her life in the throes of sickness and disease, but seemed to live out her last years on her smallish pension.

Like Cratfield, Poslingford had its own fairly representative aged pensioner. This was "old" Thomas Plume, born in 1608 and married to the widow Prudence Steven in September 1638 (see Figure 5.3). They apparently had no children of their own, nor did the Widow Steven have any from her previous union, at least not any traceable within the parish. Thomas entered the arena of organized relief well after the death of his wife, as a recipient of one of Poslingford's endowed charities. He first appeared in May 1662, receiving 4d per year from "Mistress Ashfield and Mister Strut's gift", which provided 7s annually for the poor of the parish. Thomas was then 54 years old. A few years later he received a small fortune in the sum of 5s 6d, when the will of "Frances Golding spinister ante to Thomas Golding esquire" was examined and it appeared that "she lickwise gave to the poore in monye twenty shillings and as much woode to them as came to six pound tenne shillings".[41]

After a year of relative wealth, Plume resumed his charitable dole on a much less grand scale. Drawing one at a time upon a number of different endowments, the level of his support was low, only gradually increasing to a total of 1s a year from the now combined charity of Ashfield, Strut, and Golding.[42]

At age 69 "Old Thomas" received his first pension: paid "to John Deekes for Old Thomas Plume for 54 weekes . . . 26 of them at 6 pence per weeke and 28 at 8 pence per weeke", a fairly traditional amount, totalling £1 11s 8d[43] The fact that this sum was not paid directly to Old Thomas was also traditional in Poslingford. In this case, it was paid to John Deekes. Thomas Plume lived out the remainder of his life receiving a theoretical 8d a week through the hands of John Deekes, with the cost of his burial sheet, 3s 6d, added on at the end.

As pensioners, Mary Tallant and Thomas Plume were similar. Both entered organized poor relief in their widowhood and received similar-sized pensions. They were also representative of the other collectioners in their community. Plume and Tallant followed a standard relief pattern and received their village's standard pension sum, 8d a week for Plume and 1s for Tallant. Yet, a comparison of the two visual representations of their poor relief careers powerfully confirms what a reading of their biographies suggest: the sizeable and sustained availability of non-stipendiary charity in Cratfield's greater poor relief scheme produced strikingly higher levels of old age support.

VI

The pressing question is whether these aged and poor pensioners laid a heavy financial burden upon their parish or community. Did they, in spite of their small numbers, cost the parish a great deal of money? Were they the fiscal sore which the statutes and contemporary literature lead us to believe was the case for all poor people? In point of fact, aged collectioners were more the proverbial "mere flea-bite" on the leg of rural society than literature's open wound.

The average annual cost of maintaining a single dependent elderly person in Cratfield increased over the course of this study, from £1 5s during the last quarter of the sixteenth century to £2 7s 9d a century later (see Table 5.2).

Table 5.2   Average annual cost of maintaining an aged pensioner.

Community	1575–99	1600–24	1625–49	1650–74	1675–1700
Cratfield	£1:05:00	£1:05:05	£2:10:05	£2:02:00	£2:07:09
Poslingford	—	—	—	—	£1:07:08

Source: Cratfield and Poslingford Churchwardens' and Overseers' Accounts.

These figure represents all income, including odd jobs, and it covers their entire poor relief career. On average the cost of keeping an old person doubled from the beginning of the observed period to 1625–49, vividly reflecting the effects of inflation during this time. The less dramatic increase in the inflation rate after 1650 is also illustrated here in the strikingly consistent cost of maintaining an aged pensioner for the remainder of the century. But, the average annual cost of keeping up Cratfield's total poor relief scheme increased over time as well. From the beginning of the rate book in 1625 we can trace a cost rising annually from £22 16s 3d during the second quarter of the century to an annual average of £54 9s 11d during the last quarter. This annual average expenditure seems generous for its size. Cratfield's population was one-third the size of Newman Brown's Aldenham, Hertfordshire, which averaged annual poor relief costs of £74 1s 6d in the 1670s and £78 2s 2d in the 1680s.[44]

The relative cost of keeping and supporting an elderly person, however, fell dramatically over time as the bulk of the collection was directed into the hands of the labouring poor (see Table 5.3). The aged pensioner accounted for 39 per cent of Cratfield's relief in the years between 1625 and 1649. In the next quarter it fell to a mere 21 per cent of the total budget and in the period after 1675 accounted for 19 per cent of each year's expenditures. The level of assistance received by the elderly was disproportionately low compared to their presence among the poor. Until 1675, approximately half of Cratfield's pensioners were elderly, dropping to roughly 40 per cent during the last quarter of the century. In Poslingford, the aged comprised over 30 per cent of all pensioners.

Table 5.3   Percentage of average annual expenditure spent on aged pensioners.

Community	Quarter century	Average annual cost of one aged pensioner	Average number of aged pensioners	Average annual expenditure	Annual expenditure on all elderly (%)
Cratfield	1625–49	£22:10:05	3.5	£22:16:03	39
Cratfield	1650–74	£2:02:00	4.0	£40:05:02	19
Cratfield	1675–1700	£2:07:19	3.8	£54:09:11	15
Poslingford	1675–1700	£1:07:08	1.7	£25:19:02	9

Source: Cratfield and Poslingford Churchwardens' and Overseers' Accounts.

Yet, they received far less of the available relief. Clearly, the needs of other, competing groups of poor people had become more pressing and their relief a correspondingly higher priority for the parish officers. The elderly were never Cratfield's biggest poverty problem, even at 39 per cent of total spending, and certainly by the end of the period they hardly represented a problem at all.

Looking at Poslingford in this light, one is struck again by the differences in the very nature of the elderly's parish pension. While Cratfield averages nearly £2 8s annually per elderly person, Poslingford averages a full pound less a person, £1 7s 8d, including whatever they might have received from the endowed charities. Equally contrasting is the small proportion of Poslingford's relief that was spent on the elderly, 9 per cent compared to Cratfield's 19 per cent. While poverty was undeniably a problem both in terms of numbers and in terms of public funding, the elderly poor were certainly not the main burden.

VII

The interplay between economics and religion may help to explain Poslingford's smaller parish-provided old-age provision, both in terms of its amount and its overall distribution. Unquestionably, Poslingford's relatively few pensioners were a direct result of its poverty. The village simply could not afford to support more individuals than they did. Poverty is a double-edged sword. It creates needy people while at the same time restricting the ability of others to respond positively to their need. The economic limitations on both parish and parishioner undoubtedly played a decisive role in determining the number of Poslingford's pensioners.

Clearly Poslingford had more needy people than it could pension, and a culling process was required. Unfortunately, the vestry minutes do not survive to illuminate their decision-making process. However, I would like to consider the possibility that the means of selection may have been religiously influenced. Was it possible that the overseers assisted particular aged poor individuals because of shared religious views or a "respectable" lifestyle? The possibility is intriguing given the work of Keith Wrightson and David Levine, Valerie Pearl, and Paul Slack on the poor relief component of social policy in "godly" communities.[45]

Poslingford was situated in what Slack has identified as a triangle of "godly" communities with "godly" poor relief.[46] While it was a religiously conforming parish, within that collective conformity its leading men favoured the "hotter" sort of Protestantism. Likewise, aspects of Poslingford's poor relief resembled the schemes of the more outwardly "godly" cities of Salisbury and Norwich though, not surprisingly, in a diminutive version. The village employed a house of corrections, stocks, and whipping post, in addition to weekly pensions, numerous endowed charities, and parish-provided spinning wheels as part of their solution to poverty. Could the third-party overseers also be viewed as a component of a deliberate social policy designed to regulate pauper behaviour, in addition to its obvious cost-reducing effect?

Because of its limited resources, the parish could not assist all those in need of relief and a culling procedure was employed, probably one that pivoted upon perceived "worthiness" as much as upon need. Given the "hotter" type of Poslingford's religious conformity, the scaled-down version of a recognizable social policy, the village's location in the triangle of "godly" poor relief, and its financial need to be selective, we must consider the possibility that the overseers' selection mechanism was at least partly based on religious values and driven by contemporary conceptions of moral worth.

While the value of the actual pension differed by only a few pence in each parish, the additional assistance provided in Cratfield undeniably and significantly increased the value of its total relief package, even making allowances for the potential in Poslingford of generating additional income through spinning. Relative wealth and perceptions of poverty may go farther than a simple, accounting-sheet explanation towards explaining the dramatically different amounts spent on poor relief. Poverty, as every student soon learns, "is a relative and not an absolute concept". "Perceptions of it change," writes Paul Slack, "as assumptions about what is an adequate standard of living change."[47] Cratfield, with its relative wealth, may well have had a higher minimum standard of living than Poslingford, as well as the resources to do something about it. Furthermore, its economic prosperity meant that Cratfield, unlike Poslingford, was not forced to be as selective in the relief it dispensed, and was thus able to cast its net over a wider pool of potential pensioners.

Two points clearly emerge from this analysis of elderly pensioners in Poslingford and Cratfield. The first is the danger involved in generalizing from single communities and extrapolating such findings to the bigger arena. A generalization drawn from only Poslingford or Cratfield would be misleading, presenting a skewed and over-simplified image of what is a highly complex picture. The second is the combined importance of economics and religion, as well as perceived need, in determining the nature of old-age provisions provided by the parish. Old-age pensions in Cratfield and Poslingford were in fact shaped by a balance between Wrightson and Levine's cultural and religious factors and Martin Ingram's emphasis on economic determinism. Poverty and poor relief were not in a simple, cause-and-effect relationship. Though discussing medieval Cambridge, Miri Rubin neatly sums up the situation:

> economic factors will determine the ability to give and the need to receive, but will not guarantee charitable disposition nor prescribe the forms in which relief will be dispensed, considerations largely governed by non-economic, religious and cultural values.[48]

The contrasting examples of Poslingford and Cratfield verify that Rubin's observations are as true for early modern Suffolk as they were for medieval Cambridgeshire.

Notes

1. W. Shakespeare, Sonnet 22, in *Complete poems*, C. More, (ed.) (Avenel, NJ, 1993), p. 135.
2. H. Cuffe, *The differences of the ages of mans life* (London, 1607), p. 132. The Diary of Lady Sarah Cowper, Hertfordshire Public Record Office, Penshanger MSS, D/P F32 (hereafter, D/EP), p. 190. I would like to thank Anne Kugler for this and other references to the Cowper diary. See *Prescription, culture and shaping identity: Lady Sarah Cowper (1644–1720)*. (PhD thesis, University of Michigan, 1994). See also *Times alteration: or, the old mans rehearsall, what brane [sic] dayes he knew, a great while agone, when this old cap was new* (London, n.d.), The Pepys Ballad Collection,

Magdalene College, Cambridge, for an example in the popular press.

3. J. Strype, *Lessons moral and Christian for youth and old age. In two sermons preach'd at Guildhall Chappell, London*. (London, 1699), pp. 71–73.

4. Diary of Lady Sarah Cowper, D/EP F30, p. 227; F32, p. 60.

5. Shakespeare, Sonnet 63, *Complete poems*, p. 156.

6. *Statutes of the Realm*, I Edward VI, c. 3.

7. K. Wrightson, "The social order of early modern England: three approaches" in *The world we have gained. Histories of population and social structure*, L. Bonfield, R. M. Smith, K. Wrightson (eds) (Oxford, 1986), p. 202.

8. See also T. Wales, "Poverty, poor relief and the life-cycle: some evidence from seventeenth-century Norfolk" in *Land, kinship and life-cycle*, R. M. Smith (ed.) (Cambridge, 1984), p. 385.

9. D. Thomson, *Provision for the elderly in England, 1830–1908*. (PhD thesis, University of Cambridge, 1980); P. Laslett, "The study of social structure from listings of inhabitants" in *An introduction to English historical demography*, E. A. Wrigley (ed.) (London, 1966), pp. 160–208; R. Wall, "Mean household size in England from printed sources" in *Household and family in past time*, P. Laslett & R. Wall (eds) (Cambridge, 1972), pp. 163–203; M. Pelling, "Old age, poverty, and disability in early modern Norwich: work, remarriage, and other expedients" in *Life, death, and the elderly: historical perspectives*, M. Pelling & R. M. Smith (eds) (London, 1991), pp. 74–101. For unpublished work, see M. Barker-Read, *The treatment of the aged poor in five selected West Kent parishes from settlement to speenhamland (1622–1797)*. (PhD thesis, Open University, 1988).

10. Cratfield Parish Register, Suffolk Record Office, Ipswich (hereafter, SROI), FC62/A6/23, beginning 1539, and Poslingford Parish Register, Suffolk Record Office, Bury St Edmunds (hereafter, SROB), FL615/4/1, beginning 1559.

11. E. A. Wrigley, "Family reconstitution" in *An introduction to English historical demography*, p. 96.

12. For example see K. Wrightson & D. Levine, *Poverty and piety in an English village. Terling 1525–1700* (London, 1979); C. [Davey] Jarvis, *Reconstructing local population history: the Hatfield and Bobbington districts of Essex, 1550–1880*. (PhD thesis, University of Cambridge, 1990).

13. Barker-Read, *The treatment of the aged poor*, pp. 27–30.

14. See also Wales, "Poverty, poor relief and the life-cycle", pp. 351–404.

15. D. Defoe, *A tour thro' the whole island of Great Britain* (London, 1968), p. 53.

16. B. A. Holderness, "Chapter 7. East Anglia and the Fens: Norfolk, Suffolk, Cambridgeshire, Ely, Huntingdonshire, Essex, and the Lincolnshire Fens" in *The agrarian history of England and Wales* [vol. 5], part I, J. Thirsk (ed.) (Cambridge, 1984), p. 220.

17. For a full discussion of the background of both parishes, see: L. Botelho, *Provisions for the elderly in two early modern Suffolk communities*. (PhD thesis, University of Cambridge, 1996).

18. T. Gray, *Elegy in a country churchyard*, st. 8 (eighteenth century), as quoted in *Dictionary of quotations* [vol. 1] (London: Everyman's Library, no. 809, n.d.), p. 107.

19. See also Wales, "Poverty, poor relief and the life-cycle" pp. 354, 387.

20. Poslingford Town Book (hereafter, TB), SROB, FL615/7/1.

21. "You shall rise up before the hoary head, and honour the face of an old man". Leviticus 20:32. See also Proverbs 16:31: "The hoary head is a crown of glory".

22. Examples include T. Arkell, "The incidence of poverty in England in the later seventeenth century", *Social History* **12**, 1987, pp. 23–48; A. L. Beier, "Poor relief in Warwickshire 1630–1660", *Past and Present* **35**, 1965, pp. 77–100; E. M. Hampson, *The treatment of poverty in Cambridgeshire, 1601–1834* (Cambridge, 1934); E. M. Leonard, *The early history of English poor relief* (Cambridge, 1900); and M. McIntosh, "Local responses to the poor in late medieval and Tudor England", *Continuity and Change* **3**, 1988, pp. 209–45.

23. J. Walter, "The social economy of dearth in early modern England" in *Famine, disease and the social order in early modern society*, J. Walter & R. Schofield (eds) (Cambridge, 1989), p. 122.

24. *Ibid.*, p. 122.

25. M. Pelling, "Healing the sick poor: social policy and disability in Norwich, 1550–1640", *Medical History* **29**, 1985, p. 121, also n18.

26. "Rates of Wages of Labarores, Articificers, Spinners and Other Working People . . . Rated and Apointed in the County of Suffolk upon Munday 12 Aprilis, . . . 1630", University of Cambridge Library, Add. MS 22, f. 73v.

27. For gender discrimination amongst servants in husbandry, see: *ibid.*, f. 73v. See also Wales, "Poverty, poor relief and the life-cycle", p. 378.

28. "Running errands", Cratfield Churchwardens' Accounts (hereafter, CWA), SROI FC62/A6/17; "stowing wood for the poor", Cratfield CWA, SROI FC62/A6/17 "mending the guildhall", Cratfield CWA, SROI FC62/A6/117; "Tending the sick" Cratfield CWA, SROI FC62/A6/154; and "washing the dead", Cratfield, CWA, SROI FC62/A6/334.

29. Cratfield CWA, SROI FC62/A6/154.

30. Cratfield CWA, SROI FC62/A6/334. See also C. Gitting's, *Death, burial and the individual in early modern England* (London, 1984).

31. I. Archer, *The pursuit of stability. Social relations in Elizabethan London* (Cambridge, 1991), p. 193.

32. Cratfield CWA, SROI FC62/A6/162, 334.

33. Cratfield CWA, SROI FC62/A6/162.

34. See also V. Pearl, "Social policy in early modern London" in *History and imagination. Essays in honour of H. R. Trevor-Roper*, H. Lloyd-Jones, V. Pearl, B. Worden (eds) (London, 1981), p. 123.

35. Cratfield CWA, SROI, FC62/A6/1.

36. See also Cratfield CWA, SROI FC62/A6/131.

37. Cratfield CWA, SROI FC62/A2/1. Cratfield Overseers' Accounts (hereafter, OSA), SROI, FC62/A2/1.

38. Illness payments: Cratfield OSA, SROI FC62/A2/1, passim. Cash payments: Cratfield CWA, SROI FC62/A6/268, 270.

39. Cratfield CWA, SROI, FC62/A6/246.

40. Cratfield OSA, SROI FC62/A2/1. Cratfield CWA, SROI FC62/A6/212, 246, 270.

For the employment of the poor, see M. Pelling, "Illness among the poor in an early modern English town: the Norwich census of 1570", *Continuity and Change* **3**, 1988, pp. 273–90, and D. Willen, "Women in the public sphere in early modern England: the case of the urban working poor", *Sixteenth Century Journal* **19**, 1988, pp. 559–76.

41. Poslingford TB, SROB, FL615/7/1.
42. Poslingford TB, SROB FL615/7/1.
43. Poslingford TB, SROB FL615/7/1.
44. W. Newman Brown, "The receipt of poor relief and family situation: Aldenham, Hertfordshire 1630–90", in *Land, kinship and life-cycle*, R. M. Smith (ed.) (Cambridge, 1984), p. 412, Table 12.3.
45. Wrightson & Levine, *Poverty and piety in an English village*; V. Pearl, "Puritans and poor relief: the London workhouse, 1649–1660" in *Puritans and revolutionaries. Essays in seventeenth century history presented to Christopher Hill* (Oxford, 1978), pp. 206–32 and Pearl, "Social policy in early modern London", pp. 115–131; P. Slack, "Poverty and politics in Salisbury, 1597–1666" in *Crisis and order in English towns, 1500–1700. Essays in urban history*, P. Clark & P. Slack (eds) (London, 1972), pp. 164–203 and *Poverty and policy in Tudor and Stuart England* (London, 1988), pp. 149–55. For a dissenting view, see M. Ingram, "Religion, communities and moral discipline in late sixteenth- and early seventeenth-century England: case studies", in *Religion and society in early modern Europe, 1500–1800*, K. von Greyerz, (ed.) (London, 1984), pp. 177–93 and M. Spufford, "Puritanism and social control", in *Order and disorder in early modern England*, A. Fletcher & J. Stevenson (eds) (Cambridge, 1987), pp. 41–57.
46. Slack, *Poverty and policy in Tudor and Stuart England*, p. 150.
47. *Ibid.*, p. 2.
48. M. Rubin, *Charity and community in medieval Cambridge* (Cambridge, 1989), p. 15.

6

Old people and their families in the English past[1]

Pat Thane

Plato's *Republic* opens with a discussion between Socrates and an older man, who comments on the conviction among his friends that younger people were more neglectful and disrespectful of their aged parents than they used to be. He strongly disagrees.[2] Such assertions and disagreements recur so regularly through the centuries to the present that they suggest the significance of this aspect of intergenerational relationships in western culture and continuing insecurity and uncertainty as to its character.

Similar disagreements have been evident among historians concerned to explore the survival strategies of older people in the English past. As is evident in other contributions to this volume, throughout recorded history many older people, like many younger people, survived in what early modern historians call an "economy of makeshifts" and modern economists, less picturesquely, "income packaging"; that is, they put together an income from a variety of sources. The relative weighting of the components of the "package" may have shifted over time but the main components themselves have not. In the fifteenth century, as now, older people drew support in cash or services, to degrees that varied among individuals and over place and time, from earnings from work, from savings, public welfare, charity, from family and friends.

The problem for historians seeking to unpack these packages in order to understand the relative importance of each of the components is the extreme unevenness with which they enter the records. Above all there is a danger that we overestimate the importance of the one which was most consistently recorded because it was a public institution, poor-law relief. Although poor relief records, especially before 1834, survive only patchily, their survival rate is immensely greater than that of charities, employment information and, most elusive of all, evidence of support from family and friends, activities which no-one had any reason to record systematically. This undoubted over-representation of poor relief in the historical record is a problem because, although at most times the "aged and impotent" were among the main recipients of relief, most studies conclude that most old and poor people did not receive relief, or received it at most irregularly and/or at too inadequate a level to provide subsistence.

So how did old people survive? This is too large a question for a single chapter, which will confine itself to the relationship between family support and poor-law support.

The Cambridge Group, Laslett and the family

The argument that the family made a much less important contribution than poor relief to the survival of old people has been promoted most systematically and valuably in the work of scholars associated with the Cambridge Group for the History of Population and Social Structure. Peter Laslett's early work on household and family was an invigorating and necessary challenge to commonplace stereotypes of a "past" in which old people normally spent their declining years under the same roof as, and in the care of, their adult offspring or other close relatives. The data collected on household structure in "the past" called this is in question as part of the general unpacking of the notion of an extended family norm in pre-industrial northwest Europe.

From quantitative data about household structure Laslett deduced a set of norms about intergenerational obligations: once children had left the parental home as servants, and certainly after marriage, they rarely returned to it to live for any extended period, and there was no obligation upon them to contribute from their earnings to the support of their parents. Parents who could afford to do so would continue to give support to offspring when needed, and, when possible, would set them up with property on marriage. The line of material obligation was downwards not upwards through the generations. The bonds of mutual intergenerational dependence and obligation were relatively weak compared with the commonly held stereotype.[3]

Laslett and, more forcefully, Richard Smith have linked these insights into family structure to observations about the long history of collective provision for poor relief in England: that because the extended family was not customarily available as a resource in times of hardship, due for example to old age, the community (generally the parish) from very early times, predating the Elizabethan poor law, took on a high degree of responsibility for the needy, by means of either voluntary charity or compulsory contributions from parishioners. This is the so-called "nuclear hardship" hypothesis which seems to assume that the poor law arose to do what the family did not.[4]

Nevertheless in 1977 Laslett pointed out that "the fragmentary though suggestive evidence . . . indicates that the aged in pre-industrial England were more frequently to be found surrounded by their immediate family than is the case in the England of today".[5] This did not contradict statements about the rarity of the extended family because the situation described was not due to elderly parents sharing a house with married offspring, but to the fact that elders were more likely to have unmarried children living with them than in modern times. This was owing to the combination of the relatively high marriage age and the longer period of childbearing compared with the twentieth century. If a woman bore her last child in her forties that child might still be at home when the parents were defined as "old" in their late fifties or sixties. Also higher rates of widowhood and the relatively high re-marriage rates, especially of older widowers to women of childbearing age, meant that ageing men would have sometimes very young children around them, and, more problematically, become dependent upon them as they aged.

Laslett concluded in 1977 that there was

> no clear pattern of failing fathers and mothers joining households of married offspring or requesting it and parents did not strive to keep children at home. Where the elderly shared households with the young it was because they were useful or were head of the household.

Such co-residence, he argued, was based on sentiments of affection, duty or charity rather than on

> any socially sanctioned expectation that such an action should take place. . . . It would certainly not be justifiable, however, to suppose that the story of welfare relationships between the young and the old, between children and their ageing and infirm parents in traditional English society was one of indifference or neglect.[6]

This characterization of intergenerational relations as often close, but voluntaristic rather than rule-bound, opens the path to a range of possible relationships, co-residential and otherwise; and indeed it seems that over time Laslett has shifted, as has Richard Wall, to an increasing emphasis on the variability of family forms around the nuclear norm, to emphasizing that "the nuclear rules were not rigid"; to a greater stress on the possibility that even where the generations did not live together kin connections were important especially in major life crises and life course transitions, although how important in relation to other sources of support remains debatable.[7]

Laslett – whose perception of intergenerational relations has always been more subtle than is always recognized – has rightly stressed, as have others, that where old people are found living alone in the past or in the present this should not necessarily be interpreted as evidence of loneliness and neglect. There is in all times strong evidence of older people *choosing* to keep an independent household for as long as they are able, although exchanging emotional and material support with kin and friends; and of a long-established, deep-rooted cultural awareness and fear of the conflicts that can arise when generations live together and the old give up their independence, power or property to the young. This is vividly expressed in a long line of north European folk-tales, which reach their sublimest expression in *King Lear*. Of course, some old people really have been neglected and lonely at all times.

What is emerging from recent work is increasing emphasis on the variety of intergenerational relationships in the past and the present and an increasing awareness of the importance of family in the material and emotional support of older people, following a long period in which the role of family has been rather down-played in relation to that of collective poor relief. A large area of debate remains about the relative importance of the two and of other sources of support for old people.

The role of the poor law

The belief that it has long been a cultural norm that "it is unEnglish behaviour to expect children to support parents"[8] is most vigorously promoted by David Thomson. Thomson's conviction that support from the family was of minor significance in the lives of old people at all social levels over a long period of English history derives from his studies of the treatment of old people by the provisions of the new poor law in the nineteenth century.

This belief might seem to be contradicted by the clear provision in the poor law statute of 1601 that

> The father and grandfather, mother and grandmother and children of every poor, old, blind, lame and impotent person, or other poor person not able to work, being of sufficient ability, shall at their own charges relieve and maintain every such poor person, in that manner, and according to that rate, as by the justices . . . in their sessions shall be assessed. (43 Eliz. I c. 2)

This remained in force until the mid-twentieth century.

Thomson argues that this clause was rarely enforced and that its interpretation was progressively narrowed by court decisions over the seventeenth and eighteenth centuries. He takes this as strong evidence that family support for the elderly poor was not an English norm, pointing to the absence of evidence that the law was implemented and to contemporary comment that it was not. Historians have to be wary of confusing absence of evidence with absence of research, and this is a field in which there has been little research. Such as there is calls Thomson's interpretation into question and the contemporary commentaries on which he relies do not unambiguously support him.

He relies in part on eighteenth- and nineteenth-century digests of the law relating to poor relief.[9] These indeed point out how restricted were the circumstances in which the "liable relatives clause", as it was called, could be applied. It is questionable whether we can generalize societal norms about family relationships from a series of technical legal decisions in cases arising from a statute designed to deal with the very poor, especially when it is clearly stated, in one of these digests, published in 1830, that

> The poor laws were never intended to supersede the obligation which the ties of kindred impose upon all mankind to support the helpless and destitute members of their family . . . the statute which forms the groundwork of the whole system expressly recognizes the primary right of the indigent to claim support and assistance from their relatives and affords its sanction to this moral duty.[10]

A reference to this "moral duty" appears also in the other eighteenth-century digest which Thomson cites: "By the law of nature a man was bound to take care of his own father and mother."[11] We need to consider taking seriously such statements as being representative of general cultural expectations about family responsibility for the elderly.

The need to do so seems stronger if we examine more closely how the poor law actually operated. Thomson's assertion that the "liable relatives clause" was rarely implemented before the 1870s – when there certainly was a vigorous effort to implement it as Thomson and others (especially, and with greater subtlety than Thomson, Williams) have described[12] – derives partly from his own limited study of poor-law administration in the rural south of England in the nineteenth century;[13] partly from the assertion in the Report of the Royal Commission of the Poor Laws of 1834 that the clause was not implemented. This dramatically – indeed absurdly – claim that

> The duty of supporting parents and children, in old age or infirmity, is so strongly enforced by our natural feelings that it is often well-performed, even among savages, and almost always so in a nation deserving the name of civilized. We believe that England is the only European nation in which it is neglected.[14]

We have long known that the Report of the Royal Commission bore at best a selective relationship to the evidence on which it was supposedly based. It is interesting that the passage couples neglect of children equally with neglect of parents.

As the assistant commissioners went around the country investigating the administration of the old poor law in 1832, they enquired, some more assiduously than others, about the implementation of the "liable relatives clause". The picture that emerges from their reports, as about all things to do with the poor law, is complicated. As might be expected, the comments of the assistant commissioners reveal a range of preconceptions, from sympathy to extreme censoriousness, towards the aged poor and their relatives.

Their reports indicate that the clause was implemented, though hardly on a day-to-day basis and variably from place to place. It was enforced vigorously in Southwell (Nottinghamshire), that model of "perfect parochial management"[15] which helped to inspire the poor-law reforms to come; hardly at all in many other parishes. The relative infrequency of implementation was said to be due in part to poor-law officials using the *threat* of calling in the magistrates as an effective means to persuade those whom they believed could afford to support elderly people. Officials preferred this approach because it was simpler and cheaper than to resort to the costly and not always predictable quarter sessions; it was unlikely to be recorded. Also it could be difficult to prove that a liable relative had sufficient means; and a magistrates' order could be difficult and costly to enforce upon reluctant relatives.[16]

It was also observed that poor-law officials did not invoke the law against liable relatives who lived near or even with old people where those relatives, as was often the case, were themselves so poor that they could not afford to give more. A number of commissioners commented sympathetically on the great poverty of the relatives of the aged poor. Hence the willingness of the poor relief system well into the nineteenth century to pay outdoor relief to old people living with or close to married offspring; this was regarded as a normal, acceptable and necessary supplement to the best efforts of younger people struggling to bring up a family in severe poverty and giving the older people what they could.[17]

This picture is supported by the only substantial study of the treatment of old people under the old poor law, Mary Barker-Read's thesis on five west Kent parishes in the eighteenth century. She comments that although cases of prosecution were indeed few it was not because the law was disregarded or thought inconsistent with custom; rather officials thought the procedure costly or futile. She suggests that where locally resident relatives were judged not to be giving as much help as they could afford, the parish would put them under strong moral pressure; where they could not afford full assistance, the parish encouraged them by abating rate payments, by paying daughters to take parents as lodgers; or they would supplement the family income with poor relief while the old person lived with them.[18]

This giving of poor relief to old people living near or with relatives has sometimes been interpreted as further evidence of a limited cultural expectation that relatives should support elderly people.[19] The evidence seems far stronger that such relief was intended to encourage and support such family care by supplementing the little that families could afford to give.

The crucial phrase in the "liable relatives clause" of the old poor law was "*being of sufficient ability* . . . to relieve and maintain every such poor person"[author's italics]. This was taken seriously by magistrates and poor-law officials. They rarely pursued the pointless goal of expecting adult children to render themselves destitute, and thus also in need of relief, in order to support their elderly parents. A likely reason why Thomson finds so few cases of implementation of the law in the few unions he has investigated is that they were precisely the sort of poor rural districts in which there was no point in pursuing poor men for payments they could not afford.

The poor law, its implementation and contemporary comment upon it should not be interpreted as indicating that it was "unEnglish to expect children to support parents". Rather such support was indeed expected of adult children, but only if they could afford it without impoverishing themselves and their own children. Obligations downwards to children did come before those upwards to parents. Where the obligation to elderly parents could not be fulfilled, or not fulfilled to the extent of giving full support, then the poor relief system would provide supplementation, not always generously or willingly – how willingly varied from place to place and from time to time. It was provided only when it was clear that old people had no other resources from family, friends, charity, work or begging. The latter continued to be sanctioned for respectable old people in parts of England and Wales until well into the nineteenth century.

Thomson has argued that poor relief provided the largest component in the income package of a very high proportion of the aged poor in the 1830s and 1840s and implies that this was long-established practice. Again this rests on slight evidence. More convincing is the testimony of contemporary sources and historical studies of the old and the new poor laws which point out the high proportion of the aged poor who can have received no relief at all, or amounts so small and irregular that they cannot have provided subsistence, while only a small minority received anything approaching full subsistence.

Steven King's careful reconstruction of the poor relief experience of a rural industrial area of west Yorkshire between 1650 and 1820 shows that long-term regular relief payments to old people were almost non-existent; that payments were extremely rarely as high as 2s or 2s 6d per week and usually very much less and considerably below a possible subsistence income; and the relief was more likely to be required by in-migrants who were less likely to have relatives in the neighbourhood. He finds a similar pattern elsewhere in northern England and links it to interconnected economic structures and cultural traditions. In this area of west Yorkshire a cohesive land-based kin system created a tenacious kin-based survival structure, in which "co-residence of young and old families as a coping strategy for both appears to have been common". Co-resident or not, relatives provided mutual support by means of exchange of cash, experiencing a "'lived' sense of duty felt between the generations".[20] For people living at a very low level of subsistence such support was, literally, a vital component of their survival package.

This may have been an unusually ungenerous region. In few others do we hear of parishioners stoning paupers on the way to church. Other sources, such as Barker-Read's work on west Kent, Frederick Eden's survey of poor relief in the 1790s and those of the assistant commissioners in 1832 suggest somewhat more generosity in parishes, particularly in the south, which were not necessarily richer than those studied by King. However, the number, levels and regularity of payments which they report still indicate that the poor law was normally a residual provider supplementing other sources of income and a major resource for only a small minority of the aged poor.[21] Clearly there were important local and regional variations which require exploration. The old poor law could be more generous than has been thought, but, whatever the inadequacies of modern welfare states, early modern historians may be too sanguine in describing the poor law as comparable in scope.[22] It remained overwhelmingly residual in character.

It seems, then, that poor relief generally, though with variations, made an important but not a dominant contribution to the incomes of the aged poor; and that families contributed more, not necessarily in cash, than has been recognized.

Much of the evidence so far comes from the words, or from inferences from the actions of poor-law officials. The words of the poor can rarely be heard before the later nineteenth century. Working men and their representatives who gave evidence before the Royal Commission on the Aged Poor of 1895 protested vigorously against the severe implementation of the "liable relatives clause" in the 1870s and 1880s. A possible reason for this rigour was the belief that by the 1870s British workers had become more prosperous than ever before and could be expected now to bear the full cost of the support of their elderly relatives. Witnesses protested that this belief was erroneous, especially in the case of agricultural labourers, who were still poorly paid. But their argument was not that it was wrong and against English custom to expect children to support their parents, but rather that it *was* the tradition that children did their very best for their parents. What was wrong and was protested against was the new attempt to enforce this obligation upon those who could not do more without rendering themselves, their spouses and children destitute, and the apparent assumption that they could afford cash support in addition to services. They complained that the strict enforcement of the law was insensitive to the reality of the lives of poor people to a greater degree than previous methods of administration.[23]

To quote just one example: George Edwards, General Secretary of the Norfolk and Norwich Amalgamated Labour Union faced a leading question from a Commissioner, Joseph Arch, founder of the agricultural workers union:

> And invariably you find that those children rendered their parents more help in kind than they would do if they had to pay the money. That the assistance they render in kind as well as many little things and comforts that they take their aged parents would be worth more than the one shilling per week that they pay into the union?

Edwards replied:

> Oh, a great deal. They do now assist them. I have known cases in which they assist them with reference to garden produce in the way of a few potatoes and such like and they are very anxious to assist them in any way they can outside of monetary assistance. . . . They are enabled to give far more than a shilling a week in kind. For example in garden food, and the old lady would go and see after the children and they would have them to tea and dinner with them, so they are able to and do render a large amount of assistance in kind. . . . The agricultural labourers' first duty is to take their money home to their wives and children; the children being their own must be the first that are thought for . . . even at the present rate of wages, the agricultural labourers have to get heavily into debt where there are large families.[24]

This picture was supported by Charles Booth's survey of the aged poor in the 1890s. He gathered evidence from 360 poor-law unions on, among other things, the treatment of old people by their relatives. He received almost every conceivable shade of opinion and fact on the matter. This testifies to the variety of old people's experience and of expectations about it. But he felt able to draw certain conclusions:

1. Married children and their families, if themselves poor, find it difficult to make any regular money allowance.

2. Unmarried children working at a distance – for instance a daughter in service or sons at sea – do frequently send money regularly, acting dutifully and generously.
3. Unmarried children living at home often support their parents.
4. When a home breaks up married children frequently provide a home for a widowed parent.
5. Apart from money provision or provision of a home much is done in many irregular ways for old people by their children and relatives.
6. This help is more effective in the country than the town.
7. Old women are more easily provided for than old men.[25]

With striking regularity historians of poor relief in all periods have concluded that family and neighbours must have supported the elderly in some form, for it is inconceivable that they could have survived on the amount of poor relief they received and other known resources.[26] Through the nineteenth century poor-law administrators took such support for granted and used it to justify low levels of outrelief.[27]

Co-residence

Can we go further in establishing the extent and kind of intergenerational exchange involving the aged poor? First what can be established about the extent of co-residence? One of the valuable early contributions of the Cambridge Group was to undermine the notion that normally in pre-industrial England people lived in vertically and/or laterally extended families. As already pointed out, they also emphasize the variety of family forms around the nuclear norm. This variability was true at any one time and over time. Richard Wall and Steven Ruggles, for England and the United States, have indicated that the three-generation extended family became rather more prevalent in the nineteenth century.[28] This was partly for demographic reasons: higher survival rates increased the chances of three generations of the same family staying alive together. Mid-nineteenth-century studies of the varied communities of Preston, the Staffordshire Potteries, Bethnal Green, Cardiff, industrial villages of the Midlands, and York suggests that this is so, but that the numbers co-resident were not great and varied from place to place.[29] We should not assume of course that co-residence was necessarily a happy or a strongly desired option for old people or that it delivered them the best care when they needed it.

It still is not easy to estimate what proportion of old people experienced co-residence; still less why they did so. Cambridge Group methods may have led to underestimation of functional co-residence. In 1972 Laslett published his classic definition of "households" as consisting of people wholly co-residing on a regular basis. Households in this definition excluded "kin and affines who live close by, even if they collaborate so closely in the productive work of the family that for economic purposes they form part of it and may frequently or usually take their meals at the family table". This included, he wrote,

> retired members of a former generation . . . even if supported by it and still working with it, provided that they would not be regarded by the family, or by an enquirer, as resident in the family home . . . a retired couple occupying a cottage in the yard, or "doing for themselves" in rooms set aside for them in a farmhouse, are not members.[30]

This is a wholly defensible strategy when seeking to establish rules whereby household size and structure could be compared over long time periods. It causes problems only if we try to use the results to measure things they were not designed to measure, such as relationships other than very close co-residence between old people and their relatives.

It is also a problem for these purposes that the Cambridge definition of a household excludes lodgers for, as Laslett once noted (though he interpreted it, perhaps anachronistically, as evidence of social distance between kin)[31], aged and other close relatives could be described as "lodgers" from at least the sixteenth century to the nineteenth century in censuses and other listings, diaries and memoirs. Hence the method may miss some three-generation families where surname or other evidence does not make relationships clear; as for example when an old man lived with a married daughter, as was by no means uncommon.

Thomas Sokoll has used a wider definition of the household to include lodgers, in reconstructing pauper households in Ardleigh in Essex in 1796 and Braintree in 1821. In Ardleigh, but not in Braintree, significant numbers of extended families were discovered at the social level where previously this had been thought least probable – the poorest, though he also found substantial numbers among the non-poor. The difference between the two areas is hard to account for. The economies of both parishes were in a troubled state at the time. This again suggests local variability in patterns of intergenerational support.[32]

In fact it is difficult to measure co-residence in England before the nineteenth century owing to the extreme shortage of sources providing ages. For the whole period before 1800, for the whole of England and Wales only eight censuses have been found which list the inhabitants of a particular parish or township, and record both the ages of inhabitants and adequate detail about relationships of household members to the head of household. These are all one-off, "snapshot", listings, so they give no impression of change within any household over time. They come from different parts of the country and a variety of time periods; no-one has tried to claim that they are representative of the whole population over 200 years or so. These have formed the basis of most calculations about intergenerational co-residence. Richard Wall has commented that it is "ironic" that

> households in pre-industrial England have received more attention than households in other parts of Europe, given that the census material that survives for pre-industrial England is so much more fragmentary and poorer in quality than that which is available for other parts of Europe.[33]

Painstaking linking of different kinds of record, such as that undertaken by Sokoll and King, can valuably extend our understanding of these processes, but this is difficult work and, so far, rarely done. Are there other data which will confirm, deny, amplify or help us to interpret the picture of very limited co-residence which emerges from these sources?

Margaret Spufford was puzzled to find in wills from Staffordshire and Warwickshire in the fifteenth century and from Cambridgeshire in the sixteenth century multiple examples of "old folk being provided with bed, board and access to the fire", "sleeping in the little low chamber off the hall".[34] Wills specifying that widows should be provided with house-room by the heir have been found very widely in place and time between the fifteenth and eighteenth centuries, although the variations are hard to explain.[35]

Not only the prosperous made such bequests. William Sampfield of Orwell, Cambridgeshire, a labourer, in 1588 left his cottage, garden and orchard to his only son who was to support his two sisters and give houseroom to his mother, a considerable burden on a small income.

Spufford concluded that "living with in-laws, or rather, having a widowed parent to live with one, when one was of age to inherit the farm was very much the ordinary expected thing to do". She also calculated that this does not necessarily conflict with the Cambridge Group conclusion that such co-residence was uncommon in most communities at most times in pre-industrial England. The Cambridge estimate of the average percentage of vertically extended households among all households in England between the late sixteenth and early nineteenth centuries was 5.8. On average at any one time only 6.2 per cent of the population was widowed. Hence it is perfectly possible that a very high proportion of widowed people (very many of whom of course would not have been old) lived with their offspring, yet that vertically extended households were a small proportion of all households.

Also, due to the normally late marriage age and lower life expectancy of the elderly compared with today, this three-generation phase in the developmental cycle of the family, if it occurred at all, was likely to be brief. This suggests that co-residence of elderly widowed parents with children was normal in some places at least, but relatively infrequent and that it might be brief.

Diaries, memoirs, autobiographies, biographies and historical studies of communities provide further evidence of intergenerational co-habitation and other forms of support. Patchy and unrepresentative such data may be, but certainly no more so than the available quantitative data. Such sources are constructed mainly by the literate and comfortably off. As such they can supplement the evidence from poor-law records and wills to assist in constructing a picture of expectations about intergenerational relationships at all levels of society.

There is insufficient space to summarize such sources here. Taken as a whole,[36] they suggest that the generations moved in together, not necessarily as a matter of routine though in some agricultural areas this may have been so, but often in response to need on the part of one or other generation, and not always that of the older generation. Need could be of various kinds, such as that of ageing landholders experiencing difficulty in working their land or the younger generation needing help with child care. We should not see the flow of assistance as being always from young to old, or the old as passive, helpless and incapable of determining their own fate. It was very much not so: old people could use their material or emotional leverage over the younger generation very effectively in their own interests.

In the seventeenth century, for example, Ralph Thoresby recalled how his prosperous father decided to "live upon his children", moving from house to house, apparently assuming it as his right. Thoresby found it expensive. He could

> by no means quit my father-in-law who gave over house-keeping and came with his wife, daughter and servant to live upon his children and though he sometimes went to brother Ws and Rs yet I think he was half if not two-thirds of his time at my house, and being of a generous spirit was so liberal of my liquor to visitants that I saw it absolutely necessary to give over wine.[37]

The diary of William Stout, the Quaker merchant of Lancaster who lived from 1665 to 1752, gives a full picture of the relationships first of his mother then of himself with their relatives as they aged. Both lived into their eighties. Stout's mother was widowed in middle age, with teenage children. She brought them up while managing her own household, later running the same house for the youngest brother, Josias, who neither moved nor married. At age 65 she began to find this too much, so Josias let the estate to a tenant and moved to live with his second brother, Leonard, while mother shared her time between Leonard's and William's houses. The tenant was disappointing, so Josias decided to employ servants under his mother's management. They moved back and managed, in William's words, "to the satisfaction of me, my sister and all our family and relations".

But when mother reached the age of 76 in 1709 she had become "very infirme and uneasy with the care of the house and was urgent on [Josias] to marry, he not being willing to keep house with a servant". Obediently Josias, aged 48, married a woman of whom his mother approved. But there were soon clashes between Mrs Stout and her daughter-in-law. After a year Josias asked William to "entertain" his mother. She remained in William's household "in much content and unity till the time of her death", aged 84, about eight years later.

William Stout was equally long-lived and also lived through a variety of living arrangements as he aged. He never married and for much of his life his house was kept by his sister. After her death, for five years his house was managed successively by two of his nieces and by a paid housekeeper. He then let it for four years to Mary Dillworth and "lodged" in it. Then aged 69, he gave over his house to the nephew to whom he had passed his business and lived in rooms over his old shop, cared for by two more nieces. This did not work out so he began to take his meals at his nephew's table, paying him £20 per annum for this and retaining his independence in other respects in separate rooms. Then his nephew went bankrupt and William moved back into his old house. He rescued the firm and lived in the house at least until the age of 79, looked after first by a servant then by a great-niece. Up to this age he was fit and active and very much in control of his life and affairs, and those of a good many other people. He had a serious accident in 1743 and the diary ends, although he lived for eight more years. The diary shows the closeness of relationships and the complexities of intergenerational exchange among this merchant and small land-owning family in eighteenth-century Lancaster.[38]

There is a great deal of evidence, for example from the censuses of the poor of the late sixteenth and early seventeenth centuries, that old people took into their homes their deserted or widowed daughters and/or their grandchildren. The Norwich census of the poor of 1570 provides many examples of grandchildren, or sometimes unrelated young children, living with old people for mutual support. Such children might be placed by the poor relief authorities but it is also probable that the poor made their own arrangements of mutual convenience. The mobility and alertness of a child could greatly enhance the viability of an ageing household while providing a home for an orphan or relieving an overburdened family.[39]

There is no evidence of a clearly established customary right of the elderly to shelter even with very close relatives, but it was equally clearly a taken for granted fact of everyday life at all social levels and occurred with some frequency – although how frequently is hard to establish since evidence is so fragmentary. It seems to have occurred most often in case of need on one side or the other: of a son for a housekeeper, a daughter for a childminder, the older person for care or shelter. Quantitatively based nineteenth-century community studies reached similar conclusions to those drawn from qualitative and quantitative evidence for pre-industrial England. They also discuss motivation for co-residence. Michael Anderson seems to be on his own in stressing "calculative reciprocity", economic rationality, as the key. Dupree, Clarke and others stress a wider variety of emotions and needs.[40]

Support other than co-residence

The nineteenth-century studies also stress the extent of intergenerational exchange where the partners were not co-resident; and the degree to which the two forms could be complementary, or situated at different points in a spectrum of forms of interaction. Anderson finds a large number of old women living in households in which mothers of young children worked outside the home and concludes that they were welcome as childminders.[41] Preston was an expanding town with high rates of in-migration. Dupree, studying the more settled communities of the Potteries, found less co-residence of this kind but believes that older mothers who lived near their working daughters provided childminding.[42] Similarly Bethnal Green, in the 1850s as in the 1950s[43], was a settled artisan community where, Clarke argues, co-residence was less probable than in Preston because less necessary, since relatives lived close by and could provide mutual assistance without change of residence.[44]

Non-residential forms of intergenerational support are particularly elusive in the sources, in part because they were so routine a part of everyday life as rarely to merit comment. Traces of it recur throughout English history.

In early fifteenth-century Coventry at all social levels, though perhaps least among the poorest, kin provided support for needy elderly relatives. Probably elderly parents lived close to such offspring as they had, though the 1523 census suggests that "only in a tiny minority of cases (invariably mothers) can elderly parents have survived long enough to become so enfeebled that they had to be taken into a filial home".[45]

An illustration from the later nineteenth century can stand as representative of the survival strategies of many old people over several centuries. Thomas Pitkin of Swanborne, Berks., told his story to the Royal Commission on the Aged Poor of 1895. He was aged 67. He had a cottage and garden, rented an allotment and kept a pig or two, both useful sources of food and of earnings and/or exchange. He had occasional earnings from roadmending (commonly an old man's task) and kept off poor relief. He had had eleven children, five of whom still survived, but he lived alone with just one daughter living nearby. When a commissioner asked whether his children gave him help he replied: "No. I have had to help them when I can. They have got large families, most of them. I do what I can in that sense. I do not get anything from them in any way. The daughter that I have lives about the length of this room perhaps from me and she looks after my house."[46] His failure to define what was evidently very considerable service from his daughter as "help" from his children again suggests that sources may often be silent about such intergenerational support because it was a taken for granted part of everyday life. In consequence historians have underestimated its importance.

Other evidence from the later nineteenth and early twentieth centuries of widespread family support for old people includes a national sample survey undertaken in 1899 for a government investigation of sources of income of old people. This found that five per cent of men and 26 per cent of women were wholly supported by family and friends.[47]

Rowntree's surveys, from that of York in 1899 onwards, provide vivid vignettes, although not useful statistics, of intergenerational reciprocity among relatives who did not share a home. Poor young people gave what help they could to poor old people; and sometimes very poor old people provided food, old clothes and services for needy children and grandchildren.[48]

Quantitatively more impressive is the evidence of the allowances granted to the dependents of servicemen who died in the First World War. These were introduced for the first time when it was recognized how many parents, in addition to partners and children, had been dependent upon the income of dead combatants. Allowances were paid on proof of such dependency. The number of payments made between 4 August 1914 and 31 March 1919 (exclusive of those to dependants of officers, for whom there were separate arrangements) was 221,692. By somewhat surprising contrast, in the same period only 192,698 allowances were granted to widows.[49]

In the Second World War allowances were available on the same terms, but the number paid to parents of dead combatants was significantly lower than to widows.[50] Between the wars and during the Second World War the value and coverage of state old-age pensions increased significantly. This suggests that pensions substituted for a previously high level of dependency upon adult children.

This brief summary of a wide range of sources covering a long time period necessarily elides shifts over time and place in the character and extent of intergenerational support. However, they are consistent in testifying to its importance.

Did old people have families?

One of the things we need to know if we are to assess the reality of intergenerational relationships is how many old people actually had children alive or in a position to help them. Given the high mortality rates characterizing early modern England, parents might well outlive children. How often they did so known sources cannot tell us. Computer simulation exercises suggest that up to one third of women living to 65 in the sixteenth and seventeenth centuries had no surviving children.[51] Michael Anderson calculated for mid-nineteenth century Preston that about 67 per cent of people aged 65 and over would have had a child still alive.[52] Dupree agrees with this for the Potteries.[53] We can safely say that over many centuries a considerable number of old people would have had no children available to look after them.

If children did survive, in the highly mobile society that pre-industrial as well as industrial England was, they might have migrated beyond reach. Hence Ruggles' suggestion that a high proportion of those who could have co-resided may well have done so seems plausible and is supported by the work of Anderson and Dupree. If we add strong signs of support between relatives who did not co-reside, a picture emerges of inter-generational support as an important though not precisely quantifiable element in the income package of old people at all times.[54]

Lack of children able to give support does not necessarily leave old people bereft of care from members of a younger generation. In societies where this is the only socially recognized form of support for the elderly, the childless have long adopted parent-less or property-less heirs who in return care for them in old age. As suggested above, there are many examples in English history of poor old people taking in orphans or the children of other poor families for mutual assistance.

There were other ways in which those lacking younger kin could acquire them. One was marriage. It could be expected to solve multiple family difficulties. In a petition to the poor-law authorities a Northumberland woman claimed in 1699 that she had been persuaded to marry a "simple man", the son of the house where she was a servant, because his parents had grown too old to "manage their concerns as they had formerly done". This would have brought her security and upward social mobility and care for the parents and in the longer run for their "simple" son. But she suffered a crippling accident and was ejected from the house and forced to return to her pauper mother.[55]

Patterns of re-marriage of older widows and widowers varied over time and place and social background, though it was generally more usual for men than for women. Re-marriage was often to someone younger and capable of providing some support. The early censuses of the poor, such as that of Norwich in 1570, list partnerships of very disparate ages, which suggest that, at least to some degree, they were inspired by mutual material need owing to age and/or physical disability.[56] Similarly we find in a poor-law listing of 1832 a man described as "very old and infirm with a young idiot wife and child five years old". They were given four shillings per week outdoor relief.

Such marriages could have their disadvantages. In west Kent and also in Colyton in the late seventeenth and eighteenth centuries a number of male pensioners had wives who were considerably younger and several small children, and found themselves raising families when their ability to labour was diminishing.[57]

At higher social levels marriage to a propertied old man could bring security to a poorer woman and give the man someone to care for him, especially if she was an experienced servant – though in two of the cases of this kind described by Gough in seventeenth-century Shropshire the wives drank away the elderly husband's property and a third disgraced and made a laughing stock of her rich "weake and old" husband by murdering her lover's wife.[58] It might be less risky for the better-off to employ a servant as carer, as William Stout did when necessary and no doubt other older people of sufficient means.

Unmarried children – or as in Stout's case other unmarried relatives – stayed in or returned to the home, willingly or not, to care for ageing relatives – a long-surviving, still familiar phenomenon. Stout describes how in 1702 Thomas Greene, a 74-year-old grocer and draper of Lancaster, sent for his two daughters then living with relatives in London "in hopes and expectations that they might be assistant to him and their mother in his trade and other ways in their old age". The need was occasioned by the fact that their son, whom they had expected to assist them in their old age, had drunk himself to death at the age of 35. The arrangement with the daughters did not work out happily.[59]

Some distinguished women experienced this carer role. Harriet Martineau was recalled from her journalistic work in London to act as companion to her widowed mother in Norwich in the 1830s; Charlotte Brontë nursed her sick father in the 1840s; Rachel Macmillan was called home from school at 18 to care for her sick mother and it was 11 years before she could embark on her career in social reform and labour politics. W. E. Gladstone's daughter, Helen, gave up an effective and fulfilled life as deputy Principal of Newnham College, Cambridge, and turned down the offer to be first Principal of Royal Holloway College, London, to fulfil her duty to care for her parents after the marriage of her sister, despite, as in all these cases, the presence of a supply of servants.[60] Where recognized family members were available to provide support, servants were evidently not an acceptable substitute. Beatrice Webb, then Potter, described at length the years spent nursing her dying father and the difficulty of fitting in serious work around his needs, despite, again, the presence of servants.[61]

Dupree comments on the number of unmarried adult children living with widowed parents in the Potteries. In the case of a father the child was usually a daughter; when a mother was widowed, sons and daughters stayed in equal numbers.[62] Well into the twentieth century it was common enough for a child, normally a daughter and normally the youngest, to be discouraged from marriage, though not necessarily from paid work if the income was required by the household, while parents survived and needed support.[63]

Also, voluntarily or not, old people in all times might share a household with others in need who were apparently unrelated to them. This might be arranged by the poor relief authorities as one of the means some parishes employed to care for old people.[64] Surveys of present-day Britain suggest that older people who lack close relatives, or even those who do not, may construct networks of support with unrelated people with whom they form close ties:

> People do not seem to turn to others simply because they are related to them, or have no-one else to turn to; they turn overwhelmingly to people they live very close to and see regularly, although those people may be friends, neighbours or other relatives rather than close family relations . . . support networks of people without key relatives are not necessarily less well defined, or more diffuse than those of people who have both a spouse and children.[65]

There is no obvious reason to believe that this was not so in the past.

Conclusion

For all the variability in experience over place and time there were some generally observed social rules about family support for the poor in England from at least the late sixteenth century:

1. There was no obligation to shelter an elderly relative, though it clearly occurred where the generations felt that they could get on together or where there was simply no alternative. But there was deep awareness of the dangers of such a course. It was most likely to occur at the very end of the older person's life and might be for a brief period before death. When older people lived independently of kin it was not necessarily because they were neglected but, then as now, because they preferred it. And generations might support one another even if they lived apart.

2. There was a strong sense of obligation to give what material and emotional support one could to elderly relatives, within reason – but not so as to drive oneself and family into destitution. The obligations of married sons and daughters were first to their spouses and their children and only secondarily, if they had resources to spare, to their parents.

3. When relatives could not help, or were non-existent and an old person could find no substitute, rendering her or him destitute, the poor-law system would support them with as much generosity as local resources and custom would allow, although generally at a minimal level and strictly on condition of inability to acquire resources through work or any other means. Family support and poor relief were not alternatives but both were shifting and variable components in the "economy of makeshifts" in which poor old people have long struggled.

Rather than characterizing family support for the elderly as "unEnglish" it is more appropriately described by Leopold Rosenmayr's phrase, "intimacy at a distance"; but perhaps historians should stress "intimacy" rather more than we have and "distance" rather less.

Notes

1. Various versions of this chapter have been given to a number of seminars, including at the Cambridge Group for the History of Population and Social Structure. I am grateful for comments made at that seminar, especially by Richard Wall.
2. Plato, *The Republic* (tr. D. Lee, 2nd edn (Harmondsworth, 1974), pp. 61–5.

3. P. Laslett & R. Wall (eds), *Household and family in past time* (Cambridge, 1972).

4. R. M. Smith, "Some issues concerning families and their property in rural England, 1250–1800", in *Land, kinship and life-cycle*, R. M. Smith (ed.) (Cambridge, 1984), pp. 68–73. P. Laslett "Family, kinship and collectivity as systems of support in preindustrial Europe: a consideration of the 'nuclear-hardship' hypothesis", *Continuity and Change* **3**, 1988, pp. 153–76.

5. P. Laslett, *Family life and illicit love in earlier generations* (Cambridge, 1977), p. 176.

6. *Ibid.*, p. 177.

7. See also Zvi Razi, "The myth of the immutable English family", *Past and Present* **140**, 1993, p. 3–44.

8. D. Thomson, "The welfare of the elderly in the past: a family or community responsibility?" in *Life, death and the elderly. Historical perspectives*, M. Pelling & R. M. Smith (eds) (London, 1991), pp. 194–221 is his most recent exposition of this view.

9. *Ibid.*, p. 198.

10. J. Steer, *Parish law. Being a digest of the law* (London, 1830), p. 455.

11. E. Bott (ed.), *A collection of decisions of the Court of King's Bench upon the Poor Laws down to the present time* (London, 1773), p. 87.

12. D. Thomson, "The decline of social security: falling state support for the elderly since early Victorian times", *Ageing and Society*, **4**, 1984, pp. 451–82. K. Williams, *From pauperism to poverty* (London, 1981) pp. 96–107.

13. D. Thomson, *Provision for the elderly in England 1830–1908.* (PhD thesis, University of Cambridge, 1980).

14. *The Poor Law Report of 1834* (ed.) with an introduction by S. G. & E. O. Checkland (Harmondsworth, 1973), p. 115.

15. *Royal Commission on the Poor Laws (RCPL), Report* Appendix 1, Part 11, PP(1834) [vol. 29], p. 104.

16. *Ibid.* [vol. 29], p. 17 (evidence from Dorset); p. 249 (Cambs.); p. 324 (Carlisle); p.543 (Surrey); pp. 729, 783, 831, 865 (West Riding of Yorks).

17. *Ibid.*, p. 135 (evidence from Northumberland and Durham); p. 292 (Suffolk); p. 338 (Norfolk); p. 486 (Devon); p. 538 (Sussex); p. 659 (Hunts., Ely and Cambridge).

18. M. Barker-Read, *The treatment of the aged poor in five selected west Kent parishes from settlement to speenhamland (1662–1797).* (PhD thesis, Open University 1986); *RCPL* report, cited in n15–17; Sir Frederick Norton Eden, *The state of the poor* (London, 1797). P. Sharpe, *Gender specific demographic adjustment to changing economic circumstance: Colyton, 1538–1837.* (PhD thesis, University of Cambridge, 1988), pp. 262–3, gives examples of implementation of the liable relatives clause in Devon in the 1840s. Marguerite Dupree gives examples of enforcement in the Staffordshire Potteries in the 1860s, before enforcement became widespread. She also points out how difficult enforcement could be and that families could not always afford to comply. M. Dupree, *Family structure in the Staffordshire Potteries, 1840–1880* (Oxford, 1994), pp. 309–10.

19. Thomson, "The welfare of the elderly", p. 203.

20. S. King, "Reconstructing lives: the poor, the poor law and welfare under rural industrialization 1650–1820", unpublished paper (University of Central Lancashire) S. A. King, *Poverty and welfare, 1700–1870* (Manchester: forthcoming). T. Wales "Poverty, poor relief and the life-cycle: some evidence from seventeenth century Norwich" in Smith, *Land, kinship*, pp. 351–405, also provides a good reconstruction of how the aged poor packaged their incomes.

21. M. Barker-Read, *West Kent; RCPL report*, cited in n15–17 and 18.

22. P. Slack, *Poverty and policy in Tudor and Stuart England* (London, 1988), p. 206. T. Sokoll, *Household and family among the poor* (Bochum, 1993), p. 293.

23. Royal Commission on the Aged Poor (RCAP) report. PP(1895) (XIV). Evidence of George Edwards qq.6454ff, 67145; Zacharias Walker, Agent for National Agricultural Labourers Union, 7101–7118, 7165–68; Thomas Pitkin, 14105–14137; Henry Allen, carpenter, 16561; John Valentine Stevens, tinplate worker, 17287.

24. *Ibid.*, qns 6715, 6801

25. C. Booth, *The aged poor in England and Wales* (London, 1894) pp. 425–6.

26. C. C. Dyer, *Standards of living in the later middle ages. Social change in England c. 1200–1520* (Cambridge, 1989) p. 25. Slack, *Poverty and policy*, p. 83ff. Barker-Read, *West Kent*, p. 273ff.

27. RCAP report pp.xix–xx.

28. R. Wall, "Regional and temporal variations in English household structure from 1650", in *Regional demographic development*, J. Hobcraft & P. Rees (eds) (London, 1977), pp. 89–116; "Relations between generations in British families past and present", in *Families and households: divisions and change*, S. Arber & C. Marsh (eds) (Basingstoke, 1992), pp.63–85; S. Ruggles, *Prolonged connections. The rise of the extended family in nineteenth century England and America* (Madison, 1987).

29. M. Anderson, *Family structure in nineteenth century Lancashire* (Cambridge, 1971); Dupree, *Potteries*; M. Clarke, *Household and family in Bethnal Green, 1851–1871. The effects of social and economic change.* (PhD thesis, University of Cambridge, 1986); C. G. Fraser, *The household and family structure of mid nineteenth century Cardiff in comparative perspective.* (PhD thesis, Cardiff University 1988); J. Quadagno, *Ageing in early industrial society* (New York & London, 1982); W. A. Armstrong, *Stability and change in an English county town. A social study of York, 1801–51,* (Cambridge, 1974).

30. Laslett & Wall, *Household and family*, p. 27.

31. Laslett, *Illicit love*, pp. 178–9.

32. Sokoll, *Household and family*.

33. R. Wall, "Elderly persons and members of their households in England and Wales from preindustrial times to the present", in *Ageing in the past: demography, society and old age*, D. Kertzner & P. Laslett (eds) (California, 1995), pp. 82–3.

34. M. Spufford, *Contrasting communities* (Cambridge, 1974), pp. 88–90.

35. A. L. Erickson, *The property ownership and financial decisions of ordinary women in early modern England.* (PhD thesis, University of Cambridge, 1989), pp. 305–6. C. Howell's study of wills in her "Peasant inheritance customs in the Midlands, 1280–1700" in *Inheritance and rural society in Western Europe, 1200–1800*, J. Goody,

J. Thirsk, E. P. Thompson (eds) (Cambridge, 1976), pp. 113–50, has found it to be common in a region of Leicestershire in the sixteenth and seventeenth centuries. Using quite different sources S. King has found co-residence to be normal in west Yorkshire between the seventeenth and early nineteenth centuries. Both attribute it to patterns of landholding and inheritance. S. King, "Reconstructing lives".

36. They include R. Gough, *History of Myddle* (London, 1993); A. Macfarlane (ed.), *The diary of Ralph Josselin, 1616–1683* (Oxford, 1976); W. Plomer (ed.), *Kilvert's diary. Selections from the diary of Rev. Francis Kilvert* (London, 1969); N. Mackenzie & J. Mackenzie (eds), *The diary of Beatrice Webb* [vol. 1] (London, 1982); J. D. Marshall (ed.), *The autobiography of William Stout of Lancaster, 1665–1752* (Manchester, 1967); R. Parkinson (ed.), *The life of Adam Martindale* (Chetham Society, Manchester 1895); J. Beresford (ed.), James Woodeforde, *The diary of a country parson 1758–1802* (Oxford, 1978).

37. A. Macfarlane, *Marriage and love in England, 1300–1840* (Oxford, 1986), p. 112.

38. Marshall, *Stout*.

39. M. Pelling, "Old age, poverty and disability in early modern Norwich: work, remarriage and other expedients" in Pelling & Smith, *Life, death*, pp. 74–101.

40. Anderson, *Family structure*, p. 111ff.

41. *Ibid.*, pp. 139ff.

42. Dupree, *Potteries,* pp. 328–33.

43. P. Willmott & M. Young, *Family and kinship in East London* (London, 1957).

44. Clarke, *Bethnal Green,* pp. 80ff.

45. C. Phythian-Adams, *Desolation of a city. Coventry and the urban crisis of the late middle ages* (Cambridge, 1979), p. 150. J. Boulton, *Neighbourhood and society. A London suburb in the seventeenth century,* (Cambridge, 1987) provides examples from seventeenth-century Southwark.

46. RCAP qq. 14103–37.

47. *Report of the departmental committee on the financial aspects of the proposals made by the select committee of the House of Commons of 1899 about the aged deserving poor.* PP (1900) [vol. X] Appendix II.

48. B. S. Rowntree, *Poverty: a study of town life* (London, 1901); (with May Kendall) *How the labourer lives* (London, 1914), *Poverty and progress* (London, 1941).

49. Second annual report of Minister of Pensions. Cmnd. 39.1920) (PP (XXII) p. 373).

50. 23rd annual report of Minister of Pensions. Cmnd. 10. 1948 (PP (II) p.77).

51. E. A. Wrigley, "Fertility strategy for the individual and the group", in *Historical studies in changing fertility*, C. Tilly (ed.) (Princeton, 1979), pp. 2355–54; J. Smith "The computer simulation of kin sets and kin counts", in *Family demography: methods and their applications*, J. Bongaarts, T. Birch, K. Wachter (eds) (Oxford, 1987), pp. 261–5.

52. Anderson, *Family structure*, p. 40.

53. Dupree, *Potteries*, p. 333.

54. Ruggles, *Prolonged connections.*

55. P. Rushton, "Lunatics and idiots: mental disability, the community and the poor

law in north-east England, 1600–1800", *Medical History* **32**, 1988, p. 39.

56. Pelling, "Norwich", p. 85–90.
57. Barker-Read, *West Kent*, p. 284; Sharpe, *Colyton*, p. 56.
58. Gough, *Myddle*, pp. 120–21.
59. Marshall, *Stout*, pp. 140–41.
60. P. Jalland, *Women, marriage and politics, 1860–1914* (Oxford, 1986), pp. 292–4.
61. Mackenzie, *The diary of Beatrice Webb* [vol.1].
62. Dupree, *Potteries*, p. 333.
63. D. Gittens, "Marital status, work and kinship, 1850–1930", in *Women's experience of home and family, 1850–1940*, J. Lewis (ed.) (Oxford, 1986), pp. 249–67.
64. Slack, *Poverty and policy*; Barker-Read, *West Kent*.
65. C. Jarvis, *Family and friends in old age, and the implications for informal support: evidence from the British Social Attitudes Survey of 1986* (Age Concern Institute of Gerontology, King's College, London, 1993), p. 20.

7

The *"mixed economy of welfare"* in early modern England: assessments of the options from Hale to Malthus (c.1683–1803)

Joanna Innes

The sixteenth century saw attempts in many European countries to systematize giving to the poor. It was suggested that accumulated funds should
be put under central direction, perhaps of bodies of men appointed by
municipalities, and that casual alms should likewise be directed to such
bodies for distribution. In practice such consolidation was certainly rarely –
probably never – achieved in communities of any size, neither in England,
nor elsewhere in Britain, nor on the Continent. Although public bodies or
officers – in England, churchwardens and "overseers of the poor" – did gain
control of some funds, even in some states the right to tax (much more
extensively employed in England than elsewhere), they did not achieve a
monopoly of relief, but rather joined the ranks of other official, collective
and individual donors. The seventeenth century was, indeed, marked by
a proliferation of relief sources: in Catholic countries, in the context of
counter-Reformation mobilization of both clerics and pious laity; in
England, in the context of a wave of charitable giving within the framework of the developing law of trusts, lovingly chronicled in this century by
W. K. Jordan. The invention of the "subscription charity" in late seventeenth-century England – a kind of charity relying more or less heavily for
its funds on regular or occasional donations by a body of supporters – added
a powerful new type to the existing range of relief-distributing entities.
None of these developments displaced the individual donor, doling out
alms face-to-face or in response to "begging letters".[1]

Was it desirable that relief should flow through diverse channels? Should
a judicious public policy favour some modes of giving over others? Was the
collection and distribution of relief monies best systematized, and, if so,

how was that systematization best achieved? Sixteenth-century observers made a crucial mental leap when they began to try to conceptualize relief flows as a totality, to measure their extent, to assess their relative merits, and to devise systems of incentives and sanctions to promote some forms of charitable giving over others. Against that background, we should not be surprised to find successor generations recurrently asking themselves such questions. In Western Europe, at least, a "mixed economy of welfare" has persisted from that era to this – with, of course, changes both in the nature of constituent agencies and practices, and in the balance between them. Recent questioning of the efficiency, viability and even desirability of welfare states has helped to give older concerns about the character and balance of this "mixed economy" new resonances, and to sharpen curiosity about the ways in which such matters were conceptualized and addressed in the past.

In what contexts were such issues addressed in early modern England? Parliament provided an important forum for discussion. It assumed responsibility for co-ordinating aspects of poor relief from the 1530s. Thereafter, the merits and demerits of different ways of regulating and relieving the poor repeatedly figured on its agenda. Relief strategies were also undoubtedly the subject of discussion at municipal and parish level during the sixteenth and seventeenth centuries; preachers too expatiated on the nature of charitable obligations.[2] In the early and mid-seventeenth century, occasional publications addressed these issues. From the 1670s, there developed a steady flow of discussion in print. Economists, projectors, magistrates and preachers set out their thoughts in book or pamphlet form. Some such writings were primarily directed to MPs; some to local opinion-formers; some to potential donors. The need to retain old and attract new subscribers made subscription charities especially voracious of publicity: from their first appearance in the late seventeenth century, they frequently published fundraising sermons and reports of their transactions.[3]

Fragmentation in the practice of relief-giving was mirrored in fragmentation of discussion: most printed discussion focused primarily on parliamentary legislation, municipal initiative or on one or another form of voluntary charity; characteristically, alternative forms of relief attracted, at most, only fleeting consideration. Often enough, none the less, these publications embodied ideas as to the relative merits of different forms of giving, even positive suggestions as to how patterns of relief should be reordered. A careful reading of these writings makes it possible to chart shifting assumptions, and to track the moving frontier of debate.

This chapter attempts to chart shifting patterns of thought on these themes from the late seventeenth through to the end of the eighteenth century: through the first period in which a significant proportion of discussion took place in print. Its account of debate is prefaced by a rough sketch of diversity and change in relief practice through the early modern period. The chapter carries its account of debate into a period when opinion had swung far away from its early to mid-sixteenth-century origins: to a time when the merits of the intuitive individual as donor were much trumpeted, and state-sponsored welfare subject to vigorous attack.

The chapter charts a complex story, depicting a debate which went through a sequence of phases, and in which there were always competing voices. The range of options in play was always considerable – greater than most commentators managed to acknowledge in the course of a single discussion. A property-tax-based, parochially administered relief system was established throughout England in the sixteenth and early seventeenth centuries. Some later observers were substantially content with this. Others, although they favoured deriving the bulk of relief funding from taxes, none the less believed that existing administrative arrangements should be varied. Others again would have preferred to see a greater part, even the whole, of relief funding drawn from voluntary donations. But those who shared this view differed among themselves as to who should have the disposal of voluntary funds. That task might be conceived as a public trust, best discharged by a public body. Alternatively (the subscription-charity model suggested), self-constituted, special-purpose bodies might compete for donations. Some would have left as much as possible to be disbursed by donors themselves. Commentators varied in the importance they attached to, on the one hand, the manner in which relief monies were raised, on the other, the manner in which they were spent. Few argued that, of all the possible modes of relief, one only should prevail; most contemporaries were either resigned to diversity, or positively appreciative of it. But tolerance of diversity was compatible with the conviction that there should be some change in the mix.

This subject has attracted strikingly little attention from historians. If contemporary discussion was fragmented, the historiography is yet more so. A voluminous literature on statutory relief co-exists with a substantial literature on voluntary charities – but few historians have contributed to both enquiries, or attempted to combine accounts of the two into a single synthetic overview.[4] The fact that statutory relief and organized charities have left separate archives has no doubt helped to discourage research into the ways in which the two interacted in practice. Contemporary printed material, as we have seen, was not so organized as to have thrust strategic issues upon historians' notice. In this context, this chapter is inevitably exploratory and tentative in character. No doubt further research will make it possible to refine and improve upon the story it tells.

I

All moderately well-informed seventeenth- and eighteenth-century observers knew that the statutory relief system of their own day was a relatively recent invention, having been authoritatively codified as recently as 1601, by "43 Elizabeth". Before that date, it was commonly assumed, private charities must have played a much greater role in the relief of the poor. One mid-eighteenth-century writer hypothesized that relief must have come from incumbents of benefices, abbeys and monasteries on the one hand, private donors on the other. Some assumed that "old English hospitality", dispensed by nobility and gentry not huddled into towns as in latter "polite" days, must have afforded an important source of support. That the first vagrancy laws had been passed in the fourteenth century none the less suggested that the pre-Reformation era had been no golden age for the poor. They also illustrated (as some commentators noted) early involvement on the part of the state.[5]

Modern research has brought relief patterns "before the poor laws" into sharper focus. Much aid for those least able to support themselves was no doubt informally supplied through family or neighbourly networks. Such support networks were sometimes formalized: "help ales" might raise funds to bail out people in difficulties; religious gilds supported needy members. Alms were sometimes bestowed on individual supplicants; sometimes selectively distributed among the poor of the neighbourhood; sometimes more widely broadcast, at funerals, or on fixed days by monastic houses. Relief was sometimes institutionalized in the form of housing for travellers, the sick or aged. Revenues from land might be left to be administered in perpetuity for one or another of these purposes.[6]

The sixteenth century saw major changes in practice, in part as a result of the Reformation, in part as a local manifestation of Europe-wide shifts in thought. Monasteries were dissolved; religious gilds too (a development less remembered two centuries later but now judged by historians likely to have made a significant impact in this context). Funds administered by these and other bodies were critically evaluated within a new classificatory scheme: were they devoted to "superstitious" or "charitable" uses? If the former, they were subject to confiscation; if the latter, their administration might be transferred to trustees.[7] A statute of Henry VIII ordered church-wardens vigorously to solicit alms for the relief of the poor in their parish. Under Elizabeth, new "overseers of the poor" were conjured into exist-ence, with the power – indeed, the duty – to raise money by rate to relieve the impotent poor and set those able but unemployed to work. After some experimentation, the parish emerged as the standard administrative unit in which overseers would operate.[8]

The spirit of the sixteenth-century reformers' drive for "total alms con-trol" certainly informed some of these changes. Parliament clearly intended to discountenance begging – although in the early legislation, interestingly, it was implied that parish officers might authorize begging by local poor.[9] Churchwardens and overseers were relatively well placed to co-ordinate parish-level relief activity: as well as collecting rates, they had control over the proceeds of sacramental or other church collections, and might be *ex officio* trustees of local charitable funds.[10] In towns, powers that did not accrue to parish officers sometimes came to be more or less closely attached to municipal corporations: *de jure* or *de facto*, their members might serve as charitable trustees, or on the governing bodies of hospitals – as they did in the case of London's Royal Hospitals, remodelled in accordance with new conceptions of the public interest in the mid-sixteenth century.[11]

Rationalization only proceeded to a limited extent, however: power and initiative remained diffuse, and relatively unco-ordinated. National, municipal and parochial structures were superimposed upon one another, supporting a complex matrix of resources and practices. Thus, almshouse places might be in the royal gift; collections in parish churches might take place by royal brief or order; corporations or county magistrates might levy rates throughout a district for the support of the poor in the hardest pressed parishes.[12] Furthermore, the repudiation of the notion of salvation by good works did not lead governing authorities to wish to discourage charitable activity as such – nor does it seem to have done much to check the charitable impulse. Since only so much could be elicited by taxation before taxpayers' goodwill was lost, voluntary donations remained an extremely attractive source of social capital.[13] The courts recognized donors' rights to name the administrators of their own gifts. That willing-ness opened the way for the multiplication of fundholders. Finally, private individuals clearly continued to give directly to the poor: on their door-steps, in the streets, even distributing largesse on special occasions in the traditional way. As late as 1764, Westmorland magistrate Richard Burn wrote that "a funeral in the country is a kind of fair for beggars".[14] The begging letter probably gained currency as a mode of supplication through the early modern period.[15] In the eighteenth century the pious and chari-table might have to devote considerable time to considering and evaluat-ing such applications. Some retained their own almoners to assist them in distributing bounty.[16]

In the course of the seventeenth century, the statutory relief system came to operate in well-nigh every parish in the country, and totals raised and expended in this framework increased. In the course of the eighteenth century, they may have increased as much as tenfold – from £400,000 at the start to some £4 million at the end. Population less than doubled over that period, nor can price rises account for all of the increase. Probably there was an increase in both the scope and the scale of statutory relief.[17]

Yet "legal charity" (as contemporaries sometimes termed it) did not crowd out "voluntary charity", and contributory relief schemes also prolif-erated. W. K. Jordan has charted the continuing flow of gifts and bequests through the seventeenth century. Subscription charities multiplied from the 1690s. Charity schools and hospitals often drew an important compo-nent of their incomes from subscriptions. In the mid-eighteenth century, an impressive array of (substantially) subscription-funded charitable insti-tutions appeared in the metropolis: the Foundling Hospital, the Lying-in Hospital, the Marine Society, the Lambeth Orphan Girls' Asylum, the Lock Hospital, the Magdalen Hospital. By the end of the century metropolitan and provincial subscription societies catered to a bewil-dering diversity of needs, including artificial resuscitation (the brief of the Humane Society), children in need (the brief of the Philanthropic Society), and distressed authors (the brief of the Literary Fund).[18]

Meanwhile, institutionalized self-help, hard hit by the abolition of the gilds, had re-emerged from the mid-seventeenth century with the appear-ance of "box clubs" or "friendly societies". By the end of the eighteenth century perhaps one in six of the adult population, men and women, were members of such clubs. In some trades, rights to draw on such funds were transferable from one place to another: the "tramping artisan, perhaps armed with a certificate, presented himself at the appropriate public house in a new city, and could expect assistance".[19] The precise nature and limi-tations of the statutory relief system helped to determine some of the forms assumed by non-statutory relief. Poor rates funded a wide but not unlimited range of kinds of assistance. Most commonly paid in the form of cash doles, parish relief might be granted for the purchase of food, fuel, clothing, lodging, nursing in sickness or childbirth, the apprenticeship of children, burial expenses, and sometimes (although not as often as many critics of statutory practice would have liked) the provision of work for those poor people able to contribute at least something to their subsistence. From the 1720s, rates could be used to build and maintain workhouses. They could not lawfully be used to establish schools or infirmaries (although workhouses might serve some of the functions of both). Schools and infirmaries consequently emerged as favourite objects of voluntary charity.[20]

Although formally independent of ecclesiastical governance, the statutory relief system was closely associated with the Church of England: "pensions" were, for example, sometimes paid outside church after the Sunday service. Unsurprisingly, therefore, dissenting sects often strove to maintain their own poor. From the early eighteenth century, Methodist societies did the like. The needs of foreign immigrant communities were sometimes catered to by their own religious societies.[21]

Under the statutory system, as modified by the 1662 Settlement Act, relief was payable only to those with a "settlement" in the parish, although parishes sometimes paid to maintain their own "settled" but non-resident poor at a distance.[22] The proportion of inhabitants in a parish not settled there might be high: surveys of Stratford-upon-Avon and Norwich in the eighteenth century both suggested something on the order of a quarter of inhabitants were not "settled".[23] In this context, non-statutory welfare sources had decided attractions. Voluntary hospitals, for example, dedicated, as they often were, to getting the sick and injured poor back into the workforce as quickly as possible, could not have played this role so effectively had their operations been hampered by settlement laws (their criterion for admission was in fact usually recommendation by a governor).[24] Friendly societies must have attracted the working poor in part because contribution determined entitlement. Certainly one reason why some employers encouraged such societies among their workers was to give them access to relief without threat of removal.[25] In practice, the unsettled poor were so many, and the difficulty of denying them all access to relief so great, that – especially in cities – extra-legal practices developed within the statutory relief framework: parish officers made payments even to the non-settled, terming them the "casual poor".[26]

CHARITY, SELF-INTEREST AND WELFARE IN THE ENGLISH PAST

Oriented as it was to the support of the poor in their parishes, the statutory relief system had little to offer to poor travellers. The absence of statutory provision for the relief of poor travellers is especially striking given that they had been among the favoured objects of pre-Reformation charity. The expansion of the commercial lodging sector – in the form of alehouses letting beds, or shares in beds – perhaps helped fill the gap, but poor travellers still had to subsist. It seems clear that they often begged their way, and that, despite the fact that this put them in breach of Vagrancy Acts, the respectable often regarded them as proper recipients of alms. In fact, as with the non-settled poor, such was the evident pressure of demand that local officials developed extra-legal relief customs to cater to travellers. Constables' books reveal that constables often paid out a few pence to travellers "with passes", recouping the money from the rates, although this widespread practice had no statutory basis.[27]

As well as having a variety of formal limits, statutory relief was often not the favoured resort in periods of special crisis: harvest failure, exceptionally severe winters, trade depressions and the like. At such times, wealthier inhabitants often preferred to build up special crisis funds from voluntary donations. In the high-priced 1790s, some benevolent groups operated on a permanent crisis footing: a form of charitable mobilization encouraged by the propagandistic Society for Bettering the Condition of the Poor.[28] One reason for developing alternatives to statutory relief at such times was that the same circumstances which increased poverty often pressed hard upon poorer ratepayers. By raising relief funds on a voluntary basis, elite groups *de facto* shifted towards more progressive forms of taxation, but because they did not institutionalize these, left the way open for a return to the fiscal *status quo ante* when the crisis had passed. A further consideration encouraging the raising of special funds in these circumstances was probably the desire not to undermine the self-respect of those who had never yet applied for parish relief, so as to maintain their commitment to supporting themselves and their families without parish aid. A third consideration, especially pressing in the 1790s, was the hope that charity might encourage the poor to regard the better-off with gratitude in times that might otherwise have disposed them to discontent. Ostentatiously voluntary donations dramatized the generosity of the rich as the payment of rates did not.

The limitations of the statutory relief system help to explain why voluntary charity took particular forms, and, especially in those forms, survived and flourished. But many of these limitations were not intrinsic to the very nature of a statutory system, and had rather been designed into this one. It should in theory have been possible to change the law, so that rates might have been used to relieve more people, in more diverse ways. Why was this not done? Not because change was inconceivable. Reform of the poor laws was proposed in the Interregnum and immediately after the Restoration; reform schemes were propounded in print from the 1640s, and were recurrently considered by parliament every ten or twenty years thereafter. Some of these proposals are considered in what follows. Impelled by a variety of considerations, some had among their objects broadening the scope of the statutory system by, for example, including hospitals for the sick within its ambit; distancing it from the Church and doing all that could be done to make provisions acceptable to Dissenters; or, most commonly and most importantly, liberalizing formal criteria of eligibility, by reformulating the law of settlement.[29] Parliament's failure to endorse any general measures implementing such changes is explicable in part in terms of the – sometimes contingent – difficulties which impeded the mobilization of sufficient support to carry such proposals through both of its houses. Relevant too was probably the fact that vastly more money was spent on poor relief than on any other operation conducted under the auspices of local government. MPs and others were consequently wary of the possible repercussions, administrative and otherwise, of redistributing power and responsibility in this sector of public activity. But reservations about the capacities of any and all *public* bodies in this sphere also undoubtedly operated to inhibit the enthusiasm of some for any extension of the statutory system. Conflicting and shifting views on these matters are further explored in the remainder of this chapter.

From the later seventeenth century onwards, several attempts were made to estimate how much money was being channelled through the statutory relief system, on the one hand, and through various forms of "voluntary charity", or contributory relief schemes, on the other. Historians have not improved on these estimates, which are reproduced in the Table 7.1. All the estimates of rate-based expenditure draw on returns from local authorities, and are probably fairly reliable. Estimates of monies flowing through other channels are much more speculative. Some information was available on which to base estimates of metropolitan expenditure. In the 1790s, William Eden drew on these to arrive at a national estimate. It will be apparent that estimators had somewhat different ideas as to what was worth estimating.

The table suggests how significant rate-based expenditure was, by all

Table 7.1 Tax-based and "voluntary charity" expenditure estimates 1696–1803 in £000s.

National	1696	1748–50	1780s	1790s/1803
Rates:	400	690	2,004	4,268
Miscellaneous endowed charities	—	—	259	⎫
Hospitals etc.	165	—	—	⎬ 6,000
All other charities	—	—	—	⎭

Metropolis	1696	1738		1796
Rates	40	90	—	245
Dissenting meeting	—	31	—	—
London companies	—	26	—	75
Trinity House	—	6	—	—
Miscellaneous endowed charities	—	—	—	150
Hospitals etc.	45	79	—	75
Charity schools	—	18	—	10
Other miscellaneous	—	—	—	9
Private charities	—	—	—	150
Friendly societies	—	—	—	36

Sources of estimates:

National: 1696 rates: Board of Trade, based on returns from *c*.50% parishes (PRO: CO 388/5/ 194–210; CO 389/14 f.109; 128–9).

Hospitals: Gregory King, commissioned by Board of Trade (PRO: CO 389/14 f.114–15).

1748–50 rates: Parliament, based on near-complete parish returns PP (1818) (V), Appendix 1) (I have omitted from the table a similar 1776 return, suggesting a total of some £1.2m expended – *Reports of committees of the House of Commons* [henceforth *Commons Reports*] vol. 9).
1780s rates: Parliament, as above (*Commons Reports*, vol. 9).

Miscellaneous endowed charities: Parliament, based on incomplete returns to a national survey covering only charities adminstered by feofees or trustees i.e. excluding those administered by corporations PP (1816) (XVI).

1796 voluntary charities: F. M. Eden, *The state of the poor* (London, 1797), vol. 1, p. 465.

1803 rates: Parliament PP (1803–4) (XIII).

Metropolitan: 1696: Board of Trade and Gregory King, as above.

1738: William Maitland, *History of London* (London, 1739), p. 800.

1796: Patrick Colquhoun (extent to which based on empirical research unclear), *Treatise on the police of the metropolis* (London, 1796), pp. 379–80.

estimates, among all the heterogeneous forms of charity; secondly, how significant none the less the total contribution of "voluntary" charities was supposed to be – and almost certainly was. Gregory King in the 1690s assumed (plausibly enough) that proportionately more was spent on hospitals in London than in the country at large, and indeed in larger towns in general than elsewhere. William Eden in the 1790s made the same assumption, but hypothesized a smaller differential. As a relatively conservative writer, writing in the shadow of the French Revolution,

Eden was undoubtedly disposed to estimate voluntary relief at a high level
– although the considerations that made him do so also operated in that
era (as we have noted) to encourage charitable exertion in practice.[30]
Overall, comparison between successive estimates suggests an upwards
trend in both statutory and voluntary spending we know contemporaries
did suppose to be taking place.

II

When public debate as to the pros and cons of existing and possible alternative relief regimes first emerged into print in the later seventeenth century,
the rate-based relief system had been in operation for a century – although
probably only some half a century had passed since its nationwide adoption. Contemporaries supposed that spending levels within the system were
rising, and historical research tends to support their conclusion.[31] Developing relief practice was attracting a good deal of criticism. In particular there
was concern that, against the apparent intent of the Elizabethan statute,
cash doles were being given to the able-bodied, rather than any serious
attempt being made to employ them in petty manufactures. A 1697 report
by the newly founded Board of Trade endorsed the view that, far from contributing to national wealth to the extent that their capacity to labour
should have enabled them to do, the poor were all-too-characteristically
sunk in idleness and vice. This analysis suggested the need for a reduction in
cash relief (perhaps associated with some shift towards relief in kind), more
spending on work-creation, and a crackdown on idleness and vice (a "reformation of manners" campaign did get under way in that decade.)[32]

Some late-seventeenth-century observers blamed the very existence of
the rate-based system for these ills. As they saw it, parish officers had all too
little incentive to resist the clamours of the poor. Naturally spending went
up – but was channelled rather to the clamorous than the needy. At the
same time, it was sometimes suggested, the requirement that householders
contribute to the relief of the poor sapped the charitable instincts of the
better-off, so that low-born parish officers were left in sole possession of
the field.[33]

If the public interest lay above all in setting the poor on work, and the
parish-based system had been revealed as ill-contrived for that end, what
was the best way forward? Individuals and groups differently placed within
the polity developed differing views about this. Socinian Thomas Firmin,

veteran fundraiser for Protestant causes, established a workhouse on the basis of his own and others' charity. London Quakers, ignoring the Anglican parochial network, established work-creation funds, and subsequently a workhouse, for Quaker poor only.[34] The projecting spirit of the age encouraged some to look for some form of mutually beneficial marriage between private speculators and government. In the 1690s especially, when war disrupted foreign trade and left investors short of investment opportunities, schemes of this sort found eager proponents. Pamphleteer Laurence Braddon urged such a scheme again in 1721, in the context of the speculative fever associated with the South Sea Bubble.[35]

Some thought public authorities might do an effective job – if only they were reconstituted. Those who took this view – Hale, Child and Cary – were the men whose proposals were most commonly cited in the next century.[36] Sir Matthew Hale, whose views were published posthumously, had been Lord Chief Justice: it is perhaps predictable that he should have favoured proceeding through reconfigured public authorities. He suggested that benches of magistrates should divide the country into districts, each of which should be supervised by a body of men of higher social standing than ordinary parish officers. An attraction of increasing the size of the basic unit of administration was that it would open the way for the construction of large public workhouses, where the poor might be employed.

Merchants Sir Josiah Child and John Cary, while sharing many of Hale's views, focused on the urban environments they knew best. Unlike Hale, Child did not confine his discussion to the statutory sector. Meeting one of the arguments of the critics of statutory relief, Child denied that the charitable impulse had withered. If this seemed to be so, he argued, that was primarily because potential donors were inhibited by uncertainty as to how to put their alms to good use. Noting that the London companies had an outstanding reputation as administrators of charitable trusts, Child suggested that some of their members should be appointed to a corporation which should assume responsibility for relief administration throughout the metropolitan region. These men would have the disposal both of such rates as they judged it necessary to raise and of whatever voluntary donations were directed to them. Some of these funds should be employed to construct and maintain a workhouse.

John Cary had the opportunity to participate in the launching of a scheme somewhat along these lines in Bristol. In 1696, in response to a petition, Parliament passed an act establishing a "Corporation of the Poor" in Bristol, consisting of the mayor, aldermen, churchwardens and elected members. They had the right both to collect rates and to receive gifts and bequests, and were to use these to establish a workhouse, as well as providing other kinds of relief, and indeed, correction for the idle and vagrant poor. Cary helped to publicize this venture, which was imitated in London and in 13 other provincial towns within the next two decades.[37] The fact that both Thomas Firmin's nephew and business partner Jonathan James and John Bellers (treasurer of the Quaker scheme) served as "assistants" on the London corporation suggests the potential of such public schemes to attract heterogeneous support.[38]

Corporations of the Poor were *public* welfare projects in two senses. First, the holding of office in them was clearly a public trust: characteristically their governors were either public officeholders serving *ex officio*, or were elected. Secondly, these bodies had the power (by virtue of the acts which established them) to raise rates to support their activities. Although they always co-existed with a variety of other, variously funded and governed welfare institutions, they themselves were ambitiously conceived, offering a variety of forms of relief to a variety of recipients. Their ability to attract charitable gifts and bequests in support of their work – gifts which effectively reduced the demands they had to make on ratepayers to support their ambitious operations – was undoubtedly seen by their supporters as an important part of what they had to offer. In its early years the London Corporation of the Poor received up to 30 per cent of its income from these sources.[39] (A minority of acts went so far as to empower corporations to administer all charitable gifts made thenceforth.)[40]

In the 1690s and in the first years of the eighteenth century, Parliament repeatedly considered proposals to remodel the whole of the statutory relief system after the example of the corporations. At least one such bill would have pushed to its logical conclusion the notion of the multi-functional public welfare body bestriding the public and voluntary sectors: it would have given JPs responsibility for overseeing not only (what would have remained of) parish relief administration, but also all hospitals and almshouses.[41]

Yet none of these bills passed. And, although distractions and divisions arising from parliament's other concerns may have had something to do with that, it also seems clear that they encountered opposition – as indeed did the Corporations of the Poor themselves, some of which were within a few years cut back, even wound up. Opposition came in part from those reluctant to cede or share power with the new bodies – sometimes therefore having a religious or party edge to it. Tory Anglicans with power bases in parish administration sometimes saw Corporations as dissenting strongholds (in London, at least, with some justice). But simple competition for local resources and power was probably enough to create tension. From Hull, Trinity House, the seamen's charity, petitioned Parliament to complain that the recent act founding a Corporation of the Poor for Hull (one of the minority of acts giving the Corporation command of all future charities) had cut them off from funds at a time of special need: when war was causing acute distress for seamen and their families.[42]

By 1704, revised relief bills under consideration in Parliament evinced more willingness to work within existing structures, but, in the Commons at least, ingenious new form was also being given to the desire to ensure the effective deployment of voluntary charity. A bill promoted by industrial entrepreneur and pious Anglican Humphrey Mackworth proposed to strengthen the powers of parish officers to set the poor to work, including the right to rent workhouse space. More innovatively, it proposed a variety of new arrangements for the administration of voluntarily funded projects. Ministers, constables and parish officers were to take over the administration of all apprenticeship charities, unless the donor had specifically otherwise provided. The formation of corporations at parish level to maintain charity schools, and the incorporation of hospitals were also to be facilitated, while JPs were to gain power to establish commissions to enquire into the misuse of charitable gifts.[43]

Mackworth was at one with other reformers of the day in assuming that the best way to safeguard the effective administration of charitable funds was by entrusting their management to some form of local authority – though his proposal differed from Child's in that it would have kept tax-derived revenues and voluntary gifts distinct. The Lords, while not averse to any measure of reform, none the less set their faces against that part of the plan that would have provided for local authority supervision of charities – perhaps because the judiciary objected to any encroachment upon Chancery's supervisory powers.[44] In the event, no reform at all was enacted, and charitable bodies were left free to multiply largely or wholly independently of local government control, answerable only to Chancery.

Meanwhile, the broader project of employing either public or charitable funds to set the poor to work – the project that informed so many late-seventeenth and early-eighteenth-century initiatives – itself came under attack, most notably from Defoe, in his 1704 *Giving alms no charity*. There was no shortage of work available, Defoe averred. The poor should go where the work was: artificially to create work would be to upset the natural play of economic forces.[45] Though "workhouses" were to survive as an important tool of social policy for two centuries more, the notion that public employment might drive forwards the nation's economic development does seem to have lost such credibility as it had ever had from this date.

III

The 1690s saw the first efflorescence of subscription charities, which flourished alongside other forms of subscription association, such as reformation of manners societies and the Society for the Promotion of Christian Knowledge (SPCK) – which, among its other activities, campaigned with varying success on a range of welfare issues down to the 1730s. "Charity schools" were the first widely popular form of subscription charity. Their influence on Mackworth's thinking is suggested by his singling them out for special mention.[46] Voluntary hospitals, which multiplied in London and the provinces from the 1720s, were the next set of institutions to flourish on a subscription basis, to be followed in their turn by such mid-century metropolitan charities as the Foundling and Magdalen Hospitals. As the century proceeded, increasing numbers of subscription charities were devoted to the support of non-residential institutions. Examples include the mid-century Marine and Humane societies and the Thatched House Society for the relief of persons imprisoned for small debts, as well as the end-of-the-century propagandistic and lobbying body, the Society for Bettering the Condition of the Poor.[47]

The distinction between subscription and earlier forms of charity should not be overstated. Institutional charities, such as the Royal Hospitals, had long received gifts and bequests, had drawn income from collections in parish churches, and had sermons preached for their benefit. New subscription charities sometimes relied heavily on large gifts and bequests, as well as regular subscription income.[48] Certain features none the less tended to mark the new charities out. First, they were not linked by any formal ties into the apparatus of local government: local officeholders were not *ex officio* among their governors, and they drew no revenue from any form of taxation. Secondly, they devoted considerable care and energy to wooing subscribers, often publishing, in support of this effort, annual reports, giving an account of their activities, money raised and spent, and publicizing subscribers' names. Thirdly, they commonly gave subscribers a voice, even outright control over their management.[49]

The rise and proliferation of subscription charities changed the environment in which questions of welfare strategy were debated. One crucial effect was to boost confidence in the nation's disposition to give. In the late seventeenth and early eighteenth centuries, it was common for people to bewail the superior charity of Catholic countries. By mid-century, it began to be claimed that Britain was proving itself the equal of its Continental neighbours in point of charity. By the end of the century, Britain's charitable record induced complacency.[50]

Many contemporaries' views were clearly affected by the efflorescence of new forms of charity. They none the less drew differing conclusions as to the best way forwards. Some continued to think that efforts should be made to create public bodies that could effectively harness the charitable spirit, even move into the territory the new charitable bodies were effectively marking out as their own. Some thought that the statutory relief system should be left much as it was, and saw the best way forwards as lying in a partnership between the public sector and voluntary charity. Some thought that statutory relief should be radically cut back, and a larger field left to voluntary endeavour.

Continuing commitment to enhancing public management of welfare provision is perhaps best illustrated by the case of William Hay, Chairman of the East Sussex bench, MP and associate of the Sussex-based Duke of Newcastle (which undoubtedly bolstered his standing). Hay campaigned for poor-law reform between the mid-1730s and early 1750s. Echoing earlier proposals (but having an exceptionally exalted vision as to the class of person who might effectively execute this public trust), he proposed that each county should have its own corporation, empowered both to levy rates and to receive charitable benefactions. The corporation was to take over all charities assigned to the parish poor unless specifically otherwise appropriated, and to set up collecting boxes in all parish churches. Monies received were to be used to establish workhouses, "hospitals" for children and other impotent or infirm poor, and houses of correction for idlers and vagrants. (Corporations might also, at their discretion, direct that some poor families be relieved outside the workhouse.) After batting the bill around for a while, Parliament in 1740 approved only new vagrancy provisions.[51]

In 1747, searching for a more acceptable way forwards, Hay radically revised his scheme, suggesting that his proposed new authorities should concentrate on the relief of the poor "by voluntary charities".[52] Like his previous scheme, but to somewhat different effect, his new scheme combined elements of previous thinking about improving the administration of poor relief with elements of previous thinking about improving the administration of charitable funds – spiced with the hope, inspired by recent experience with infirmaries and the Foundling Hospital, that the elite might be made to engage with the task of giving relief to the poor. The preamble to Hay's draft bill noted that "several hospitals and infirmaries have of late been established by voluntary charities, to the great comfort of the poor". Such charities, it argued, would surely become more general if only men of great credit were appointed in each county to receive contributions. Hay proposed to form such "men of great credit" – all local peers, the lord lieutenant, *custos rotulorum*, sheriff, knights of the shire, bishops, deans, archdeacons and all with estates worth £300 or more who chose to put their names forward – into a corporation empowered to receive gifts and bequests, to be employed in relieving and employing any poor people belonging to the county or found within the county, such provision as they might make to co-exist with whatever parishes chose to continue to provide. Hay's hope was that the new voluntarily funded body would in time take over all parish welfare functions. An interesting provision in Hay's bill (anticipated in some earlier local acts) states that any who gave substantial benefactions – at the very high rate of £100 a year – might become guardians for so long as they continued to give. Here the subscription charities' device of giving managerial powers to voluntary contributors was to be actualized in public adminstration.[53] Passed by the Commons, Hay's bill was defeated in the Lords.

Hay's intention was plainly that a limited number of formally constituted bodies should harness the charitable impulse: modes of administration were his main concern. Others were much more preoccupied with modes of giving – and with the diversification of relief practice that voluntary giving made possible. Careful as they might be to avoid any "popish" hint that one might earn salvation by good works, many pious Anglicans and Dissenters none the less wished to maintain that voluntary charities were pleasing to God in a way that the mere payment of taxes to support welfare activity was not.[54] To such people, the distinction between legal and voluntary giving – no more than a pragmatic consideration to Hay – was freighted with special significance. Importantly, such people did not commonly urge that public welfare projects be disbanded. They accepted these as having their place (indeed in Cambridge, and no doubt elsewhere, the establishment of a new town workhouse was the occasion for a commendatory sermon).[55] But they did think it vital that voluntary effort should supplement public provision.

The practice of directing voluntary charity especially to objects not catered for by public funds had clearly been developing in the seventeenth century. In the eighteenth century, preachers for charitable causes (responding of course to the special needs of the occasion) can be found sketching out the elements of a theory of the division of charitable labour. Voluntary charities, such preachers often suggested, could helpfully play a prophylactic function, helping to keep people off relief rolls – by, for example, educating them when young into habits of self-reliance and industry, or helping them to recover their health in the aftermath of accident or sickness. Within this matrix of provision, the role of the poor laws was to provide a safety net or backstop: to succour the chronically ill or aged, or force work on the work-shy.

Were voluntary charities meritorious *only* when they were carefully aligned with some larger vision of the public good? This probably was the dominant view. Preachers on behalf of subscription charities often urged it as a special virtue of these organizations that they *organized* charity, ensuring that donations were employed to good effect. "Alms control", in this sense, was as much the objective of this part of the voluntary sector as of public welfare bodies. Individual acts of charity were not ruled out: most major donors to public charities probably also gave sustantial sums to individuals in need. Indeed, experience in dealing with individual cases probably often played a vital part in alerting charitable activists to possible new objects of organized charity. But – in this theory of things – the public-spirited individual donor had to allocate his or her bounty with a careful eye to the greater good. For those without energy or opportunity to develop philanthropic expertise, donations to a subscription charity might provide a welcome, conscience-squaring alternative.[56] There were those – as John Walsh and others have recently reminded us – who stood out against fashion and, following the example of the early Church fathers, deliberately practised indiscriminate giving. John Wesley was one such; Anglican mystic William Law another. But in their positive advocacy of this course, they were highly eccentric.[57]

The case of the SPCK, in its campaigning mode, illustrates the willingness of some pious people in this era to promote, almost indifferently, legal and public activity on the one hand, voluntary endeavour on the other. SPCK members supported the work of some Corporations of the Poor.

Mackworth was a member, as was Sir Edward Knatchbull, whose 1723 Workhouse Act empowered ordinary parishes to establish workhouses. But the Society was also to the fore in promoting the establishment, on a voluntary basis, of charity schools; also, the first of the new breed of voluntary hospitals.[58] The Society's attitude to law and government seems to have been essentially pragmatic. It favoured them when it suited its purposes, not when they threatened to obstruct them. From its foundation to the failure of Mackworth's bill (and even beyond) the society lobbied for charity schooling to be placed on a statutory basis. At one point, it hoped to require that the Anglican catechism be taught in such schools – but had to abandon that as too controversial. The Society was well disposed to William Hay's poor-law reform proposal – until it became aware that it was envisaged that the proceeds of sacramental collections would be funnelled towards Hay's guardians. Since such collections were sometimes employed for the support of charity schools, it lobbied against that clause.[59]

The case of Jonas Hanway, merchant, philanthropist and philanthropic publicist, further illustrates willingess to operate in more than one mode. Hanway was closely associated with many of the new mid-century metropolitan charities, from the Foundling Hospital on. He was also a Governor of the Poor in his own incorporated parish of St Andrew, Holborn. Experience in the Foundling Hospital having helped to alert him to the vulnerability of poor infants, he became concerned about high infant death rates in parish workhouses, and succeeded in legislating to monitor and improve standards of care in these. In his published writings, Hanway offered miscellaneous reflections on the complementarity of public and private charity. The poor laws, as he saw them, supplied breadth of coverage and ensured the desirability of certain forms of welfare provision. Private charity, by contrast, lent itself to steadier administration, simpler government, and concentration on particular ends. Developing the "prophylactic" theme that was a commonplace of charity sermons, he suggested that private charity might function like preventive medicine: timely involvement in prophylactic charity might be expected to pay for itself inasmuch as it averted relief dependency.[60]

Dislike of public provision for the needy poor *as such*, associated with the belief that it created the very problems of idleness and poverty it purported to address, can be traced back (as we have noted) at least to the late seventeenth century. For a few years in the early 1750s, this persistent strand of thought achieved unusual prominence in public debate. It is not entirely clear why this was so. Relatively few people were involved, and it may be that they influenced each other's thinking. Growing awareness that England was unique – even within the British Isles, let alone within Europe – in the scale and character of its public relief provision may also have been a factor. Thomas Alcock, cleric and former fellow of an Oxford college, one of the pamphleteers of the period, certainly showed keen awareness of that fact.[61] The immediate context for debate at this period was provided by the ending, in 1748, of the War of the Austrian Succession. In what was to prove a brief interlude of peace, Parliament and public turned their attention to the domestic scene. Awareness that Britain was effectively locked into continuing conflict with other major European powers encouraged sensitivity to questions of comparative strength and weakness. Since the withering of the hope that public employment might prove a powerhouse of economic growth, it had become common to stress the economic cost of the poor laws. As Sir Matthew Decker expressed it in his *Essay on the causes of the decline in foreign trade*, poor rates were "a tax on the industrious". Could a struggling power afford to load itself with such burdens?[62] A final important factor may have been growing confidence in the charitable propensities of the English – given public demonstration in that very span of years with the foundation of new high-profile metropolitan charities. Given that it was widely accepted that, although their excessively swollen numbers might be reduced, the poor would always be "with us", it would scarcely have been possible to propose the withdrawal or radical retraction of public relief unless it could plausibly be supposed that something would fill the gap. Trends in recent decades had made it increasingly easy to suppose that some combination of forms of voluntary charity might be counted on to play that role.

Pamphleteers went furthest in making their antipathy to public provision explicit. Thomas Alcock, publishing early in 1752, was the most explicit of all. He suggested that it was contrary to the practice of almost all nations and ages to force charity. His account of the effects of legal on voluntary charity was not entirely coherent. On the one hand, he wanted to argue that voluntary charity had dwindled: church collections and poor boxes yielded less than they once had; and bequests had fallen off. On the other hand, he wanted to argue that the English were outstandingly charitable by temperament, as evidenced by their support for charity schools. He did not believe that public relief could be suddenly withdrawn – but suggested as an interim measure that hospitals for the impotent, workhouses for the able and houses of correction for the workshy should be established in every county. (Evidently having noted the gap in existing provision, he suggested that such hospitals might also give shelter to all "distressed travellers".)[63]

In the following year, recently appointed Westminster magistrate Henry Fielding (perhaps significantly, a promoter and supporter of new metropolitan charities) put his somewhat similar, although previously conceived, thoughts in print. Fielding proposed to restrict public provision to penal and disciplinary institutions: county houses of correction for the workshy, workhouses, intended to maintain habits of labour, for the unemployed. Young, disabled, sick and aged, and the victims of transient bad luck, might, Fielding thought, all safely be left to the charity of the benevolent.[64]

Topics the pamphleteers were agitating were also being aired in Parliament. Early in 1752, two bills were brought into Parliament, each of which was interestingly marked by recent trends and shifts in thought. The two bills emerged out of discussions within a Commons committee set up to consider how to deal with a post-war upswing in robberies and murders. Clearly, part of the roots of the problem were thought to lie in institutions and practices which nurtured bad habits among sections of the poor. Hay and others with independent interests in this sector of public policy had been drawn into the discussion, however, which had broadened out from that relatively narrowly conceived starting point. The Solicitor-General, Sir Richard Lloyd, who had chaired the committee on crime, brought forward one of the two bills; the other was introduced by Lord Hillsborough, a rising Whig politician. Each bill pulled in two directions. On the one hand, each proposed a reorganization and reform of public provision, building on a tradition of thought which now stretched from Hale to Hay. On the other hand, each was also clearly designed to make possible – in the longer or shorter term – a reduction in the range and scale of public expenditure.[65]

Lloyd's bill would have left the parish-based system in being, but established alongside it new corporations of guardians, charged with maintaining hospitals-cum-workhouses for all poor children whose parents could not support them from their own earnings. Parish officers were in this context to cease granting relief to assist the able-bodied to rear their children. The expectation seems to have been that that would permit the cutting back of parish relief to the truly impotent. Certain features of Lloyd's bill suggest an interest in increasing the significance of voluntary contributions in the funding of public relief efforts. The costs of maintaining poor children were to be defrayed by a combination of rates and charitable donations. Following Hay (although radically lowering the qualifying threshhold), Lloyd proposed that anyone donating £20 or more might thereby qualify to serve as a guardian.

Hillsborough's more radical bill proposed the abolition of 43 Elizabeth Corporations – comprising all who donated as little as £5 or more to the cause – were instead to raise rates to establish hospitals for children, the disabled, the aged, the sick (who were to receive medical care), and "no other kind of poor people whatsoever". The corporations (like voluntary hospitals and other subscription charities) were to produce yearly reports on their proceedings, with lists of donors which were to be submitted to Parliament. Overseers would survive as co-ordinators of charity at parish level. They would solicit alms monthly in church, quarterly door-to-door, and would also receive bequests. They would use these monies to provide work for poor children and others, and to relieve such acute distress as might arise from epidemic disease or other calamity.

Neither bill passed, perhaps in part because of timetabling and political pressures, in part because Parliament was hesitant radically to alter so entrenched and ramified a series of institutions and practices. Charles Gray, a Colchester MP who took part in parliamentary deliberations, went into print in the midst of discussion to advocate the retention of parochial relief – although his arguments earned him ridicule from an anonymous respondent. Thomas Alcock, by contrast, was (predictably) sympathetic to the general thrust of Hillsborough's scheme in particular. Interestingly, from their different perspectives, both Gray and Alcock found fault with proposals to extend public provision into areas currently catered for by voluntary charities. Gray did not believe that hospitals for the sick should be included in such schemes: he thought these best "constituted on a voluntary charity only". Alcock criticized Lloyd's desire to institutionalize poor children, not only because, as he said, he did not think most parents would wish to see their children confined in workhouses, but also because (he claimed) in most parishes there were already in existence charity schools where such children might be clothed and perhaps fed.[66]

IV

A shift in the character of debate on public policy from the mid-century through the 1760s, 1770s and 1780s is nicely reflected in the shifting orientation of Richard Burn's polemic. A Westmorland cleric, magistrate, and author of a very successful magistrate's handbook, Burn in 1764 published a *History of the poor laws,* in an attempt to ensure that ignorance of the history of public policy did not lead people to repeat old errors. In writing that book, Burn appears to have had the challenge presented by mid-century critics of public relief very much in mind. Against such criticisms, he asserted the propriety of public action, and impropriety of private action, in the strongest terms. Those who would see private charity play a greater role, according to Burn, effectively aspired to set their private judgement against public law. The previous year, he had written to his bishop in terms striking between two such parties: Burn averred that it was "absurd" to continue with private charity from religious motives when the state had effectively superseded the efforts of religion. Burn would have had both begging and giving to beggars made penal offences. Recognizing that the existing system effectively excluded some from help, he urged that those without a settlement be relieved from some general fund, such as the land tax.[67]

By the mid 1770s, by contrast – responding to a new generation of legislative proposals – Burn left the case for public relief as such unstated, and focused his energies rather on a question which had also attracted a portion of his attention in the earlier decade: the question of whether public relief was best administered in large districts equipped with workhouses, or by parishes. (He stood forth as a staunch advocate of the parish system, as more practicable, flexible, economic and humane.)[68]

A new wave of local legislation relating to poor relief had got under way in the late 1740s. Upon the failure of attempts to reform the poor laws at a national level in the early 1750s, the localities became for a while the sole focus for experiment. A new wave of incorporations in provincial towns was initiated by Bury St Edmunds in 1748. Some London parishes had sought incorporation for poor relief purposes from 1750; 1756 saw the first of a pioneering series of rural incorporations in two Suffolk hundreds. The outbreak of war in 1757 slowed this activity, but with peace in 1763, incorporations in all categories picked up again.[69]

The local incorporations of this period have not been researched as a group. It seems probable that research would reveal issues agitated in parliamentary debate being differently resolved in different places. There was no uniform practice as to who might serve as guardians, as to what categories of poor might be confined in workhouses – or as to whether charitable monies were to be concentrated in the hands of guardians, or left in the hands of trustees, whether parish officers or otherwise.[70]

Of the various local incorporations, what developed as a series of East

Anglian rural incorporations generated the most lively controversy in print. Here, attention focused on the issues which were also to dominate national debate for the next few decades, and which latterly dominated Burn's discussion: What were the relative merits of large districts versus parishes, and of workhouses versus home relief?[71]

One man who did more than any other to set the agenda for *national* debate from the 1760s to the 1780s was Thomas Gilbert, land agent in charge of Earl Gower's Staffordshire and Shropshire agricultural and industrial estates, and MP for Lichfield. From 1764 to 1788, Gilbert took up the mantle from what was by that time a long line of reforming forebears, and strove to persuade Parliament to enlarge the basic unit of relief administration.[72] Gilbert argued that experience accumulating in the local context showed both the viability and the desirability of this approach. His primary objective was to improve the quality of relief administration. So much was this his central concern that, although in his early projects, in what was by then the traditional fashion, he envisaged prescribing to guardians that they must erect large workhouses, by the late 1780s he envisaged compelling only administrative reorganization: guardians were to be given discretion to pursue whatever relief policies in their judgement best fitted local circumstances.[73]

Gilbert gave his own twist to poor-law reformers' long-standing secondary concern with the optimal deployment of charitable funds. He expressed doubt as to whether many of these were being well administered by existing trustees, and argued (in traditional form) that such mismanagement must be operating to discourage giving. As early as 1764, he proposed that there should be a public enquiry to locate and list such funds, and enquire into their administration. By the early 1780s he was advocating a variant of Hay's scheme. In every county, a body of gentlemen should be elected annually to administer charitable funds, which might be used to maintain hospitals, schools and seminaries. Gilbert did eventually succeed in persuading Parliament to sponsor an enquiry, which was completed in 1788, but no action to ensure the better administration or employment of such funds ensued.[74]

In 1765 one of Gilbert's early bills actually passed the House of Commons – only to founder, partly for party-political reasons, in the Lords.[75] In the following decades Gilbert was scrupulously careful to canvas the views of those involved in the local administration of the poor laws. The effect of that consultation was, however, to evoke much criticism – such as Burn's – of the central features of his scheme.

In fact, as we shall see, changing fashions in thought were increasingly inimical to Gilbert's, in many ways, traditional assumptions and aspirations. Permanent charitable foundations, the bureaucratization of relief, large-scale residential instititutions, all attracted mounting criticism – as indeed did all forms of relief practice which did not put the nurturing of self-reliance on the part of the poor close to the heart of their concerns. In this changing context, Gilbert's concern to enlarge and strengthen the powers of public authorities had a somewhat old-fashioned air. Perhaps new trends in thought did affect the final redaction of his scheme, in 1787–8. At this time, he proposed not only giving guardians discretion to erect more or fewer, larger or smaller workhouses as they saw fit, but also urged that poor-law reform be associated with a host of other measures, including not only the encouragement of voluntary charity (which might in the long run, he suggested, displace rates altogether), but also of contributory friendly societies.[76]

V

Changes in thought in the later eighteenth century led to a revaluation of options within the mixed economy of welfare. Perhaps most strikingly, individual acts of charity were positively re-evaluated: even hard-hearted writers of political-economy bent can be found hailing them as perhaps the most publicly beneficial form of charitable giving. Expectations derived (at least in part) from the managerial routines of subscription charities were turned against public relief administration, which was faulted as insufficiently sensitive to the interests of those whose hard-earned money financed its operations, and insufficiently public – and therefore accountable – in its modes of proceeding.

Yet, something more complex than just a simple shift in favour of voluntary, as against publicly funded and administered, forms of welfare was in question. Many of the older subscription charities also fell foul of new standards and aspirations. It came to be supposed that any charitable enterprise, voluntary or public, with anything approaching guaranteed funding was likely to fall into one or another form of abuse. Administrators would tend to grow careless and spendthrift; the charity's beneficiaries, complacent. Opinion swung similarly against almost all forms of large-scale residential institution, however funded and managed. It came to be supposed that such institutions were unlikely to be well run for any length of time.

It was feared that they harboured and nourished disease. Even if well run, they involved high per capita outlays: "domiciliary relief" was likely to be cheaper. The old fear that relief might encourage dependency and the notion – by this time well-established – that the best charities were pro-phylactic flowered into a driving determination to multiply forms of relief fostering self-reliance.

One spur to this shift was probably disillusionment with the fruits of new initiatives launched earlier in the century. The Foundling Hospital, for example, had stood at the peak of its reputation in the 1750s and 1760s, when it was awarded parliamentary grants to help it extend its serv-ices to infants throughout the nation. But that experiment was pro-nounced a failure; the grant discontinued; the Hospital's provincial annexes closed down and sold off. Similarly, once the first flush of enthusi-asm had faded (it was said), management of the new incorporations had tended to pass once again into the hands of low-born people, deficient in public spirit. Outbreaks of disease in giant new workhouses provided ammunition to their critics.[78]

Various cultural shifts also helped to shape this process of change. The growth of radical and "economical" critiques of government gave new life to old doubts about the wisdom of vesting power in public institutions.[79] Conversely, the fashion for "sensibility" encouraged the positive revalua-tion of the more personal forms of charitable relationship. Sentimental imagery and rhetoric appeared in subscription charity sermons from an early date. Adherents of the cult of sensibility valued highly the kind of interaction involved in an individual donor's immediate, sympathetic response to another's display of need.[80]

Traditionally, much informal, local charity had been the responsibility of women: it was regarded as an aspect of household management. As more women ventured into print, this form of charitable activity was given a higher public profile.[81] A striking feature of the second half of the eighteenth century was women's growing role in managing, and indeed in bringing into being, new charitable institutions, including day and Sunday schools and visiting societies. Women had fewer such opportunities in the public sector.[82]

Changes in English thought and practice echoed, and surely must have been affected by, broader European trends. The last few decades of the eighteenth century saw a pan-European rethinking of relief strategies unparalleled since the Reformation. Enlightenment thinkers raised doubts about the wisdom of permanently endowing charity (they of course had foremost in their minds the "hospitals" and other residential institutions, sometimes run by religious orders, which played so large a part in Continental relief practice.) This period, one of rising population and prices, saw a widespread drive to bring some form of relief within the reach of more of the poor – but at the same time (necessarily) to find more cost-effective forms of relief. Schools, "spinning schools"and other non-residential employment schemes, and new forms of out-patient medical care proliferated throughout Europe.[83]

Within the context of this pan-European discussion, both British and Continental commentators seem to have become increasingly aware of the unique character of England's public relief system. Nowhere else was tax-funded relief doled out on so extensive a scale. Most (although not all) of those who noted English exceptionalism concluded that the English had made a bad choice. Like the administrators of large endowments, the administrators of tax revenues had (as these critics saw it) all too few incentives to economize, or to target relief where it might do most good. Public relief systems were likely to work effectively (such critics supposed) only if they could be organized so as to incorporate the best features of voluntary charity. There must be high levels of involvement on the part of the tax-paying community. Officials must make it their business to acquaint themselves with the personal circumstances of relief applicants, preferably by home-visiting. Recipient lists should be open to public scrutiny. Due attention should be paid, moreover, to ensuring that the form of relief was not in itself demoralizing. Whenever possible, it should be associated with work.[84]

The case against public relief was powerfully developed by three British writers in the last decades of the eighteenth century. The first was the Scottish enlightened jurist, Lord Kames, who included an essay on the poor in his 1774 *Sketches of the history of man*. The second, a Wiltshire clergyman, Joseph Townsend, did not adequately acknowledge his debt to Kames in his 1786 *Dissertation on the poor laws*. The third, another cleric, Robert Malthus, read Townsend's work between writing the first and second editions of his *Essay on the principles of population* (1799, 1803), and warmly welcomed what he recognized to be important points of overlap with his own thinking. Kames must have been influenced both by his acquaintance with Continental thought, and by his awareness of contrasting Scottish practice. In Scotland, although kirk sessions might raise rates if they saw fit, they tended to prefer to support the poor from the proceeds of voluntary collections. Even Edinburgh and Glasgow city workhouses were largely supported by voluntary charity.[85] Kames preferred Scottish practice to both English and French, seeing each of the latter as profligate, and tending to encourage dependency. Townsend was similarly critical of the effect of the known availability of public relief on the calculations of the poor. Preferable, he argued, were individual acts of charity, which he evoked in strikingly sentimental terms: poor cottagers would, he thought, respond to the visit of a benefactor with "sparkling eyes . . . bursting tears . . . uplifted hands . . . [and] artless expressions of unfeigned gratitude for unexpected favours". Although cautiously noting that benefactors would need to be adequately instructed in the basic principles of political economy, Malthus quoted this passage verbatim in the second edition of his *Essay*.[86]

One interesting effect of the rise to an ascendant position of these preoccupations was that different aspects of past debate began to attract attention. Hale, Child and Cary, the proponents of large administrative units and workhouses, had been the authors most commonly cited. But in 1787, *A collection of pamphlets* disinterred a series of past publications critical of institutionalized charity: Dunning's *Bread for the poor* of 1698, which advocated a reduction in cash doles; Defoe's *Giving alms no charity* and, tellingly, a Scottish pamphlet: the 1783 *Letter to the citizens of Glasgow, containing a short view of the management of the poor's funds.*[87]

In her recent study, *Philanthropy and police*, Donna Andrew has charted the effect of new thinking not only on the foundation of new charities, but also in the pattern of donations to older ones.[88] No-one has as yet comprehensively explored the fortunes of old-style municipal charities in this period, but there are indications that at least some of these were subjected to vigorous criticism and reforming effort. In London, there were attempts to rationalize and rethink the functions performed by the old Royal Hospitals, and the much reduced but surviving Corporation of the Poor. Evangelicals were drawn into enquiries into corruption in hospital management. In Norwich, radical Edward Rigby, elected a Guardian of the Poor in 1783, at his very first meeting attacked the Corporation's high expenditure and inadequate accountability.[89]

New attitudes also made their mark on legislative proposals. Even in Gilbert's heyday, some MPs' thoughts were moving along rather different lines. In the early seventies, William Dowdeswell, a former Chancellor of the Exchequer, brought forward a scheme devised by lawyer and mathematician Francis Maseres for the establishment of a national fund, into which charitable contributions might be made directly, and in which all trustees of charitable funds might invest (being empowered to sell any lands they possessed for that purpose). From this fund, annuities were to be paid to small investors. Burke attacked the scheme with that characteristic combination of appeal to principle and intellectual fast footwork which earned him the distrust of some. He first pronounced "permanent charities" undesirable – then argued that, were it desirable to have a permanent fund, government stock was not permanent enough: the monies should rather be invested in land.[90]

The intended beneficiaries of Maseres's scheme were probably people of small property, rather than the labouring poor. However, attempts were also made to place on a public footing contributory schemes accessible to the latter. One such scheme was authorized in 1768 by a local act applying to the county of Devon (a region with a long-established friendly society tradition). Confidence in that venture rapidly collapsed, and the scheme was abandoned, but in 1787, Devon MP John Rolle, acting, as he said, at the express desire of his constituents, proposed legislation to authorize nationwide contributory relief.[91]

When repeated frustration and old age finally induced Gilbert to cease his efforts, a long tradition of reforming advocacy halted – not to be revived for over 40 years. No parliamentary spokesman emerged to press the case for large-scale, rationalizing public authorities, commanding tax revenues and voluntary charity alike, in the welfare field. Instead, public debate increasingly focused on ways of indirectly relieving poverty: by minimum wage legislation, education, moral discipline, or the encouragement of friendly societies. MP and JP Samuel Whitbread, putting forward his own scheme for the reform of the poor laws in 1807 (a scheme entailing both public schooling and a national insurance scheme), remarked that the past few years had seen a revolution in thinking on this subject. No longer was "43 Elizabeth" regarded even as a proper starting-point for thought. The question was, rather, how to hasten the era when the poor laws could be superseded.[92]

In practice, the economy of welfare remained mixed. The high-price, troubled 1790s saw not merely an efflorescence of voluntary charity but also sharp rises in rate-based spending. What does seem to have been universally accepted, none the less, was that public relief should form, at most, no more than part of a broader spectrum of provision. Even Thomas Paine – not representative even of radicals in his bold advocacy of an array of welfare benefits to be funded by national taxation – envisaged total public welfare spending somewhat below the current total, supplemented by substantial payments by friendly societies financed by the working poor themselves.[93]

VI

Contemporaries often drew a broad distinction between "legal" and "voluntary" charity, although the forms of relief they included under that latter heading – bequests, charitable subscriptions, alms, and even contributions to self-help schemes – were so diverse as to place a question-mark over the utility of this simple dichotomy. If not asked to do too much work, however, the distinction has its uses. Some of the main conclusions which arise from this discussion can be summarized within its terms.

This chapter has emphasized a point that previous historiography has already amply supported: that the growth of rate-based relief in England from sixteenth-century origins to a scale unparalleled elsewhere in Europe did not displace voluntary charity, which survived and indeed – in some forms and at some periods – flourished, diversified and expanded.

In the course of the seventeenth and eighteenth centuries, a rough-and-ready division of labour developed between statutory and voluntary sectors. The location of the dividing line was largely determined by the limits of statutory relief. The Elizabethan poor laws had set out to establish a nationwide system of basic provision. They did not provide for capital expenditure on institutions. The 1662 Settlement Act, by strictly limiting eligibility for relief, further limited the utility of the public system.

It was not inevitable that these restrictions would survive – and indeed in the long run, of course, public provision was to be further extended. Voluntary charitable activity time and again indicated areas in which a case could be made for an extension of public provision, notably, although not uniquely, in the fields of education and health. Some reformers would have liked to see the rate-based system take at least some of these responsibilities on board. That this did not happen surely owed something to the very effectiveness of voluntary activity, and to its ability to satisfy a variety of aspirations. Experience of the statutory relief system helped to foster reservations about the effectiveness of parish-based, if not all, public administration. For all that early-modern English local government *was*, for most practical purposes, self-government, voluntary charitable institutions seemed to some observers to set standards in respect of participation and effective public accountability that formally public institutions rarely met. In a religiously divided society, the flexibility voluntary association offered was surely another of its attractions. Voluntary associations could provide a meeting-ground for different denominations, or could serve exclusive denominational purposes. Since they had no power to tax or otherwise compel those not spontaneously moved to support them, it was not necessary to fight for their control. A further attraction of voluntary charitable activities for those who valued the charitable impulse as such was that they were thought to give it purer expression than public tax-based charitable activity ever could.

This chapter has attempted to demonstrate that at all times in our period there were differences of opinion as to the merits of current practice, and as to the best way forward. On the whole, as it has also tried to show, the trend over the period was in favour of "voluntary" rather than "legal" charity – and, within "voluntary" charity, in favour of less institutional-ized, more individualized forms of giving. This did not of course entail a triumph of private over public *interest*. The period rather saw a shift in thought as to the most promising means of promoting the public interest.

The period surveyed ended with public relief under attack, and volun-tarism riding high in favour. But public relief was not in practice retracted at this time. New modes of thought had more effect on its form and organization than on its scale. So long as the charitable project was con-ceived, in whole or in part, as an expression of the interest of the commu-nity as a whole in the welfare of all its members, moreover, ideological space remained within which ideals of law-based, universalized public provision, and public oversight over all forms of charitable endeavour, could yet take root and flourish. If experience of parish-based and even reformed "incorporated" varieties of local administration highlighted the possible shortcomings of public control, experience of the maladmin-istration of charitable bequests provided an insistent reminder of the potential shortcomings of the voluntary mode. In the early nineteenth century, the Whig Henry Brougham's campaign for a fresh enquiry into the administration of charitable trusts[94] was to presage Whig reassertion of a reconceptualized version of the state's responsibilities in the field of poor relief.

Notes

1. R. Jütte, *Poverty and deviance in early modern Europe* (Cambridge, 1994); P. Slack, *Poverty and policy in Tudor and Stuart England* (London, 1988) and *The English poor law 1531–1782* (London, 1990); W. K. Jordan, *Philanthropy in England 1480–1660* (London, 1959); D. Owen, *English philanthropy 1660–1969* (Cambridge, Mass., 1964).

2. J. Kent, *Social attitudes of MPs 1590–1624 with special reference to the problem of poverty.* (PhD thesis, University of London, 1971); Slack, *Poverty and policy*, ch. 2.

3. Early pamphlets are discussed by M. James, *Social problems and policy during the puritan revolution 1640–60* (London, 1939), ch. 7; see also V. Pearl, "Puritans and poor relief: the London workhouse 1649–1660", in *Puritans and revolutionaries,* D. Pennington & K. Thomas (eds) (Oxford, 1978), pp. 206–32. S. Webb & B. Webb, *The old poor law* (London, 1927) surveys much pamphlet literature on public policy; D. Andrew, *Philanthropy and police* (Princeton, 1989) similarly on charity, and see also D. Andrew, "On reading charity sermons. Eighteenth-century Anglican solicitation and exhortation", *Journal of Ecclesiastical History* **43**, 1988, pp. 581–91. Sermons (among other sources) are more extensively examined in S. Lloyd, *Perceptions of poverty in eighteenth-century England.* (DPhil thesis, University of Oxford, 1991).

4. Slack, *Poverty and policy* (pp. 162–73) assesses the relation between "public and private" relief; see also his *English poor law,* pp. 49–52, and local studies cited by him. M. Barker-Read, *The treatment of the aged poor in five selected West Kent parishes 1662–1795.* (PhD thesis, Open University, 1988) helpfully stresses the different charitable endowments of her different parishes. For a close study of recipients, see A. Tomkins, *The experience of urban poverty: a comparison of Oxford and Shrewsbury 1740–70.* (DPhil thesis, University of Oxford, 1994).

5. T. Andrews, *An enquiry into the causes of the encrease and miseries of the poor of England* (London, 1738), pp. 23–8; T. Alcock, *Observations on the defects of the poor laws* (London, 1752), pp. 39–43; R. Burn, *The history of the poor laws* (London, 1764), chs 1–5 (see esp. pp.7–8, 106 for his emphasis on the limitations of monastic charity); T. Ruggles, *The history of the poor* [2 vols] (London, 1793), vol. 1, pp. 14–80. The varying accounts of the past supplied by these different writers correlate with their varying diagnoses of the present.

6. J. Bennett, "Conviviality and charity in medieval and early modern England", *Past and Present* **134**, 1992, pp. 19–41; see also response by M. Moisa, *Past and Present,* (forthcoming); F. Heal, *Hospitality in early modern England* (Oxford, 1990); G. Rosser, "Communities of parish and guild in the late Middle Ages" in *Parish, church and people,* S. Wright (ed.) (London, 1988), pp. 29–55; M. Macintosh, "Local responses to the poor in medieval and Tudor England", *Continuity and Change* **3**, 1988, pp. 209–45; B. Harvey, *Living and dying in England 1100–1540* (Oxford, 1993), ch. 1; M. Rubin, *Charity and community in medieval Cambridge* (Cambridge, 1987).

7. G. S. Jones, *History of the law of charity 1532–1837* (Cambridge, 1969), pp. 11–15. Similar rethinking was undertaken in relation to charitable briefs, once authorized

by the Pope or ecclesiastical authorities; at the Reformation, brought under the control of the state (see M. Harris, "'Inky blots and rotten parchment bonds': London charity briefs and the Guildhall Library", *Historical Research* **66**, 1993, p. 98–110.)

8. Slack, *Poverty and policy*, ch. 6, surveys legislative change in this formative period.

9. 39 Eliz. *c.* 3; note also Slack, *Poverty and policy*, pp. 127–8.

10. Harris provides some information on church collections: "'Inky blots'", pp. 102–3. For parish charities, see W. E. Tate, *The parish chest* (Cambridge, 1969), pp. 109–19.

11. For the remodelling of royal hospitals, see P. Slack, "Social policy and the constraints of government 1547–58", in *The mid-Tudor polity*, J. Loach & R. Tittler (eds) (London, 1980). The hospital charters provided that City of London aldermen should nominate all governors, some of whom were to be drawn from among their own number, some not.

12. Examples in Tomkins, *Experience of urban poverty*, pp. 278ff. Harris, "'Inky blots'", pp. 100–3. See I. Archer, *The pursuit of stability* (Cambridge, 1991), pp. 158–63, for Christ's Hospital's original dependence on poor rates.

13. Slack, *Poverty and policy*, p. 165 notes statutes of 1572, 1576 and 1598 to encourage the charitable funding of hospitals, almshouses and houses of correction. See also Jones, *Law of charity*, p. 22ff.

14. Burn, *History of the poor laws*, p. 119.

15. E. Larson, "A measure of power: the personal charity of Elizabeth Montagu", *Studies in eighteenth-century culture* **16**, 1986, pp. 197–210. D. Andrew, "*Noblesse oblige*. Female charity in an age of sentiment", in *Early modern conceptions of property*, J. Brewer & S. Staves (eds) (London, 1995). The practice of begging by inserting paragraphs in newspapers, noted by Andrew, was also satirized in Sheridan's *The critic* (1779), where Mr Puff boasts of having formerly made a living by this means.

16. In 1815, the secretary to the Ladies Charitable Society stated that his grandfather had been almoner to John Thornton and other gentlemen who gave very largely, and that he himself had been "in the habit of making enquiries since his infancy". PP (1814–15) (III), p. 249. Andrew, "*Noblesse oblige*", p. 292, discusses the use of a variety of agents in investigating applications; see also p. 296nn 24, 26.

17. Slack, *English poor law*, p. 30.

18. Jordan, *Philanthropy* – and for references to debate on his conclusions, Slack, *Poverty and policy*, pp. 162–3; Owen, *English philanthropy*, part I; M. G. Jones, *The charity school movement* (London, 1964); Andrew, *Philanthropy and police*; F. K. Brown, *Fathers of the Victorians* (Cambridge, 1961) ch. 9, "Ten thousand compassions and charities".

19. P. Gosden, *Self-help* (New York, 1974), ch. 1; R. P. Hastings, *Essays in North Riding history 1780–1850* (Northallerton, 1981), ch. 7; R. Leeson, *Travelling brothers* (London, 1979), ch. 4.

20. For the objects of charity, Jordan, *Philanthropy*, ch. 5; Owen, *English philanthropy*, part I. For workhouses and education, see R. J. Robson, "The SPCK in action: some episodes from the East Riding of Yorkshire", *Church Quarterly Review* **156**, 1955, pp. 266–78; for workhouses and the care of the sick: M. Fissell, *Patients,*

power and the poor in eighteenth-century Bristol (Cambridge, 1991), p. 118; Tomkins, *Experience of urban poverty*, pp. 192–5. In this paragraph, I take the limits of the law as given – but arguably, it was *because* it proved possible to fund schools and infirmaries in other ways that they remained outside the scope of the law. Proposals for changing the law, and their fate, are further considered below.

21. E. Bebb, *Nonconformity and social and economic life* (Bedford, 1935), pp. 137–44; A. Lloyd, *Quaker social history 1669–1738* (London, 1950), ch. 3; W. J. Warner, *The Wesleyan movement in the industrial revolution* (London, 1930), ch. 7; C. F. A. Marmoy, *The French Protestant hospital* (London, 1977) and *The case book of the Maison de Charité de Spittlefields 1739–41* (London, 1981). See also M. F. Lloyd Prichard, *The treatment of poverty in Norfolk 1700–1850.* (PhD thesis, University of Cambridge, 1949), ch. 9.

22. J. S. Taylor, *Poverty, migration and settlement in the industrial revolution: sojourners' narratives* (Palo Alto, 1989), N. Landau, "The laws of settlement and the surveillance of immigration in eighteenth-century Kent", *Continuity and Change* 3, 1988, pp. 391–420 and "The regulation of immigration, economic structures and definitions of poverty in eighteenth-century England", *Historical Journal* 33, 1990, pp. 541–71.

23. J. M. Martin, "Rich, poor and migrant in Stratford-on-Avon", *Local Population Studies* 20, 1978, pp. 40–43, reports that 21–27 per cent of household heads had settlements elsewhere; P. Corfield, *Social and economic history of Norwich.* (PhD thesis, University of London, 1976), p. 493, reports that a 1786 investigation showed that 26 per cent were alien.

24. J. Woodward, *To do the sick no harm* (London, 1974) provides a general account; Fissell, *Patients, power* provides a local study.

25. *Journals of the House of Commons* (henceforth JHC), vol. 43, p. 167. "County societies", which existed from at least the late seventeenth century, and which relieved certain poor from their members' counties, and "Strangers' Friend Societies", established from the later eighteenth century and associated especially with Methodists, addressed the same difficulty.

26. Silas Told, a Methodist, describes trying at some time in the 1750s or 1760s to secure the admission to the London Lying-in Hospital of the widow of a hanged man: since she did not know her husband's parish he was "obliged to commit her as one of the casual poor on the parish of Shoreditch" (*Life of Silas Told* [1786] (London, 1954), p. 94). Islington secured statutory authorization for procedures to relieve the "casual poor" (clearly distinguished from the resident poor on outdoor relief), 17 Geo. III c. 5. In a debate in the Commons (April 1800) on a bill to prevent the removal of the casual poor, the *relative* cheapness of supporting the non-resident poor was cited as a reason for keeping the settlement laws in being: it was said that in a parish four miles from London, £8034 had been spent in the past few years on maintaining 555 resident poor, as opposed to £171 3s 4d spent on 571 non-resident poor (cited *Parliamentary Register*, vol. 11, p. 180).

27. Tate, *Parish chest*, pp. 183–5. Statutes suggested the need for special tolerance for certain classes of poor traveller: those robbed on the way; harvesters; soldiers and sailors.

28. G. B. Hindle, *Provision for the relief of the poor in Manchester 1754–1826* (Manchester, 1975), chs 6–8 ; for the 1790s more generally, R. Wells, *Wretched faces* (Gloucester, 1988), pp. 310–11.

29. Hillsborough's 1752 bill, further discussed later in this chapter, had the first two features; [T. Gilbert], *A scheme for the better relief and employment of the poor* (London, 1764), pp. 12–13, would have provided public infirmaries and indeed lunatic asylums; all proposals for larger administrative districts would effectively have liberalized settlement laws.

30. Colquhoun in his 1806 *A treatise on indigence* (London, 1806), pp. 60–62, guesstimated a somewhat lower national charitable total of £4million.

31. Slack, *Poverty and policy*, pp. 173–81.

32. PRO: CO389/14 fols128–38. Developments in this decade are discussed by T. Hitchcock, *The English workhouse 1696–1750*. (DPhil thesis, University of Oxford, 1985), ch. 2.

33. Critical commentators included Roger North (whose *Discourse on the malicious tendency of the laws for the maintenance and settlement of the poor* was not published until 1753); R. Dunning, *Bread for the poor* (Exeter, 1698); and F. Brewster, *Essays on trade and navigation* (London, 1695), p. 58. For an MP who believed that the poor laws had helped to create poverty, and that what was needed was to "affright" the poor, see Bodl. Ms. Eng. Hist. b209 81v. Joyce Appleby, *Economic thought and ideology in seventeenth-century England* (Princeton, 1978), ch. 6, seems to me to underrate this strand of criticism – although it is true that few if any envisaged being able to shed all public expenditure on the poor.

34. S. Macfarlane, "Social policy and the poor in the late seventeenth century", in *London 1500–1700*, A. L. Beier & R. Finlay (eds) (London, 1986), p. 259; H. W. Stephenson, *Thomas Firmin 1632–97*. (DPhil thesis, University of Oxford, 1950); T. Hitchcock (ed.), *Richard Hutton's complaint book. The notebook of the steward of the Quaker workhouse at Clerkenwell 1711–37* (London, 1987); G. Clarke (ed.), *John Bellers. His life, times and writings* (London, 1987); Lloyd, *Quaker social history*, pp. 40–41, on workhouses in both London and Bristol.

35. The Webbs (*Old poor law*, pp. 105–14) cite numerous instances of the "projecting" approach. See also Hitchcock, *English workhouse*, p. 79; [L. Braddon], *A proposal for relieving, reforming and employing all the poor of Great Britain* (London, 1721).

36. M. Hale, *Discourse touching provision for the poor* (London, 1683); J. Child, *Proposals for the relief and employment of the poor* (n.d., but probably early 1690s); J. Cary, *An essay on the state of England in relation to its trade* (London, 1695). These publications were summarized by Burn, *History of the poor laws*; Ruggles, *History of the poor*, and F. M. Eden, *The state of the poor* [vol 1] (London, 1797) and were cited by many others.

37. E. E. Butcher, *Bristol Corporation of the Poor 1696–1834* (Bristol, 1932); Webbs, *Old poor law*, ch. 3 (a slightly expanded version of a chapter from their earlier *Statutory authorities for special purposes*), surveys incorporations in general; pp. 116–23 focus on early urban incorporations.

38. Macfarlane, *Social policy*, pp. 262, 266. See similarly for Bristol, Clarke, *Bellers*, p. 5.

39. Macfarlane, *Social policy*, pp. 267 – although he puts the emphasis elsewhere, thus:

"gifts from benefactors rarely exceeded 30% of total income between 1700 and 1713".

40. The Tiverton act of 1698 was the first to make such provision. A clause in the Tiverton act gave the Bristol Corporation similar powers. Their example was followed only by Hull and Worcester. I owe this information to Paul Slack.

41. Hitchcock, *English workhouse*, ch. 2. The bill mentioned is summarized in Bodl. Ms. Eng. Hist. b210 58v.–59.

42. Macfarlane, *Social policy*, pp. 265–70, explores opposition to the London scheme. See also J. Barry, "The parish in civic life: Bristol and its churches 1640–1750", in *Parish, church and people*, Wright (ed.), pp. 168–71. For Hull, *JHC*, vol. 13, p. 167, and G. Jackson, *Hull in the eighteenth century* (London, 1972), pp. 321–6. The Hull act was amended.

43. *Historical Manuscript Commission (HMC) House of Lords mss*, vol. 6, p. 273ff (a bill brought up from the Commons).

44. Contrast the Commons bill with another, apparently the work of the judges, originating in the Lords at the same period: *HMC, House of Lords mss*, vol. 6, p. 245ff. In the following session, the Commons essentially accepted the Lords model: *HMC, House of Lords mss*, vol. 7, p. 46–7. For the role of Chancery, see Jones, *Law of charity*, esp. pp. 54–6, 160ff. SPCK members were involved in promoting a later bill focusing on the safeguarding of charitable funds alone in 1712, but although this passed the Commons, it was lost at the end of the session. See M. Clement (ed.), *Correspondence and minutes of the SPCK relating to Wales 1699–1740* (Cardiff, 1952), pp. 48, 52, 86.

45. [D. Defoe], *Giving alms no charity* (London, 1704). Defoe also attacked the proposed legislation extensively in his *Review*, which began publication in the same year. Similar comments were made earlier, for example by Sir Richard Cocks, in Bodl. Ms. Eng. Hist. b209 81v.

46. Mackworth himself was a member of the SPCK, which played a central role in promoting charity school foundations. The SPCK took a close interest in poor relief legislation from its foundation through to the mid-eighteenth century. For the SPCK, see n58.

47. See n18.

48. For the financing of the royal hospitals, see Archer, *The pursuit of stability*, pp. 158–63, pp. 170–76; for voluntary hospitals, A. Berry, *Patronage, funding and the hospital patient*. (DPhil thesis, University of Oxford, 1995).

49. Owen, *English philanthropy*, p. 3, stresses the novelty of "associated philanthropy", but spends little time analyzing its distinctive organizational features. Andrew has more to say: *Philanthropy and police*, pp. 44–54, 79–92. See also R. Porter, "The gift relationship: philanthropy and provincial hospitals in eighteenth-century England", in *The hospital in history*, L. Granshaw & R. Porter (eds) (London, 1989), pp. 149–78; K. Wilson, "Urban culture and political activism in Hanoverian England: the case of voluntary hospitals", in *The transformation of political culture*, E. Hellmuth (ed.) (Oxford, 1990), pp. 165–84 and P. Langford, *Public life and the propertied Englishman 1689–1798* (Oxford, 1991), pp. 490–500.

50. Andrew, *Philanthropy and police*, pp. 20, 60, [J. Duncan], *Collections relative to the*

systematic relief of the poor, at different periods and in different countries (London, 1815), p. 174ff.

51. [W. Hay], *Remarks on the laws relating to the poor* (London, 1735), reprinted under his name with the same title but additions (1751). Hay's parliamentary diaries, in Northamptonshire Record Office (L[C] 1733), include some relevant material. It is of interest that Joseph Jekyll, Master of the Rolls, who worked closely with Hay, introduced mortmain legislation (to limit deathbed bequests of land to charity) in 1736, in the session following that in which Hay first advanced his proposal. Although Jekyll himself was actively involved with various city hospitals in a way that scarcely implies hostility to charitable foundations, in debate in the Lords the Mortmain bill was *opposed* in the name of the importance of charitable giving; *supported* on the grounds *inter alia* that the poor were best supported by their parishes, and that magnificent hospitals were monuments not to charity but to worldly pride and ambition. See *Parliamentary history* , vol. 9, cols. 1121–56, and for the legislation, Jones, *Law of charity*, ch. 7.

52. Hay, *Remarks* (1751 edn), pp. v–vi, 29ff.

53. Most (11 out of 14) local acts establishing corporations of the poor had provided for the co-option of benefactors giving more than a certain amount, usually £50–£100. I owe this information to Paul Slack. A plan to introduce such a provision for London was defeated in 1700 (Macfarlane, "Social policy", p. 267). Mackworth's 1704 bill had included a provision that all who contributed 20s. a year or more to support charity schools should be admitted to their governing corporations (*HMC, House of Lords mss,* vol. 6, p. 280). Hay was already considering empowering benefactors in 1735: *Remarks*, p. 49.

54. Religious exhortations to charity are explored by Andrew, *Philanthropy and police*, esp. ch. 1, and in her "On reading charity sermons", and by Lloyd, *Perceptions of poverty*, ch. 5. I am grateful to Sarah Lloyd for discussing this subject with me. Her comments inform especially the following paragraphs.

55. J. Mickleborough, *The great duty of labour and work* (Cambridge, 1751).

56. Fissell, *Patients, power,* p. 76ff develops the theme of the subscription charity as a solution to the would-be philanthropist's problems. Robert Nelson's "Ways and means of doing good", Appendix to his *Address to persons of quality and estate* (London, 1715), addressed the same problem with a menu of worthy causes.

57. For some of John Walsh's thoughts on the topic, see J. Walsh, "John Wesley and the community of goods", in *Protestant evangelicalism: Britain, Ireland, Germany and America c.1750–c.1980* K. Robbins (ed.) (Oxford, 1990), pp. 25–50; E. Duffy, "Religion and the counter-reformation", in *Revival and religion since 1700,* J. Garnett & C. Matthew (eds) (London, 1993), pp. 1–19. John Walsh tells me that Wesley favoured a variety of approaches to charity: he thought that there was a place both for targeted and for indiscriminate giving.

58. The most accessible survey of the SPCK's activities is probably now T. Hitchcock, "Paupers and preachers: the SPCK and the parochial workhouse movement", in *Stilling the grumbling hive*, L. Davison, T. Hitchcock, T. Keirn, R. B. Shoemaker (eds) (Stroud, 1992), pp. 155–6. He interestingly explores the way in which the society's interest in charity schools developed into an interest in workhouses.

59. W. Allen & E. McClure, *Two hundred years: the history of the* SPCK (London, 1898), p. 25; Hitchcock, *English workhouse*, p. 244. In 1716, the society *opposed* a proposal to put London schools under the control of elected vestries – perhaps because, in the political circumstances of the time, the proposal appeared hostile to the schools: see Jones, *Charity school movement*, p. 115ff. From that point on, the voluntary character of the schools seems to have gone unquestioned.

60. J. S. Taylor, *Jonas Hanway* (London, 1985), ch. 8.

61. Alcock, *Observations*. Comparative issues, and awareness of them, are more fully explored in my forthcoming article, "The state and the poor. Eighteenth-century English poor relief in comparative perspective", in *Rethinking Leviathan*, J. Brewer & E. Hellmuth (eds) (forthcoming).

62. Decker began writing in 1739; the tract was first published in 1743; I quote from the 1749 Dublin edition, p. 9. See more generally Andrew, *Philanthropy and police*, chs 2–4.

63. Alcock, *Observations*.

64. H. Fielding, *A proposal for making an effectual provision for the poor* (London, 1753). Fielding had developed his ideas as early as 1750: see C. Linnell (ed.), *The diaries of Thomas Wilson* (London, 1964), pp. 257–8. For Fielding's involvement with subscription charities, see Andrew, *Philanthropy and police*, pp. 57, 90.

65. N. Rogers, "Confronting the crime wave. The debate over social reform and regulation 1748–53", in *Stilling the grumbling hive*, Davison, Hitchcock, Keirn, Shoemaker (eds), pp. 90–91, discusses the two bills, though incorrectly says that Hillsborough's bill envisaged funding from rates only. He also somewhat oddly attributes Lloyd's bill to Gray, who chaired the committee, though contemporaries all saw Lloyd as its promoter. (The committee on Hillsborough's bill was chaired by Nicholas Hardinge, secretary to the Treasury.) The fullest account is R. Connors, *Pelham, parliament and public policy 1746–54*. (PhD thesis, University of Cambridge, 1993) ch. 5. For the draft bills, see S. Lambert, *House of Commons sessional papers of the eighteenth century* (145 vols., Wilmington, Delaware, 1975–6), vol. 9, pp. 369ff, 405ff.

66. C. Gray, *Considerations on several proposals lately made for the better maintenance of the poor* (London, 1751), esp. p. 17 (the pamphlet was reprinted with additions in 1752). He was assailed in *An impartial examination of a pamphlet intituled considerations on several proposals lately made for the better maintenance of the poor* (London, 1752). T. Alcock, *Remarks on two bills for the better maintenance of the poor* (Oxford, 1753), especially pp. 3–4.

67. Burn, *History of the poor laws*, pp. 203–9; B. Jones, "William Nicolson and Richard Burn", in *English county historians*, J. Simmons (ed.) (Wakefield, 1978), p. 176 (originally the introduction to a reprint of Nicolson & Burn's *History and antiquities of Cumberland and Westmorland*). Burn wrote to justify his decision not to revive the practice of making a collection at the offertory.

68. R. Burn, *Observations on the bill intended to be offered to parliament for the better relief and employment of the poor* (London, 1776). That this was already his view in 1764 is evident from *History of the poor laws*, pp. 232–4.

69. For the legislation see Connors, *Pelham, parliament,* pp. 180–90, 225–6. He notes

early acts for Bethnal Green (1745) and Dundee (1747). An important development of the mid-century was the takeover by incorporations of systems of statutory-authority borrowing, pioneered by turnpike trusts; this removed what had previously been a major practical obstacle to such foundations: the problem of amassing start-up costs. For Hay's thoughts on how this need might be met through a combination of taxation and voluntary giving, see *Remarks*, p. 48. A notable feature of Lloyd's bill was its provision for a national lottery to raise the necessary capital. (An earlier failed bill for a corporation of the poor at Leicester had also included such a provision: *JHC,* vol. 12, p. 657. I owe this reference to Lee Davison.) Dependence on public borrowing for start-up costs helped to ensure that incorporations were concentrated in peace time during eighteenth-century wars (in contrast to the 1690s); government demand was such as to soak up most loanable funds.

70. Webbs, *Old poor law,* p. 121ff, survey later incorporations; see also Langford, *Public life,* pp. 236, 240–43. R. Tompson, *The Charity Commission in the age of reform* (London, 1979), pp. 59–60, stresses similarity, but appears to document variation in practice as to whether or not new incorporations should be empowered to receive and administer charitable bequests; Alannah Tomkins informs me that Shrewsbury provides an instance in which the setting up of the House of Industry was associated with the takeover by its directors of all parish charities (Shropshire Record Office 83/1/309: see esp. entry for 15 November 1784). For studies of particular incorporations, see F. W. H. Sheppard, *Local government in St Marylebone 1688–1836* (London, 1938), especially chs 3, 11. H. Fearn, "The financing of the poor-law incorporation for the Hundreds of Colneis and Carlford", *Suffolk Institute of Archaeology* **27**, 1955, pp. 96–111.

71. E.g. R. Potter, *Observations on the poor laws* (London, 1775). (Potter was a Director of the House of Industry for Loddon and Clavering at Heckingham); T. Mendham, *A dialogue in two conversations between a gentleman, a pauper and his friend* (Norfolk, 1776). The issue was also debated in local newspapers.

72. For a somewhat fuller sketch of Gilbert's campaign, with an emphasis on his methods, see my "Parliament and the shaping of social policy in eighteenth-century England", *Transactions of the Royal Historical Society*, 5th series, **40**, 1990, pp. 88–9.

73. Cf. [Gilbert], *A scheme for the better relief and employment of the poor* (London, 1764) and T. Gilbert, *Considerations on the bills for the better relief and employment of the poor* (London, 1787).

74. [Gilbert], *A scheme,* pp. 14–15; Gilbert, *Plan for the better relief and employment of the poor* (London, 1781), pp. 11–12. PP (1816) (XVI) sets out information from returns to Gilbert's enquiry, not previously printed. These are discussed by C. Wilson, "Poverty and philanthropy in early modern England", in *Aspects of poverty in early modern Europe*, T. Riis (ed.) (Alphen aan den Rijn, 1981). For the effect of these enquiries on contemporary discussion see R. Tompson, *Classics or charity? The dilemma of the eighteenth-century grammar school* (Manchester, 1971), pp. 111–13. The Irish were quicker off the mark than the British here, beginning to pass new legislation from 1763: see Tompson, *Charity Commission,* pp. 81–3, and 84 for the effect

of Irish on subsequent English thinking.

75. See W. S. Lewis (ed.), *Horace Walpole's correspondence,* vol. 8 (Oxford, 1974), pp. 528–9, 534, 536.

76. Gilbert, *Considerations,* pp. 46–7.

77. The best account of this shift to date is in Andrew, *Philanthropy and police,* chs 4–6. See also my forthcoming "The state and the poor".

78. The Foundling Hospital's fortunes are most fully described by R. Perry, *Coram's children* (New Haven, 1981), especially chs 7–10. For waning enthusiasm for new incorporations, see Hillsborough in 1775 talking about the experience of St George's, Hanover Square; *Parliamentary history;* vol. 18, pp. 427–31. Pamphlets which discuss disease in the new East Anglian Hundred houses include J. Brand, *Observations on the probable effects of Mr Gilbert's bill* (London, 1776); [Anon], *Letter to Thomas Gilbert* (London, 1782); and J. Howlett, *The insufficiency of the causes to which the increase of our poor, and of the poor's rates, have been commonly ascribed* (London, 1788).

79. Langford, *Public life,* explores eighteenth-century attitudes to public authority in general (see especially chs 4 and 7). Shifts in these attitudes late in the century, and the effects of those shifts, have not been much explored outside the narrowly political context, although see F. O'Gorman, *Voters, patrons and parties* (Oxford, 1989), pp. 259–85, and H. T. Dickinson, *The politics of the people in eighteenth-century Britain* (London, 1995), pp. 112–23, for two relatively helpful recent discussions.

80. J. Mullan, *Sentiment and sociability* (Oxford, 1968); J. Todd, *Sensibility* (London, 1975); J. Dwyer, *Virtuous discourse* (Edinburgh, 1987); and G. Barker-Benfield, *The culture of sensibility* (Chicago, 1992) survey this process of cultural change. Lloyd, "Perceptions of poverty", ch. 5 notes the use of sentimental imagery in a charitable context. Jonas Hanway's *Sentimental history of chimney sweepers* (London, 1785) is exemplary. For personal charity in this context, see also Henry Mackenzie's novel, *The man of feeling* (London, 1771).

81. Hester Chapone's discussion of charity, under the rubric of "Economy" in her 1773 *Letters on the improvement of the mind* is interestingly set in context by S. Riordan, *Bluestocking philosophy: aspects of female aristocratic thought in England.* (PhD thesis, University of Cambridge, 1995). See also S. Trimmer, *Economy of charity* (London, 1787).

82. For women and charity see B. Rodgers, *Cloak of charity* (London, 1949) chs 6–7; F. Prochaska, "Women in English philanthropy 1780–1830", *International Review of Social History* **19**, 1974, pp. 426–45; and F. Prochaska, *Women and philanthropy in nineteenth-century England* (London, 1980), especially chs 1, 4; also M.-C. Martin, "Women and philanthropy in Walthamstow and Leyton 1740–1870", *London Journal* **19**, 1994, pp. 119–50. For the idealization of "visiting" as the key to effective charity, see J. Duncan, *Collections relative to the systematic relief of the poor, at different periods and in different countries* (London, 1815), pp. 121, 157, 178–92; L. Radzinowicz, *History of the English criminal law,* vol. 4 (London, 1968), pp. 42–55, and, for subsequent nineteenth-century developments: Owen, *English philanthropy,* pp. 139–43, and M. Roberts, "Reshaping the gift relationship. The London Mendicity Society and the suppression of begging in England

1818–1869", *International Review of Social History* **36**, 1991, especially pp. 205–8, 215–21, 227n.

83. See my forthcoming "The state and the poor".

84. For an early instance of local reforming effort along these lines, see [Anon.], *Observations on the present state of the poor of Sheffield* (Sheffield, 1774).

85. R. Mitchison has explored Scottish practice in a number of illuminating articles. See especially "The making of the old Scottish poor law", *Past and Present* **63**, 1974, pp. 58–93, and "North and south: the development of the gulf in poor law practice" in *Scottish society 1500–1800*, R. Houston & I. Whyte (eds) (Cambridge, 1989); also R. Houston, *Social change in the age of enlightenment. Edinburgh 1660–1760* (Oxford, 1994), ch. 4.

86. J. Townsend, *A dissertation on the poor laws* (Berkeley, California, 1971[1786]), p. 69; T. R. Malthus, *An essay on the principle of population*, 2nd edn, Book 4, (London, 1914), ch. 9.

87. (London and Edinburgh, 1787). This collection is traditionally attributed to Gilbert, but the attribution seems highly improbable. Internal evidence – including the joint place of publication – makes a Scottish editor seem more likely. Locke's report to the Board of Trade was similarly reprinted a couple of years later in *An account of the . . . society for the promotion of industry . . . in the county of Lincoln*, 3rd edn (Louth, 1789). A similar venture at mid-century had been the first publication of Roger North's (late seventeenth-century) *Discourse on the malicious tendency of the laws for the maintenance and settlement of the poor* (1753).

88. Chs 4–6.

89. S. Brown, *Politics, commerce and social policy in the City of London 1782–1802*. (DPhil. thesis, University of Oxford, 1992), pp. 252–78; R. Wilberforce & S. Wilberforce, *Life of Wilberforce* [5 vols] (London, 1838), vol. 2, p. 180; E. Rigby, *Reports of the special provision committee appointed by the Court of Guardians in the City of Norwich* (London, 1788), pp. iv–v.

90. D. O. Thomas, "Francis Maseres, Richard Price and the industrious poor", *Enlightenment and Dissent* **4**, 1985, pp. 65–82. *Parliamentary history*, vol. 17, cols. 645–8. Burke's intervention was idiosyncratic, in that attacks on "perpetual charities" in England had previously been associated *primarily* with their embodiment in land: see Jones, *History of charity*, p. 114. Was he perhaps also influenced by Continental debate?

91. W. S. Steer, "The origins of social insurance", *Transactions of the Devon Association for the Advancement of Science, Literature and Art* **96**, 1964, pp. 303–17; *Parliamentary history*, vol. 36, cols. 1059ff. – the scheme was referred to in Parliament and elsewhere as Acland's scheme, Acland having put the case for it in print in his 1786 *Plan for rendering the poor independent of public contributions*. J. R. Poynter, *Society and pauperism* (London, 1969), pp. 34–9, surveys the various national contributory proposals.

92. Poynter, *Society and pauperism*, pp. 207–22; S. Whitbread, *Substance of a speech on the poor laws* (London, 1807), p. 4.

93. Poynter, *Society and pauperism*, ch. 3, offers a general account; D. Eastwood, *Governing rural England* (Oxford, 1994), chs 5–7, is the most recent account of

policy change in this period – grounded especially in a study of Oxfordshire. The 1790s did see a falling-off in numbers of new local incorporations founded – but this must in part be attributed to the usual wartime squeeze on investment, for which see n69: the fall was especially marked after the declaration of war in 1793. For Thomas Paine, see his *Rights of man*, part 2, ch. 5. Paine thought that a reduction in taxes – to the extent of £2million – would make possible a reduction in relief expenditure. He suggested that the problem of poverty would then largely resolve itself into the problem of taking care of children and the old: "what remains will be incidental, and in a great measure, fall within the compass of benefit clubs".

94. Tompson, *Charity Commission*, provides the best account of this campaign and its immediate antecedents.

8

"Grasping gratitude": charity and hospital finance in late-Victorian London

Keir Waddington

In 1886 Guy's Hospital launched its first public appeal for voluntary con-tributions from Mansion House.[1] The previous six years had been anxious ones for the hospital. In 1880 Guy's had faced a virtual state of "civil war" over the introduction of a new system of nursing; the internal conflict that resulted brought into question the hospital's management and increased demands for a public enquiry into London's voluntary hospitals.[2] The onset of the agricultural depression in the late 1870s reduced the hospital's income from its landed estates that had since the mid-nineteenth century provided over 90 per cent of its funding. In 1883, under pressure from the Charity Commission which curtailed the hospital's ability to borrow and questioned the governors' financial management, the governors took the unpopular step of admitting paying patients.[3] The public appeal three years later ended a series of desperate attempts to reverse the hospital's precari-ous financial fortunes. Ten years later the governors launched a further public appeal. Guy's Hospital, which contemporaries considered one of London's great endowed hospitals and so independent of charitable fund-ing, had finally entered the highly competitive benevolent economy at a time when many other London hospitals were extending their financial base away from philanthropy.

Guy's 1886 appeal came at the end of a spate of major hospital appeals. In 1883 the London Hospital had launched an appeal for £150,000 and St George's Hospital was quick to follow.[4] Informed contemporary opin-ion saw this as a clear indication that the traditional charitable nexus of hos-pital funding was beginning to break down. Only those on the margins of reform adopted a collectivist approach and argued that the capital's voluntary hospitals should be rate-assisted.[5] Most hospital administrators, reformers and the subscribing public, however, were constrained by the belief that hospitals were an essential part of the philanthropic welfare system and could be legitimately funded only through voluntary action. Historians have accepted this interpretation and have not attempted to discuss charity's relationship with hospital funding or how hospitals acted as intermediaries between the benevolent and the recipients of charitable relief. In the debate over philanthropy, hospitals have been seen as an example of voluntary action and not as one of the main channels for the Victorians' benevolent zeal. The history of hospitals is dominated by the work of medical historians and the social history of hospitals and their finances have only recently become the subject of an analysis that seeks to challenge the traditional view of hospital finance.[6] What this chapter intends to illustrate is that a study of hospitals in late-Victorian London and an analysis of hospital philanthropy and finance has much to offer to our understanding of charity.

I

Hospitals, as Burford Rawlings, secretary to the National Hospital for the Paralysed and Epileptic appreciated, were involved in the constant "scramble of hungry institutions for bread".[7] Competition for charitable funds was intense, but as benevolent institutions they did not fare badly. In a country where philanthropy was seen to be a source of national pride, benevolence was felt to be limitless, though most organizers of charitable societies were all too aware that philanthropy was a finite resource. Hospital governors regarded few sources of income as reliable, but it was to charity that they turned first with an attitude of grasping gratitude. Even if the traditional view is accepted that hospitals were funded by philanthropy, charitable resources cannot be simply characterized.

Hospital governors seemed to know instinctively what would motivate benevolence. They carefully manipulated what they believed stimulated charity in their fundraising efforts, simultaneously invoking several concerns in the same appeal. Voluntarism was so integral to Victorian civil society that its nature was rarely openly discussed. By analyzing the hospitals' public appeals and the vocabulary governors used in their advertising and fundraising it is possible to extend our understanding of why money was given. Governors projected charity as a religious duty, building on the

Evangelical ethos, and benevolence was shown as an investment for the philanthropist's spiritual future. For one writer it was even the "genius of Christianity" and hospitals embraced non-sectarian religious sentiments in their appeals.[8] Religious images remained powerful and were combined with accounts of sickness and suffering to inspire compassion, especially by the Hospital for Sick Children whose emotive appeals must have touched even the most hard-hearted. Sympathy was often projected beyond the patient to the institution and hospitals were careful to stress their financial plight in the most pitiful terms. Notions of paternalism were played upon and occasionally the hospital was shown as the key to social harmony. Appeals on these terms, however, mainly appeared at times of social stress as in the harsh winter of 1885–6 which saw workers' demonstrations in the West End in February 1886.[9] Hospital governors tried to manipulate existing feelings of social tension rather than create it in their own appeals.[10] The projection of the hospital as a bulwark against revolution was only part of governors' attempts to appeal to philanthropy's more selfish and self-interested concerns. Contributions to hospitals were presented as an economical and efficient use of charity, which held benefits for all classes. It was a view neatly summarized by the *Daily Telegraph* in 1871:

> We know that they [hospitals] assist in the case of accidents that may happen to anybody in any class, we know that as schools of medical science they are equally useful to the rich and poor, and we know that they repay the cost to the community over and over again, in sending back to their work and homes, in health, men who if they had not been so attended to, would probably have left families destitute upon the world.[11]

London's hospitals, governors had the public believe, promoted national efficiency, reduced pauperism, and provided the training ground for doctors who could use the techniques perfected on the poor to aid the wealthy. If these claims of material, social and medical benefit were not enough, then governors appealed to their supporters' social snobbery. Charity was highly fashionable in Victorian society and for some it became an emblem of social prestige. The socially insecure, the aspiring, and the wealthy felt that philanthropy implied status and provided an opportunity to meet the noble and the famous at the hospitals' fundraising events. According to an acidic critic in the *Westminster Review*, many contributions were largely dependent on the names attached to the subscription lists.[12] Governors accordingly carefully acknowledged every donation and subscription in their Annual Reports no matter how small. The death of a prominent supporter could therefore have a marked effect. On the death of the Duke of Cambridge in 1850, the governors of the London Hospital mourned his passing as "a powerful and unwavering friend" and because his "benevolent influence has been the means of permanently increasing the income of this important charity".[13] Governors, however, preferred to play on religious sentiment, humanitarianism and the hospitals' social utility rather than on social snobbery. Religion may have provided a strong context for inspiration, but the philanthropic psyche contained a conflicting mix of motivations that could be both altruistic and intrinsically selfish. Perhaps by playing on all these concerns, London's hospitals guaranteed a high level of charitable support that was only rivalled by the level of contributions the foreign mission and Bible societies could stimulate.

Despite the London hospitals' ability to stimulate charitable interests they survived by "pleading in competition".[14] Governors were both the hospitals' fundholders and fundraisers. They operated in the institutional divide between the subscriber and the recipient, controlling expenditure and investments, and deciding how the money contributed by the philanthropic public would be distributed, and, more importantly, raised. Hospitals through their constant fundraising activities helped create a market for benevolent action and charitable giving. Charity in Victorian London was at best erratic and hospitals had to compete with other voluntary societies for funds. Subscriptions were therefore seen as the only reliable form of voluntary contributions, but they tended to be small, and although any amount could be given, few gave more than five guineas annually. Every effort was made to collect them, and the right to admit patients and influence the hospital's management were used as incentives, but the attraction of subscribers remained a "constant struggle".[15] To ease some of the burden, paid collectors were employed, who crossed and recrossed each others' paths reminding contributors that their subscriptions had fallen due. Governors did not want to leave anything to chance, but on the other hand they praised the value of donations. These were essentially unpredictable, but a certain amount could be realistically relied upon each year. The benevolent often found it easier to make a series of donations than the long-term commitment that subscribing entailed. Amounts varied and although all were acknowledged with enthusiasm, gifts such as the £1,000 given by Nathaniel Montefiore to University College Hospital's rebuilding fund in 1887 were more eagerly celebrated.[16] Donations were not just limited to money: flowers and paintings were regularly given, but where governors did not want to appear niggardly in their gratitude, many "prefer[ed] the simplicity of cash gifts".[17] Legacies were more troublesome and erratic and in some years no bequests would be forthcoming. The governors of University College Hospital relied too heavily on legacies to solve the hospital's financial problems, creating a permanent sense of anxiety. The promise of large amounts ensured that governors eagerly encouraged legacies and were willing to fight lengthy legal battles if necessary, though it is difficult to determine how many went as far as the governors of Guy's Hospital in applying directly to the recently bereaved for money. Hospital philanthropy was a cut-throat business; every institution wanted to ensure that it reaped the full reward that philanthropy had to offer.

Charitable contributions were not limited to subscriptions, donations and legacies. Philanthropic income through these channels can be termed "direct" philanthropy because in them the charitable motive and choice of benevolent agency can be clearly seen. Other sources of charitable income were not so clear cut and there were many ways to give. London's hospitals were in no position to wait for philanthropists to favour them, so several active ways of raising money were employed to encourage benevolence. "In order to stimulate the flow of funds," explained the *Medical Times & Gazette* in 1852, "the charitable public is called upon to dine, to act, and to pray."[18] Governors invested time and effort in raising money and hospital minute books are dominated by their fundraising activities. The philanthropic public were constantly reminded of the plight of individual hospitals and "day by day a column and a half of the most urgent advertisements" filled the press.[19] Many complained that the London hospitals' incessant publicity wearied the public and alienated support, but governors continued to feel they could not afford to ignore any financial opportunity and gradually increased the sophistication of their publicity. The most visual form of charitable fundraising was the public appeal, a tactic employed to meet debt or the cost of building. Prominent members of civil society were called upon to offer their support and appeals were launched from the steps of Mansion House and detailed lists of contributors were published in the hope that others would be persuaded to contribute. Such was the money-raising potential of appeals that the governors of the London Hospital set up a "quinquennial" appeal in 1878, allowing them to launch a major funding drive every five years to meet the hospital's accumulating deficit.[20] Other hospitals preferred to reserve appeals for a desperate financial situation.

In the absence of an appeal other means of soliciting philanthropy were used. To increase contributions, charity was made a pleasurable occupation and new devices and variations were introduced that mixed "seriousness" with "entertainment".[21] The annual dinner or ball became the social and financial highlight of the hospital's year, where a wined and dined audience would hear speeches in favour of the hospital and be motivated to new heights of generosity. Local societies, churches and working-men's associations were called upon to organize collections and although noisy street collections and the Bible societies' house-to-house collections met with disapproval, the governors of the Royal Chest Hospital had no qualms in taking any money collected in the local public houses.[22] Serious-minded philanthropists alternatively put on programmes of entertainments and plays where the profits went to the local hospital. The governors of the Hospital for Sick Children disapproved of such amateur performances and preferred one supporter's invitation to use the Gaiety Theatre for a "benefit" in 1878.[23] Not all hospitals were as choosy. Where the governors of the German Hospital insisted that they would not be liable for any "benefit" held in the hospital's name, there was always one institution that was glad to accept any money raised by these means. The charity bazaar, a benevolent variation on the popular commercial bazaars of the 1820s, could be more controversial. Bazaars became a popular and fashionable way of raising money in the nineteenth century, but they were also the subject of sharp criticism by the Church and by commercial dealers who saw them as unfair competition.[24] Governors ignored these attacks and set up committees to organize lavish bazaars. The financial rewards were invariably worth the criticism: in 1898 the London Hospital's Press Bazaar added over £12,000 to the hospital's ailing funds.[25] However, though bazaars became a regular and increasing feature of the benevolent economy, the effort needed to organize them ensured that they remained periodic spectacles for most institutions.

Not all forms of charitable income were raised by the hospital or by its direct supporters. The foundation of the Metropolitan Hospital Sunday Fund in 1873 signified a new departure in hospital funding – a form of "indirect" philanthropy.[26] It established the first in a series of benevolent funds that culminated in the Prince of Wales's Hospital Fund for London in 1897. The idea was pioneered in Birmingham in the 1860s and had a simple aim: an organization was established that collected money on a systematic basis and then distributed the collection in a series of grants. The Sunday Fund collected money from the capital's churches and chapels on one Sunday in every year, while the Metropolitan Hospital Saturday Fund, its working-class equivalent founded in 1874, organized workshop and street collections. Though the funds relied on voluntary contributions they positioned themselves between the subscriber and the hospital. Careful investigation by an independent distribution committee removed the subscribers' direct participation in how their contribution was used and which institution it would benefit. The level of the grant was worked out according to the individual hospital's management costs and the number of patients it treated. It was anticipated that the funds would not only increase the income available to London's hospitals, but also promote reform because governors would consciously improve their administration to increase the size of their grant. Both funds were only partially successful. From 1873 to 1894 the Sunday Fund, the more respectable and effective of the two movements, collected a total of £725,647 but marginalized its reformist intentions as its promoters became preoccupied with the problems of organizing collections and raising money. The Saturday Fund was widely attacked for its noisy street collections and the large amounts it spent on administration, while governors resented its heavy-handed approach and demands for working-class representation in hospital management. According to the *British Medical Journal* in 1887, "the Hospital Sunday and Hospital Saturday Funds are well-meant efforts to meet the [hospitals' financial] difficulty; but their most sanguine friends cannot pretend that they have solved it".[27] Hospitals needed more than philanthropic sources of income to keep their beds open.

II

The amount given to charity in the nineteenth century was breathtaking and Brian Harrison estimates that by the 1890s the country's benevolent societies were receiving at least £5 million in charitable contributions annually.[28] However, a survey by the Statistical Society of London in 1857 revealed that only 30 per cent of hospital income came from philanthropy.[29] In 1873 a similar investigation for the *British Medical Journal* came to the same conclusion and showed that charity was not the hospitals' main source of funding.[30] As one contemporary wrote in 1894, "a glance at the advertising columns of any of the leading newspapers reveals only too clearly that the existing [charitable] sources of hospital income are fatally deficient".[31] Given such contemporary statistical evidence, the traditional view that London's hospitals were primarily funded by charitable contributions begins to break down. The *Charity Record & Philanthropic News* felt that charitable "zeal" alone could meet all the hospitals' needs, but it is apparent from the hospitals' account books and ledgers that governors preferred to supplement this with other sources of income.[32]

Hospital accounts were notorious for their inaccuracy. Hospital reformers and the Sunday Fund campaigned for standardization to allow institutions to be effectively compared, but even by the 1890s they had made little headway, despite the Fund's financial pressure. The problems associated with hospital accounts are shown by the lax procedures used by St John's Hospital for Diseases of the Skin. In 1890 the *Hospital* reported that St John's kept its accounts "upon loose sheets of paper" which had become muddled; "amounts appeared twice" and "items cannot be traced and totals cannot be made to agree".[33] It was a common problem, but by using hospitals' annual reports and account books it is possible to reconstruct their finances. Each institution had its own structure of income, but by using the evidence available from individual hospitals it is possible to reconstruct their finances and suggest the types of resources that were used. Income from non-charitable sources falls into three categories: money from the hospital's property, income derived from the hospital as a medical institution, and loans. Rarely did institutions step outside these boundaries to solve their economic problems and the Royal Free Hospital's unsuccessful application for a government grant in 1841 remained an anomaly until the 1920s.[34] A subsidy from the state was the only source of finance that was considered totally unacceptable, although not all the other forms of income were greeted with equal enthusiasm.

After direct philanthropy the hospital's property was the main source of income and at St Bartholomew's, Guy's and St Thomas's (hospitals endowed with property and investments by their founders) it provided the mainstay of their funding. Property, often held as houses or in agricultural estates outside London, could be rented, or sold at times of financial crisis or when new wards and clinical facilities were added. Most of the property held by non-endowed hospitals was in investments, mainly in railway stock, consolidated stock (consols) and government bonds. The London Hospital, however, modified the standard practice of investments. In 1863, to increase the hospital's income, the governors decided to reinvest some of the hospital's stock in mortgages as they believed this would yield a higher rate of interest.[35] After two years of deliberation the house committee, the hospital's main managing committee, recommended that £100,000 in government securities should be sold for this purpose and in August 1865 they negotiated their first venture into the mortgage market.[36] The move, though original, saddled the hospital with unreliable borrowers that in 1897 threatened over half the hospital's investments and discouraged further mortgages. Income from investments or mortgages was considered reliable, though stock and deposits were often among the first forms of property to be sold if the need arose. Where the German Hospital built up its investments from 1867 to increase the hospital's reliable income after the governors had been shocked by the financial strain of rebuilding in the mid-1860s, the governors at University College Hospital frequently sold their invested property to cover the hospital's accumulating deficits. The governors of University College Hospital were not the only ones to do so in times of need: all governors sold invested property to cover their debts, but they did so with less frequency and were in a better position to invest any surplus income. The effect of such actions was to damage their hospital's long-term financial fortunes, but contemporary warnings to this effect went unheeded given the often urgent need for funds.

A more innovative approach to fundraising was the money derived from the hospitals' function as a medical institution. Income from patients, either through a small charge levied on outpatients for their treatment or medicine, or through the foundation of a separate paying ward for inpatients, was widely criticized. Some reformers believed that patient charges answered the need for institutional treatment for middle-class patients, but most hospitals were not motivated by such ideological arguments and introduced charges to solve their financial problems. By the 1880s it had become an acceptable means of raising income. Specialist hospitals drew a large part of their funds from their patients, but general hospitals remained cautious. Only St Thomas's and Guy's fully implemented a payment scheme as it was feared "that the more a hospital seeks to help itself out of patients' pockets the less it is helped by others".[37] Payment from patients rarely covered the cost of treatment and the governors of St Thomas's and Guy's were disappointed that more could not be raised from this source. According to the *Hospital* in 1889, the scheme adopted by St Thomas's produced an annual profit of £1,000 and at Guy's it was less, hardly enough to cover the revenue lost from the fall in land values during the agricultural depression.[38] One form of payment, however, was uncontroversial. Poor-law unions, unable to provide sophisticated medical facilities, sent their sick to the voluntary hospitals. Unions either subscribed on the same terms as an individual or agreed a set price per patient per day in a precursor to the internal market of the National Health Service, suggesting a closer co-operation between health care sectors than has previously been assumed.

Other sources of income from the hospitals' function aroused less antagonism. The move to the employment of trained nurses saw governors exploiting what became a necessity of efficient patient care. Most general hospitals established a nursing school, following the lead set by the Nightingale Training School at St Thomas's Hospital. Probationary nurses had to pay for their training and often in conjunction with the school a private nursing scheme was established. The London Hospital had 100 private nurses on duty by 1899 and charged £2 2s for per day for "ordinary cases", £1 1s for attendance at an operation, and 10s 6d per visit for leeching.[39] By 1891, 2.5 per cent of hospital income in Britain came from this "modest but reliable" source of funding.[40] University College Hospital adapted this principle. In theory the tuition fees from the hospital's medical school went directly to the University and the hospital's medical staff, but such was the hospital's desperate financial position that both the University and the doctors were persuaded to redirect these fees back to help fund the hospital.[41]

Loans, the final category of non-charitable income, were used at different points by all hospitals. In the first few years after an institution's foundation small amounts were usually borrowed from the treasurer. However, as the demands of the institution grew and new wards were built or sanitary improvements undertaken, governors began to turn to banks and building societies. Mostly loans were sought from one bank, and the hospital usually had an informal link with it through one of its governors. At the London Hospital and University College Hospital borrowing was a significant source of income, although the governors at the London Hospital were more careful in paying off their debts.[42]

III

The institutional mix of these non-charitable resources rarely remained static, and as hospitals evolved so too did their finances. Between 1850 and 1900 governors gradually moved away from their hospital's traditional resources and erratically sought new sources of funding, creating a process of financial diversification. More sources of income were used and the components in the structure of finance changed their relative importance.

Table 8.1   St Bartholomew's Hospital: income 1863–95 (%).

	1863–65	1870–75	1890–95
Balance from previous year	7.0	1.1	3.7
Direct philanthropy:			
Donations	1.5	0.9	0.5
Legacies	0.2	2.1	2.7
Hospital's property:			
Rent	78.1	56.3	75.2
Dividends	10.2	7.9	4.2
Sale of waste	0.5	0.3	—
Sale of property	—	12.8	4.5
Tax redeemed	0.8	1.3	2.0
Insurance	—	1.8	2.0
Hospital's function:			
College	0.1	0.1	0.8
Nursing	—	—	1.8
Loans	—	14.6	2.5
"Sundries"	1.6	0.8	0.1

Source: SBH Archive, General Account Books, Hb/23/3–4.[43]

The intention was never to dilute charity, only to keep wards open. This is best illustrated by Tables 8.1, 8.2 and 8.3. Although St Bartholomew's Hospital, as an endowed institution with large property holdings in London, had no pressing financial need to develop new sources of funding, the income from property did not meet all the hospital's increasing needs, and diversification occurred. Guy's Hospital in comparison provides a clear example of diversification. The German Hospital, like many hospitals, correspondingly diversified its income in response to the pressures of medical change and from a desire to avoid debt.

How can this process of diversification be explained? Contemporaries who offered an opinion did so from a perspective that emphasized an apparent endemic financial crisis in the voluntary sector and tried to account for the widespread level of debt in London's hospitals. Many blamed their economic problems on the "chaos of benevolence" and rising expenditure.[44] These two factors, although important, account for only part of the reason. Charity was unpredictable and could be fickle in its favours, but as not all hospitals were dependent on philanthropy and all hospitals diversified their income, a more complex argument is needed that analyzes the nature of the benevolent economy and the nature of the hospital and the pressures acting on it.

Table 8.2 Guy's Hospital: income 1853–95 (%).

	1853–55	1870–75	1890–95
Direct philanthropy:			
Donations	0.4	0.2	23.0
Legacies	—	2.1	—
Indirect philanthropy:			
Sunday fund	—	—	1.0
Saturday fund	—	—	1.2
Hospital's property:			
Rent	95.6	95.8	58.2
Dividends	3.8	1.5	4.2
Sale of property	—	—	0.1
Hospital's function:			
Nursing	—	—	2.6
Patients	0.2	0.4	9.7

Source: Guy's Archive, Financial Abstracts 1853–75, D19/1–3; Treasurer's Reports 1888–97, A94/1.

Table 8.3 German Hospital: income 1850–95 (%).

	1850–55	1870–75	1890–95
Balance from previous year	8.4	4.1	1.6
Direct philanthropy:			
Subscriptions	23.5	13.2	18.0
Donations	39.9	37.4	34.4
Legacies	2.1	2.5	6.3
Collections	8.3	0.2	0.5
Indirect philanthropy:			
Sunday fund	—	1.9	6.1
Saturday fund	—	0.4	1.8
Hospital's property:			
Dividends	2.0	13.8	18.6
Deposit	—	8.5	—
Rent	—	—	2.0
Sale of property1.6	13.6	0.1	
Insurance	0.7	—	—
Tax redeemed	—	0.1	0.5
Hospital's function:			
Patients	1.9	2.1	2.7
Loans	11.6	1.9	7.2
"Sundries"	—	0.3	0.2

Source: Annual Reports 1850–95.

Rising expenditure was the main reason for diversification. From the foundation of the voluntary hospitals in the eighteenth century, administrators had been anxious to defend any increase in spending to maintain public confidence. This, however, could not hide the fact that expenditure increased dramatically. Between 1873 and 1883, according to a survey in the *Charity Organisation Review*, expenditure in the general hospitals had increased by 22.6 per cent and by 1890 the London hospitals were on average spending £2,000 per day.[45] Growth rates varied considerably between institutions: at the Royal Chest Hospital expenditure rose from £775 19s 9d in 1851 to £8,481 3s in 1898, and at most institutions there was on average a 70 per cent increase.[46] It appeared that not even the most prudent of administrators could prevent an increase in spending. According to the *Hospital* the reasons for a rise in expenditure

> may be traced in all large hospitals, first to the enormous development of nursing arrangements, higher class and variety of diet of the patients, larger bed space, additional bed and ward furniture, expensive sanitary fittings requiring constant control and supervision, together with a costly assortment of new curative arrangements.[47]

The emphasis here is on extravagance, but when the governors of the German Hospital investigated expenditure in 1856 they found that it was an increase in "essential items" that was raising costs.[48] Many small extravagances can be found, but financial recklessness was uncommon. Governors, aware of their limited resources, were careful when it came to spending and attempted periodic economies, but they were also aware that they had a duty to provide "the best" for their patients.

The reasons for increased expenditure are not located, as some contemporaries felt, in the hospitals' constant advertising or in the encouragement cheap loans gave to spending, but in the changing nature of the hospital. Gradually the impression that hospitals were "gateways to death" was modified and they were increasingly seen as medical and nursing institutions.[49] This change in image encouraged a striking rise in patient numbers, fuelled by the doctors' desire for a large pool of clinical material. Although hospital reformers were convinced that the increase in admissions reflected a growth in "undeserving" patients, there is little quantitative evidence to support their view. Certainly, a rise in patient numbers did have a fundamental impact on spending. The link between an increase in admissions, doubling at St Bartholomew's Hospital between 1861 and 1881, and a rise in expenditure is not hard to make, especially when a quarter of the London hospitals expenditure went on food.[50] Between 1864 and 1891 the average weekly cost of inpatient care in London rose by 203 per cent. Changes in the practice of medicine with the development of anaesthetics, antiseptics and scientific medicine, and the growth of a trained body of nurses, ensured that "it cost more to cure a man than formerly".[51] Governors were often reluctant to embrace change, but advances in medicine and nursing could not be resisted for long as new specialist departments were added and new medical procedures were adopted.[52] Medical and institutional costs were forced up as the need for sophisticated treatment combined with the need for a "well-tempered environment".[53] To care for the sick increasingly meant new wards, more doctors, more specialism and better provision, and therefore higher expenditure. Under these conditions the traditional sources of funding, especially philanthropy, came under increasing pressure and to keep abreast of change and to prevent beds from being closed new sources of funding had to be developed.

Hospital governors' passion for rebuilding added to these pressures. The altered criteria of medical care, noted above, and the rise in patient numbers made new buildings essential, but they raised the hospitals' running costs. St Thomas's Hospital had to adopt a new financial strategy after its move to Lambeth and "the folly of overbuilding", and in 1880 it began to admit paying patients.[54] More frequently, governors borrowed money, or like the governors of the Royal Chest Hospital in 1889, sold investments to pay for the "sundry debts incurred in the building of the new wing".[55] However, as Henry Burdett, the doyen of hospital reform, recognized in 1881, the physical expansion of provision created a dramatic rise in expenditure, while the new wards were often left empty.[56]

The financial experiences of individual hospitals were influenced by their institutional nature. "Hospitals associated with medical schools [were] somewhat more expensive than others" as they had to admit a large number of patients and provide the most modern medical practices for teaching purposes.[57] Specialist hospitals were in a different position. Although they were initially denounced as a drain on charity, they seemed to have a natural appeal to philanthropists who had a personal or familial experience of sickness, and to businesses keen to exploit the care that specialist hospitals could offer to their employees. The Royal Chest Hospital attracted support from printing firms, whose employees were particularly prone to diseases of the chest, while the Hospital for Sick Children, "with so many claims upon the sympathies of the benevolent", relied on the emotive plight of its patients to motivate benevolence.[58] Specialist hospitals were always more successful than many of their general counterparts in attracting philanthropy. However, at least until the start of the agricultural depression in the late 1870s, the endowed hospitals had an income from property and investments that separated them from other hospitals and made them financially secure. Endowed hospitals did modify their economic basis in response to periodic financial problems, but at least until the early 1880s diversification was less anxious and often a response to opportunity rather than need. The image persisted that these hospitals were well financed, if poorly managed, and other hospitals sought to invest their surplus income in an attempt to mimic the same level of financial security that the endowed hospitals were believed to possess.

Whatever the hospital's nature, it could not be separated from its location or the benevolent economy. Governors expected the local community to give generously, but this was not always possible. The London Hospital was hampered by the level of poverty in the East End that ensured a large number of cases but few subscriptions. Areas in north London were notorious for their "tight-buttoned pockets" and the concentration of hospitals within two miles of Charing Cross strained the amount of money that could be collected locally.[59] To compensate, governors appealed beyond the hospital's neighbourhood to metropolitan and then national and imperial interests. Not all were successful and most were forced to supplement local philanthropy with other sources of income, but few hospitals in this period faced the serious threat of closure.

Despite the often low level of local collections, governors jealously guarded their community resources. Established hospitals resisted the foundation of any new hospital in their area. Governors were all too aware that there was "a limit to the generosity of even the most benevolently disposed persons" and that competition was best limited.[60] The benevolent economy was a highly competitive market in which the public were "dazed and stunned by [the] mass of big figures flung at its head".[61] Competition for charitable funds was intense and the growing number of voluntary agencies in London stretched philanthropic resources. Philanthropy was distinguished for its impulsive nature and it could easily be diverted by a touching story of disaster. Charity was supposed to begin at home, but foreign ventures, especially those in India, were a particular drain on resources. To counteract this, governors paraded the number of patients they treated and their level of debt in the hope of attracting benevolence.

However, even the Hospital for Sick Children, normally successful in its appeals, could complain in 1890 about the difficulties of obtaining funds in such a competitive environment.[62] Hospitals not only competed with other charities, but also between themselves. In 1888 Carr Gomm, chairman of the London Hospital, noted that the hospital's 1884 appeal had not been successful because of "the increased number of hospitals which were compelled to appeal for funds".[63] Particular hostility was reserved for the specialist hospitals, which were seen as "robbers of the poor".[64] It was widely believed that they were havens of quackery and greed that wasted charitable resources and were castigated for much of the nineteenth century by the medical profession.[65] The truth was less altruistic. Specialist hospitals were generally in a better financial situation than their general counterparts and their more aggressive fundraising tactics ensured that they were better at attracting philanthropy. They were condemned mainly because they were unwelcome competitors for already scare resources.

If competition was not enough, hospitals were prone to scandals and public censure that halted the troubled flow of charitable resources. "Voluntary hospitals," according to the *Hospital* in 1890, "live by popular favour, and to take away that is to deprive them of the breath of life."[66] It almost seemed that the public were searching for "reasons for buttoning up their pockets" and although governors tried to avoid any indication of a scandal, this was not always possible.[67] At a general level hospitals were damaged by the debate over vivisection and the Victoria Street Society accused many institutions of experimentation and cruelty to animals.[68] The public were quick to draw a comparison between experiments on animals and alleged experiments on patients, a link that harmed hospitals' reputations and their finances, as some philanthropists withheld their subscriptions. Scandal, however, was generally limited to individual institutions. The press was quick to pick up on any minor incident and bad publicity was quickly translated into a fall in income. At the German Hospital accusations of proselytism in 1893/4 after Baron Schröder's unfortunate comment that the hospital was a "Protestant institution", and claims that Jewish and Catholic patients were being forced to attend Protestant sermons, plunged the hospital into a very public crisis.[69] The dispute ended after a heated special meeting passed a motion by a narrow majority that the hospital was a nonsectarian institution, but the damage had already been done.[70] Donations fell from £3,253 16s 8d in 1892 to £2,695 14s 5d in 1893 and only slightly recovered in 1894.[71] The governors decided not to mention the dispute in their 1894 Annual Report for fear of antagonizing more of the hospital's supporters. The consequences of a scandal were rarely disastrous, but they were often serious enough to provoke a financial panic and force governors to rely on non-charitable sources of funding.

Hospital charity could be competed for, diverted and withheld, but the amount of money available within the benevolent economy was linked to Britain's economic performance. In times of depression, charitable donations were among the first forms of household expenditure to be restricted. Governors were anxious about any fluctuation in the economy, as the effect extended beyond charity. Uncertainty in the City or a fall in land values affected the value of the hospitals' investments and property and governors reinvested stock and sold property accordingly to overcome some of these problems. Guy's Hospital, however, was trapped by its founder's will into holding only landed estates and when hit by the agricultural depression it was forced to seek loans, admit paying patients, and finally to call upon the charitable public for funds.[72] Guy's Hospital's experiences were extreme, but no governor could be entirely confident that their hospital's income would not be affected one way or another by the vagaries of the national economy. To counter this, income was spread over several different sources of funding.

IV

A dilution of philanthropy's significance in hospital finance, however, did not also mean a transformation of the governors' power. Financial diversification was an adaptation to a new environment to keep the hospital open and on a voluntary basis, rather than a complete change. The level of voluntary contributions in the overall structure of income did not correlate with the exercise of authority in the hospital. The hospitals' administrative system did gradually evolve as the hospital changed its character: new committees were created and subcommittees were grafted onto existing bodies, but voluntary contributions remained the basis of management. Managerial responsibility was not based on Morris's "subscriber democracy", but on a minimum level of contribution, usually ten guineas.[73] A subscription or donation of that amount or more bought the right to influence the hospitals' administration and determine how relief would be dispensed. Management, however, was often left in the hands of a small, wealthy clique of governors, whose administrative experience was gained through commercial and banking ventures in London, as most governors remained uninterested or could not afford the time-consuming commitment that administration demanded. Governors did pass some of the more laborious administrative duties onto a paid administrator, but the level of professionalization in hospital management remained minimal by the start of the twentieth century. Voluntarism as the active citizen's social duty remained the dominant theme in hospital administration because it was integral to Victorian society and because it was seen as the best possible system, free from state interference, and capable of promoting a friendly and homely environment. Where the challenge did come from, was from an increasingly assertive and confident medical profession who claimed that the hospitals' medical nature and not its voluntary character should be the basis of management.[74] The governors' philanthropic credentials were increasingly ill-suited to the hospitals' changing environment. Gradually they had to rely on the doctors' professional knowledge to make informed medical decisions, allowing the doctors a greater degree of influence. However, although the philanthropists had entered a tenuous partnership with the medical profession by the end of the nineteenth century, they retained control of the hospital.[75]

V

An anonymous hospital secretary explained to the *Charity Record & Philanthropic News* in 1894 that governors spent too much time worrying about the future, but "somehow or other the hospitals were maintained in spite of the anxieties of the committees".[76] It is perhaps because hospitals did not rely on any one source of income but haphazardly developed a diverse financial framework that they managed to survive institutional expansion and the transition away from their philanthropic base. The implications these changes had on the development of health care in the twentieth century have yet to be assessed. However, it seems probable that the hospitals' incessant search for funds and charity's inability to meet their financial needs helped to ease the acceptance of a state-funded system by the 1940s.

Notes

1. Guy's Hospital Archive, Greater London Records Office (hereafter Guy's Archive), 1886 Public Appeal, Y74/1.

2. See K. Waddington, "The nursing dispute at Guy's Hospital, 1879–1880", *Social History of Medicine* **8**, 1995, pp. 211–30.

3. Guy's Archive, Court of Committees 1879–1883, A3/10.

4. *British Medical Journal* **1**, 1883, p. 776.

5. See R. Rentoul, *Reform of our voluntary medical charities* (1891); H. Roberts, *Public control of hospitals* (London, 1895); W. Sibly, *State aided v. voluntary hospitals* (London, 1896).

6. There are at present few published monographs on hospital finance; most of the current research is being undertaken at a doctoral level: see A. Berry, *Charity, patronage and medical men: philanthropy and provincial hospitals.* (DPhil thesis, University of Oxford, 1995) or M. Gorsky, *Philanthropy in Bristol 1800–50.* (PhD thesis, University of Bristol, 1996). G. Rivett, *Development of the London hospital system* (Oxford, 1986) does offer a brief account of the metropolitan hospitals' financial problems and the development of the Prince of Wales's Hospital Fund for London, whose history has been the subject of a recent book by F. K. Prochaska, *Philanthropy and the hospitals of London* (Oxford, 1992). K. Waddington, "'Bastard benevolence': centralisation, voluntarism and the Sunday Fund 1873–1898", *London Journal* **9**, 1995, pp. 151–67, looks at one aspect of hospital finance in detail and S. Cherry, "Beyond National Health Insurance: the voluntary hospitals and the hospital contributory schemes: a regional study", *Social History of Medicine* **5**, 1992, pp. 455–82, takes a similar theme for his study of hospital contribution schemes in the twentieth century. A. Borsay, "Cash and conscience: financing the general hospital at Bath *c.*1738–1750", *Social History of Medicine* **4**, 1991, pp. 207–29, is one of the few published studies that deals extensively with the issue of finance, but only in one hospital. Individual hospital histories also offer some passing mention of hospital finance, such as L. Granshaw, *St Mark's Hospital, London: a social history of a specialist hospital* (London, 1985) or G. B. Risse, *Hospital life in Enlightenment Scotland: care and teaching at the Royal Infirmary of Edinburgh* (Cambridge, 1986) but they provide no detailed analysis.

7. *British Medical Journal* **1**, 1893, p. 31.

8. J. Horsford, *Philanthropy: the genius of Christianity* (London, 1862), p. vii.

9. G. Stedman Jones, *Outcast London: a study in the relationship between classes in Victorian London* (Oxford, 1971), pp. 290–98.

10. Philanthropy as an instrument of social control has been a seductive view, held by historians like Stedman Jones, *Outcast London*, or more recently R. Trainor, *Black country elites: the exercise of authority in an industrial area* (Oxford, 1993), whose views counter the more sympathetic treatment of philanthropy by F. K. Prochaska, *Women and philanthropy in nineteenth century England* (Oxford, 1980). Where philanthropy might be motivated by ideas of class hegemony or social control, it is argued here that this was only one part of the motivation that encouraged benevolent action.

11. *Daily Telegraph*, 20 February 1871, p. 2.

12. *Westminster Review* **35**, 1869, p. 447.

13. London Hospital Archive, Royal London Hospital Library & Museum (hereafter

LH Archive), Minutes of the Quarterly Court 1846–52, A/2/9.

14. *British Medical Journal* **1**, 1892, p. 345.

15. *Charity Record & Philanthropic News* **17**, 1897, p.142.

16. University College Hospital Archive, Rare Manuscripts Room, D. M. S. Watson Library, University College London (hereafter UCH Archive), General Committee Minutes 1884–1890, A1/2/6.

17. *Hospital*, 6 February 1892, p. 226.

18. *Medical Times & Gazette* **26**, 1852, p. 39.

19. *British Medical Journal*, 1860, p. 458.

20. LH Archive, House Committee Minutes 1876–1878, A/5/38.

21. F. K. Prochaska, *Voluntary impulse: philanthropy in modern Britain* (London, 1988), p. 47.

22. Royal Chest Hospital Archive, Greater London Records Office (hereafter RCH Archive), Finance Committee Minutes 1878–1890, A5/1.

23. Hospital for Sick Children Archive, Peter Pan Gallery, Great Ormond Street Hospital (hereafter GOS Archive), Proceedings of the Management Committee 1878–1880, 1/2/16.

24. See F. K. Prochaska, "Charity bazaars in nineteenth century England", *Journal of British Studies* **16**, 1976/7, pp. 62–84.

25. *British Medical Journal* **1**, 1898, p. 277.

26. For a full discussion of the Metropolitan Hospital Sunday Fund, see Waddington, " 'Bastard benevolence' ".

27. *British Medical Journal* **2**, 1887, p. 474.

28. B. Harrison, "Philanthropy and the Victorians", *Victorian Studies* **9**, 1966, p. 353.

29. *British Medical Journal*, 1857, p. 355.

30. *British Medical Journal* **2**, 1873, p. 611.

31. *Hospital*, 28 April 1894, p. 83.

32. *Charity Record & Philanthropic News* **9**, 1889, p. 111.

33. *Hospital*, 1 February 1890, p. 286.

34. R. W. Chalmers, *Hospitals and the state* (London, 1928), p. 102.

35. LH Archive, Minutes of the Quarterly General Court 1861–1867, A/2/12.

36. LH Archive, House Committee Minutes 1863–1866, A/5/32.

37. Guy's Archive, Court of Committees 1879–1883, A3/10; *Lancet* **2**, 1886, pp. 1166–8.

38. *Hospital*, 19 January 1889, p. 246.

39. London Hospital Annual Report 1899.

40. P. Dingwall, A. M. Rafferty, C. Webster, *Introduction to the social history of nursing* (London, 1988), p. 59.

41. UCH Archive, General Committee Reports 1844–1896, A1/2/1–7.

42. LH Archive, House Committee Minutes 1852–1900, A/5/27–47; UCH Archive, General Committee Reports 1844–1896, A1/2/1–7.

43. Three five-year periods have been chosen to show the changing nature of hospital finance; an average over five years adjusts the often sharp fluctuations that could occur.

44. *Hospital*, 22 September 1888, p. 397.

45. *Charity Organisation Review* **9**, August 1883, p. 255; R. Pinker, *English hospital statistics 1861–1939* (London, 1966), p. 162.
46. Royal Chest Hospital Annual Reports 1851 & 1898.
47. *Hospital*, 5 January 1889, p. 214.
48. German Hospital Archive, Hackney District Records Office, St Bartholomew's Hospital, Smithfield (hereafter GH Archive), Hospital Committee Minutes 1857–1863, A/2/3.
49. J. Woodward, *To do the sick no harm* (London, 1974).
50. St Bartholomew's Hospital Archive, Hackney District Archive, St Bartholomew's Hospital, Smithfield (hereafter SBH Archive), Medical Committee Minutes 1878–1903, Mc/1/2.
51. *Charity Record & Philanthropic News* **7**, 1897, p. 147.
52. There is a wealth of literature on the history of medical advance and practice, for example see S. Resier, *Medicine and the reign of technology* (Cambridge, 1978) for the rise of clinical technology. For the growth of specialism and the change in therapeutic and surgical practice see R. Stevens, *Medical practice in modern England: the impact of specialization and state medicine* (London, 1966); A. Youngson, *The scientific revolution in Victorian medicine* (London, 1979) and C. Lawrence, "Incommunicable knowledge", *Journal of Contemporary History* **20**, 1985, pp. 502–20 for a more conflict-based analysis. More has been written on individual procedures, for example see A. Hardy, "Tracheotomy versus intubation: surgical intervention in diphtheria in Europe and the United States 1825–1930", *Bulletin of the History of Medicine* **66**, 1992, pp. 536–59 or L. Granshaw, "Knowledge of bodies or bodies of knowledge? Surgeons, anatomists and rectal surgery 1830–1985", in *Medical theory, surgical practice*, C. Lawrence (ed.) (London, 1992), pp. 17–46. Special attention has focused on the development of Listerian methods which were initially greeted with hostility; see L. Granshaw, "'Upon this principle I have based a practice': the development of antisepsis in Britain", in *Medical innovation in historical perspective*, J. V. Pickstone (ed.) (Basingstoke, 1992), pp. 232–262 or T. H. Pennington, "Listerism, its decline and its persistence: the introduction of aseptic surgical techniques in three British teaching hospitals 1890–99", *Medical History* **39**, 1995, pp. 35–60.
53. See R. Banham, *Architecture of the well-tempered environment* (London, 1969).
54. H. C. Burdett, *Hospitals and the state* (London, 1881), p. 11.
55. *Charity Record & Philanthropic News* **9**, 1889, p. 292.
56. *British Medical Journal* **2**, 1881, p. 646.
57. *Hospital*, 5 January 1889, p. 214.
58. Cited in GOS Archive, Letters and Press Cuttings, 8/153.
59. *Hospital*, 6 November 1886, p. 95.
60. *Charity Record & Philanthropic News* **3**, 1883, p. 40.
61. *Charity Organisation Review*, July 1888, p. 10.
62. Select Committee of the House of Lords on Metropolitan Hospitals, 2nd Report, PP (1890/1) XIII, p. 472.
63. *East End Observer*, 9 June 1888.
64. *Hospital*, 23 February 1895, p. 371.
65. See L. Granshaw, "'Fame and fortune by means of bricks and mortar': the medical

profession and specialist hospitals" in *The hospital in history*, L. Granshaw & R. Porter (eds) (London, 1989), pp. 199–220.

66. *Hospital*, 13 December 1890, p. 165.
67. *Lancet* **2**, 1879, p. 888.
68. See R. D. French, *Antivivisection and medical science in Victorian society* (Princeton, 1975).
69. GH Archive, Minutes of the Annual General Court 1867–1923, A/4/2; GH Archive Pamphlet, Ha/66/74.
70. GH Archive, Minutes of the Annual General Court 1867–1923, A/4/2.
71. German Hospital Annual Reports, 1892–1894.
72. Guy's Archives, Court of Committees 1870–1883, A3/10.
73. R. J. Morris, *Class, sect and party: the making of the British middle class, Leeds 1820–50* (Manchester, 1990), p. 184.
74. For the development of the medical profession in London see M. J. Peterson, *Medical profession in mid-Victorian London* (Berkeley, 1978) or for a more general account see I. Waddington, *The medical profession in the industrial revolution* (Dublin, 1984), while A. Digby, *Making a medical living: doctors and patients in the English market of medicine 1720–1911* (Cambridge, 1994) looks at the economic dimensions of practice.
75. See Waddington, "The nursing dispute at Guy's Hospital", pp. 211–30.
76. *Charity Record & Philanthropic News* **14**, 1894, p. 87; *Charity Record & Philanthropic News* **4**, 1884, p. 189.

9

Women, social work and social welfare in twentieth-century Britain: from (unpaid) influence to (paid) oblivion?

Jane Lewis

Women's relationship to welfare in the twentieth century has been complicated. Certainly there is no way that they can be fitted comfortably into prominent interpretations of welfare regimes and citizenship entitlements. For example, in response to T. H. Marshall's post-war notion of a progression from (eighteenth-century) civil rights to (nineteenth-century) political rights and (twentieth-century) social rights,[1] it has to be pointed out that women gained social entitlements in the form of protective labour legislation long before they gained political enfranchisement. And in response to more recent attempts to capture the characteristics of, and the entitlements offered by, modern welfare regimes in terms of the relationship between paid work and welfare, it has to be pointed out that such a formulation misses the unpaid contribution that women have historically made to welfare.[2] The discovery by late-twentieth-century economists that women tend to spend their time in more complicated ways than men – in terms of their mix of paid, unpaid and voluntary work, and (lack) of leisure time – also has implications for their welfare.[3]

Two basic issues are raised by inserting the variable of gender into the debates about modern welfare provision: first, the extent to which women had any say in what was collectively provided, and secondly, the nature of their relationship to welfare provision. In respect of the first, given the lateness of women's entry into full political citizenship, it seems reasonable to assume that their influence on policy making in respect of welfare provision must have been slight. This is certainly the case made by Skocpol & Ritter in respect of Britain on the basis of their analysis of the introduction of old-age pensions in 1908 and national insurance in 1911,[4] and it follows from the observation that social rights for women preceded political rights. However, this is in turn to assume that early welfare provision was indeed a matter for central government. It was becoming so in the decades before the First World War, but prior to 1908 social provision was administered and financed locally, and women's position in respect of local politics and administration was substantially different from their position nationally. Furthermore, women's entry into the arena of national politics has not resulted in conspicuous power and influence. In this respect the position of women in Britain, like that of women in the Continental European countries, has contrasted with the much greater influence wielded by Scan-dinavian women in their late-twentieth-century governments.

In respect of the second, women in the twentieth century have been disproportionately both the clients of the welfare state and the providers of welfare, paid and unpaid. While it has been common for recent literature to talk about the "feminization of poverty" during the 1980s and 1990s, women have always been the majority of welfare recipients in the twentieth century whether under the poor law or post-war social security.[5] As providers, informal care provided by family members – usually by women – has been the most stable form of social provision throughout the twentieth century, notwithstanding the tendency of post-war analyses of welfare to ignore it completely.[6] In the early part of the twentieth century, women also worked unpaid within the voluntary sector, which was relatively much more important at the turn of the century than it was to become later.[7] Much of the social-work related activity that they were engaged in early on became absorbed by the state, for example, the work of visiting mothers and children became "health visiting" carried out under the auspices of local authority health and welfare departments. In the post-war period, the dramatic rise in married women's paid work has been almost entirely accounted for by part-time jobs in the service of the welfare state.

This chapter seeks to tell a more complicated story than one that insists either that women played a major part in decision-making about welfare and in social provision, or that they played none. Their role in the early part of the century was with very few exceptions unpaid. But in the world of charity they were at the centre of the public debate on social welfare, as well as being substantially involved in its provision through their work as visitors, on poor-law boards, on boards of education and in local government.[8] It is not my intention to claim that their work had a significant effect in terms of improving the welfare outcomes for the poor women and children who were their chief concern, but rather to suggest that they

were able to exercise considerable influence on the direction of social provision. This was because provision was largely local, there was a symbiotic
relationship between the work of charity and that of the poor law, and
theories of social change privileged the work that women did to change
the habits of the individual (social work). As more and more of women's
hitherto charitable endeavours became part of the apparatus of state provision, so they tended to become residualized. The mechanisms for delivering welfare gradually shifted from poor-law provision to the ambition (if
never the reality) of accommodating all people and risks within a system of
national insurance. Women gained the status of paid workers, but were no
longer positioned in such a way as to make it possible to exert influence.

The chapter uses what might appear to be the limited example of social
work to make its case. However, it is in many ways paradigmatic. In the
early twentieth century, social work was as likely to be referred to as "social
service". By the inter-war period the term "social administration" was
becoming more evident and by the post-war years the separation of the
worlds of the (female) social worker and the (predominantly male) social
administrator was complete within the academic community as well as in
the world of policy and practice. It is not my intention that the story be
taken to mean that the kind of welfare regime that came into being at the
end of the Second World War was in some way necessarily "bad" for
women. Again, that would be too simple a story. The title of the chapter is
somewhat provocative, but there is a question mark at the end of it. While
women may not have had a large say in the building of post-war social
provision, modern welfare regimes are not necessarily antithetical to their
participation.

Women and social provision in the early twentieth century

Women provided "personal social service" in both the world of charity and
of the poor law at the local level, as elected Guardians and as "lady visitors"
to workhouses and infirmaries. Together these worlds were central to turn-
of-the-century social provision and furthermore they were to some extent
symbiotic. Voluntary organizations in the late nineteenth century were part
of the way in which political leaders conceptualized the state. Jose Harris
has described the aim of Victorian governments as being "to provide a
framework of rules and guidelines designed to enable society very largely
to run itself".[9] This did not amount to rank atomistic individualism: "the

corporate life of society was seen as expressed through voluntary associations and the local community, rather than through the persona of the state".[10] The fact that social provision was local made it easier for a measure of welfare pluralism to exist at the turn of the century.

The circumstances of the founding of the Charity Organisation Society (COS) in 1869 provide a good illustration of the nature of the relationship between the statutory and voluntary sector in this period. From the beginning, the COS's sphere of action was defined in relation to the poor law. The Goschen Minute on the relief to the poor in the metropolis, issued by the central Poor Law Board in 1869, set out the relationship between the poor law and voluntary action and was welcomed by the members of the Council of the London COS as being in complete harmony with their approach.[11] Goschen's main concern was to hold the line on poor-law relief. The role he set out for charity was to assist those on the verge of destitution, in other words to prevent them becoming a public charge, while the state was conceptualized as a provider of last resort. Sidney and Beatrice Webb referred to this as the "cowcatcher" theory of charitable action.[12] Goschen thus advocated co-operation between the statutory and voluntary sectors on similar tasks, while maintaining separate spheres of action. The ideas of Goschen and the COS were by no means endorsed by the whole of the voluntary sector, but they did constitute the dominant paradigm for thinking about social provision at the turn of the century. In a sense they gave the lead role to charity in terms of trying to prevent destitution, and, it was hoped, a residual role to the poor law. This in turn is important for understanding why women who were prominent in voluntary and poor-law work were in a position to exert influence.

Furthermore, the work women actually performed was also regarded as being of central importance. The ideas of Octavia Hill, for example, about the work of visiting in connection with housing management, were published in the major periodicals of the day because they were seen as being essential to achieving social change. The kind of work that Hill and her "fellow workers" carried out was designed to rehabilitate the individual. Personal social work or service was believed to be the means of achieving social progress. Social workers would work with individuals and their families to change their habits, build up their characters and give new purpose to their lives. Individual social work was above all a form of education. Indeed, to leading theorists of voluntary action, such as Bernard Bosanquet and C. S. Loch, it was important that social work be voluntary, whether carried out under the auspices of a voluntary organization or the state. By this means middle-class people could fulfil their citizenship obligations to the poor; the fact that such work was primarily a field of female endeavour was for C. S. Loch a matter for regret.[13] The test of charity was the successful promotion of economic independence and fully participative citizens.[14] Social work with individuals and families was the means of achieving this; no social advance was possible without individual improvement.

In friendly visiting, the visitor was supposed to gain the household's trust and then lead by example. But in the end the visitor was expected to try and get poor families to see the virtues of middle-class values and culture. In Geoffrey Best's judgement, the poor were helped if they would submit.[15] The purpose of visiting, befriending and investigating the circumstances of the household and the reasons for the difficulties that were being experienced was to work with the family in order to change their habits and behaviour. In a chapter on the meaning of social work, Bernard Bosanquet wrote that social workers usually wanted to brighten lives and improve conditions.[16] But it was important for all prospective social workers to realise that improving conditions effectively meant changing matters so that the poor were able to make more of their lives than they did before, in other words so that their characters would be able to master their circumstances: "wherever you start in social work the goal is the same – to bring the social mind into order, into harmony with itself . . . social disorganisation is the outward and visible form of moral and intellectual disorganisation".

Bernard Bosanquet and his wife Helen, who was also a pillar of the London COS and who edited its journal from 1909 to 1921, devoted considerable effort to exploring why, and to a lesser extent how, social workers should address the central issue of character. In a chapter written for a collection edited by Jane Addams, the Chicago settlement house pioneer, Bernard Bosanquet stressed the importance of working with the individual to a plan based on "respect for character".[17] He held that individual character was the most important determinant of the individual's circumstances, although he was at pains to stress that this did not mean attributing all blame for a person's position to that person and leaving him to his fate. That would have been the attitude of *laissez-faire* individualists, but idealists like the Bosanquets were eager to provide the means to help those in need by strengthening their characters, which according to their analysis was where the real problem lay, rather than in poverty *per se*. Bernard Bosanquet anticipated the need for large numbers of volunteer social workers to help their fellow citizens who found themselves in distress: "you offer everything – the whole matériel and guidance of life . . . there is as it were, an army of social healers to be trained and organised . . . disciplined and animated with a single spirit and purpose".[18]

In practice, such ideas translated themselves into the attention someone like Octavia Hill paid to the habits and character of her tenants: "the management depends very much on judgement of character. You must notice when the man is doing any better and when he is not".[19] Indeed,

> By knowledge of character more is meant than whether a man is a drunkard or a woman is dishonest, it means knowledge of the passions, hopes and history of people; where the temptation will touch them, what is the little scheme they have made of their lives, or would make, if they had encouragement, what training longpast phases of their lives may have afforded; how to move, touch, teach them.[20]

Little wonder that Octavia Hill stressed the cumulative importance of "infinitesimally small" actions. Similarly, Helen Bosanquet wrote of cases that exemplified the importance of attention to the detail of the lives of the poor. She compared five families she observed across the back garden of her East London house in the early 1890s (when she was serving as a district secretary for the COS and before her marriage to Bernard); she noted that the children of number 4 lived in the same surroundings and had the opportunity to go to the same school and yet were in a much more distressed condition than their neighbours. She concluded that it was "wholesome home atmosphere" that was wanting, clearly a case where the inculcation of good habits rather than an injection of cash was what was needed.[21]

This view of what constituted appropriate social action rested on the belief that the self-maintaining, independent citizen, possessed in other words of good character, was also the rational citizen, aware of common social purposes and struggling to realize what T. H. Green called his "best self". In the crucial process of the formation of character and purpose, mental struggle was considered the most important factor. Mind and will were the makings of character. Social workers had to understand how these might be changed and Helen Bosanquet turned to the new science of psychology for help. The first step to changing the individual's will and creating a purposeful and active citizen was to make an effort to understand the individual's perceptions of his or her condition. The social worker had to be able to work out why it was that people saw things the way they did, to appreciate the values they held and then work with them to change their views and behaviour. No misfortune, no matter how distressing, was irredeemable until the individual's will was broken.

The main site for social work intervention was the family, which Helen Bosanquet argued to be the fundamental social unit, mediating between the individual and the community. A strong citizenry and a strong state depended on the strengthening of the bonds between the individual and the family and between the family and the wider community. The family was crucial in developing character. Where family members developed their sense of responsibility one to the other, Helen Bosanquet argued, "the Family presented itself as the medium by which the public interest is combined with private welfare".[22] In this analysis, social problems disappeared when the family was strong and effective; for example, old-age pensions were unnecessary "where the stable Family combines young and old in one strong bond of mutual helpfulness".[23] Natural regard for his family's welfare was the primary impetus to the development of the adult male and his becoming a co-operative member of society:

> nothing but the considered rights and responsibilities of family life will ever rouse the average man to his full degree of efficiency, and induce him to continue working after he has earned sufficient to meet his own personal needs. The Family in short, is from this point of view, the only known way of ensuring, with any approach to success, that one generation will exert itself in the interests and for the sake of another, and its effect upon the economic efficiency of both generations is in this respect alone of paramount importance.[24]

Children also learned the meaning of responsibility and mutual service, trust and affection in their relationships with family members, and because the interests of the child and its pleasures centred on the home, the child naturally wanted to contribute to it. The hallmark of the hopelessly degraded "residuum" was lack of family feeling and a failure to socialize the young into "habits of labour and obedience".

There was therefore little material aid that could be offered to the family within this approach that would not damage family responsibility and subvert character. The most likely agent to intervene – by offering old-age pensions, for example – was the state. Achieving social change by changing individual habits and will was necessarily an inordinately slow business because the impetus for change had to come from within the individual. Successful change could only take place when the individual was ready for it; it was therefore unlikely that as crude an agent as the state could be effective in securing it. There was also the danger that the state would usurp the individual in the pursuit of his interests, for example by providing school meals for his children, thereby setting back the whole process of true social reform which depended on the individual's struggle to achieve a better life. The final test of any intervention in the life of an individual had to be whether it improved mind and character and it was unlikely that state action would ever be able to pass it.

Thus, according to the dominant social theory of the period, the woman social worker held the key position in preventing poor families becoming a public charge and, more idealistically, in promoting participative citizenship. Bernard Bosanquet had admitted that personal social service demanded "armies" of volunteer visitors. While large numbers of women engaged in voluntary social work,[25] "armies" were never forthcoming. And while evidence regarding their actual endeavours is slim, it appears that they bore little relation to what was expected. In particular, the majority of COS visitors found themselves struggling to decide whether to provide some material relief to a family, and if so how to raise the money, rather than working on the hopelessly ill-defined task of "changing habits". One young woman visitor for the COS recorded that she found it very difficult to follow COS principles: "The unfortunate part of it is, that I find it so very difficult to apply the theories of relief, as taught by the COS, to any of the practical cases I come across." She agreed that most of her cases exhibited failures of character and that money was therefore not the answer. However, she was unsure as to how then to proceed, finding COS ideas "interesting, generally convincing, but a little paralysing".[26] Nevertheless, there is no doubt as to the influence of women leaders within the world of female voluntary social action on the thinking of policy makers at the turn of the century. Both Octavia Hill and Helen Bosanquet found places on the 1909 Royal Commission on the Poor Laws.

The erosion of the influence accorded personal social service

Beatrice Webb also found a seat on the 1909 Royal Commission, and of course had rejected what Mary Richmond, the leading American authority on social work, called the "retail" method of reform, in favour of the legislative or "wholesale" method as early as the 1880s.[27] In particular, Webb became critical of the distinction between those who were deserving of charitable help, and those who were undeserving and who must therefore resort to the poor law. She noted that the deserving were often those whom it was impossible to help effectively via charity; for example, the respectable elderly person required a permanent pension, which charity was rarely in a position to guarantee.[28] In 1909, she advocated the break-up of the poor law and state intervention to remedy the ills of poverty associated with old age, childhood, ill health and unemployment.

Other critiques of the nexus of beliefs espoused by people like Hill and Bosanquet also became more prominent at the turn of the century. In evidence to the 1895 Royal Commission on the Aged Poor, Alfred Marshall, the neo-classical economist, spoke in favour of old-age pensions.[29] In face of such a prominent doubter, Bernard Bosanquet continued to defend the division of labour between the poor law and charity, whereby the former took the "hopeless", undeserving cases where there was no sign of the possibility of a return to self-maintenance, and charity the more complicated, deserving cases, where there were "points" of character or capacity to be fostered.[30] In reply, Marshall stated that he looked forward to the time when the poor law would be abolished and "higher forms" of aid of the working classes introduced.[31]

In what he termed a "friendly criticism" of the COS, Samuel Barnett also accepted that forms of state aid to working people, such as old-age pensions, were desirable.[32] As early as 1883, he began to explore the idea that the state should meet men's needs, defined as things that are "good", but which men did not necessarily recognize to be such (for example, education), while the people supplied their own wants, defined in terms of the things they recognized as necessary for life, such as food and clothing. Thus the "means of life" would be provided by the state, while citizens would have to work for the "means of livelihood".[33] Barnett admitted that these principles were too difficult to define to provide a good guide to the limits of state action. But, like Marshall, he had abandoned the idea that all forms of help outside the poor-law workhouse were wrong. His criticism was inspired by his observation that not withstanding the efforts of charity, the poor remained miserable.

The shift in ideas about the relationship between charity and state in respect of the problem of poverty gathered pace in the decades before the First World War, when old-age pensions were finally introduced in 1908 and national insurance in 1911. It became accepted by a wide spectrum of opinion that the state should provide a national minimum level of relief, while the voluntary sector continued to provide friendly visiting, but as an adjunct to state effort rather than as an integral part of the approach to poor relief. There is little evidence that women played any great part in the Liberal Government's welfare reforms of the period 1906–14. Indeed, in regard to national insurance, women's groups complained both that they were not consulted and that their needs were not addressed.[34] The closest women got to the administration of the national insurance scheme was to serve as "sickness visitors" to check on malingerers.[35]

The new view of the role of the voluntary sector was increasingly shared by those active in it, as well as by state officials. In particular, members of the new Guilds of Help and Councils of Social Welfare set up in the 1900s and 1910s favoured a reworking of the role of charity. Violet Markham, who supported their work, asked in the *Spectator* in 1911 whether it was

> not increasingly difficult to accept the view that the great forces of the state are only to be at the service of the pauper, the lunatic, and the criminal, and that the honest and deserving citizen, if he falls on evil days should be handed over to what Malthus wryly called "the uncertain support of private charity?"[36]

The Guilds and Councils remained convinced as to the importance of the role of charity, but stressed their civic ideals. They were there to serve everyone, and as part of this more positive approach, they were also prepared both to countenance state intervention in the field of social welfare and to co-operate with the state in a different way. The Guilds in particular grew fast, especially outside London. By 1911, there were 60 of them with a membership of 8,000, which surpassed that of the COS.[37] These new forms of voluntary organization continued to stress the importance of friendly visiting. Indeed, they seemed almost to rediscover it. Charity organization societies in the USA during the progressive period always traced the work of visiting back to Octavia Hill and the London COS,[38] but in their anxiety to distance themselves from the COS the English Guilds of Help very rarely made any reference to these antecedents, and were in fact more likely to refer to American or German developments as models.[39]

According to the investigation mounted by the Local Government Board in 1911, the main objects of the Guilds were to foster a sense of civic responsibility, to provide a friend or "helper" for all those in need of assistance.[40] In many respects, the Guilds wanted to return to the pure milk of COS ideas. Their leaders accused the COS of having "descended" into relief work and they picked up the kind of criticism levied by Beatrice Webb much earlier: that it was very difficult for charity effectively to provide assistance even to cases deemed deserving.[41] Too many applicants were deemed to be "ineligible" because of the COS's inability to help, rather than because of their own deficiencies. The Guilds were determined to separate relief from friendly visiting, preferring the idea of "not alms but a friend", the motto of the Boston Association of Charities. In fact a majority of Guilds were quickly sucked into the provision of material aid. However, Clement Attlee was probably right in the assessment of the Guilds' work that he included in his text on social work, published in 1920. While many of the objects and practices of the Guilds looked very similar to those of the COS, they exhibited, he felt, a different attitude that appeared both more generous and more democratic.[42]

Thus while a large role for social work, which continued to be the province of women, remained within the voluntary sector, by the First World War this work no longer assumed the same strategic importance. The shift in the balance of social provision away from the voluntary sector and towards the state was confirmed in the writings of the inter-war period. Elizabeth Macadam, for example, who came from the settlement world and who had become involved in the government's initiative to investigate social work training during the First World War, wrote of a "new partnership" between the voluntary sector and state, whereby voluntary effort was most appropriate in schemes that were experimental, in activities that called for flexibility or highly individualized work, or in specialized watchdog activities.[43] In other words, the work of the voluntary sector became defined as complementary and supplementary. Constance Braithwaite felt that as a citizen she had become "conscious of the superiority of state action over philanthropy in its universality of provision and democratic spirit" and she felt that the state must take responsibility above all for alleviating poverty.[44] High mass-unemployment during the 1920s and 1930s had, she felt, clearly removed this task from the purview of charity. This left voluntary action with the task of providing a more flexible "personal service" in the form of "casework". In one of the few philosophical contributions on the role of social work during the inter-war years, R. M. MacIver welcomed the increased role of the state in the prevention of poverty in particular, but pointed out that this meant that there were now limits as to what could be hoped for from social work. It could no longer be "an uplifter" and the sole means of achieving social change, but should rather see its role as providing expert aid to the maladjusted.[45]

E. J. Urwick, who had been head of the COS's School of Sociology in the pre-war years, and who by the 1930s was a professor in the Department of Social Service at the University of Toronto, mounted a passionate attack on social work as casework. His attack undoubtedly gained in force from his being located in North America, where psychiatric social work was already the norm. Urwick had no quarrel with the extension of state action in the field of social provision. His concern was focused entirely on the meaning of social work, which he insisted on locating in the discourse on citizenship. Citizens, he argued, were born debtors, not creditors, and citizenship had no meaning unless it was earned by personal service to others. He deplored the idea that the science of psychology could supply a sufficient rationale for social work, for it amounted to "the belittling – the appalling belittling – of all that we mean by social work and by social life and its difficulties".[46] For Urwick, social work could never be just a simple matter of diagnosis and treatment; to make it such was to reduce it to "the ancillary of specialised medical treatment".[47] Urwick was perceptive in linking the eclipse of older ideas as to the importance of the place of social work to a growing impatience with the injunction to duty and service which late Victorians had found so powerful. His real protest was against social work becoming a set of skills divorced from larger social principles and an end in itself rather than a means to a greater end. He was prescient in seeing that the new social work, defined as casework and based on psychodynamic principles, would have difficulty in supporting a social work profession.

The residualization of social work

During the inter-war years, there was unanimity among commentators on the place of voluntary agencies and on personal social work belonging in the voluntary rather than in the public sector.[48] By the 1930s American commentators had to be careful to explain to their audiences that social service in the British public sector was called social administration, not social work.[49] They might have added that it was also largely carried out by men rather than by women.

The post-war settlement consolidated the position of the voluntary sector as complementary and supplementary to the state, although William

214

Beveridge himself was a stout defender of voluntary action and sought to reassure voluntary providers that there would always remain scope to provide individual care for those who needed something more or different. Beveridge intended state provision as a national minimum, which left plenty of room for social provision above that minimum. In particular he believed that many things could not be accomplished simply by the redistribution of resources. Money was not everything and there was a need for services "which often cannot be bought with money, but may be rendered from sense of duty".[50] Increasingly the role of personal social work was conceptualized as helping those people who were unable to take advantage of the help provided by the state.

Even though large numbers of social workers remained within the voluntary sector until the Seebohm reforms of the early 1970s, which created the personal social service departments in local authorities, they were increasingly paid professionals rather than volunteers. British post-war social work professionalized on the back of psychology in the manner deplored by Urwick, and it was a professionalization spearheaded by women. The post-war welfare state left the woman personal-service worker with a reduced sphere of action. Psychology may have been a narrow basis on which to build, but it spoke to the importance of personal relationships with which women social workers had always been involved and it proved sufficient to broaden the constituency for casework such that it could be carried into the statutory sector. The problem was, as Urwick had spotted, that it provided no link to wider social problems and policies. Indeed, social work moved from its turn-of-the-century position where it had been deemed central to social reform, to a position where it was accused by social administrators of having very little to do with social policy.

The professionalization of social work had begun earlier in the United States. At the American National Conference of Charities and Correction in 1915, Abraham Flexner, noted for his recommendations regarding the reform of the medical profession, asked whether social work could be regarded as a profession. He came to the conclusion that while social work was intellectual in character and involved discrimination, analysis and judgement, the social worker was essentially a middleman. His contact with a case had no definite end and no delineated scope. The social worker co-ordinated and co-operated with others, but the enterprise was "vague" and indeed, often voluntary. Flexner concluded that it could not be considered a profession.[51] Mary Richmond took up the challenge to systematize the body of knowledge that comprised social work in her book *Social diagnosis*, published in 1917. The book elaborated in extraordinary detail the process of investigation, analysis and treatment that comprised the practice of casework. She acknowledged that social questions could be approached via the individual or via the manipulation of larger units; casework was committed to the former and had the possibility of bringing about better adjustments in the social relations between men, women and children. Soon, she felt, social workers would be recognized by other professionals as people who dealt with the social relations of human beings and would take their place as the natural complement of medical practitioners.[52]

Una Cormack, writing in 1945 from the perspective of psychodynamic caseworkers, felt a certain distaste for the rigour of Richmond's exposition: "Throughout the whole book the interviewer, as it were, shoots a sitting duck, plucks him, trusses him, bastes him, and dishes him up finally settled 'in his right relation to society'".[53] Indeed, Richmond's method merely codified COS best practice, shorn of the COS's particular aims and objectives related to its operation alongside the poor law. American casework went on to seek theoretical legitimacy for its work in the new psychology and psychoanalysis. Virginia Robinson, for example, described the way in which analytic therapy was seized upon to provide knowledge of family relationships in terms of the emphasis it put on needs rather than character. This meant that casework proceeded to search for the individual's needs as a first step in diagnosis, and to focus then not on material provision but on the symbols by which needs had expressed themselves.[54] Case papers informed by psychoanalytic principles were very different from the older, more sociological documents. There was increasing detail on behaviour, attitudes and relationships between family members, and less on social and economic circumstances.

Psychodynamics made little inroad into British social work before the 1950s.[55] Eileen Younghusband's second report on social work for the Carnegie UK Trust in 1951 called for social work training to provide a better understanding of human motivation and experience because social work was centred on human relationships.[56] Younghusband cited the American literature in arguing for the importance of self-awareness and for the connection between accepting others and facing oneself, although she stopped well short of suggesting that social work training be dominated by psychology and psychoanalytical methods. However, by the end of the 1950s, casework had become synonymous with social work among leaders of the profession.

Eileen Younghusband's generic social work course, begun at the London School of Economics in 1954, was important in seeking to unify social work around the concept of casework. Younghusband brought Charlotte Towle from the University of Chicago to assist in setting up the course. In an appreciation of Charlotte Towle, Helen Harris Perlman suggested that Towle believed that all casework – that is social work – students should be inducted into "the psychosocial forces and mysteries governing everyday life".[57] Interestingly, Younghusband sought to link Towle to the British tradition via Octavia Hill and the development of the understanding of personal social work.[58] The LSE course represented an attempt to universalize the casework method across social work settings, relying on a conceptualization of casework as a *professional* relationship between client and worker that was no longer class-related.

The lead provided by Younghusband proved influential in determining the direction of social work. It is possible to interpret the developments in training during the 1950s and 1960s as the successful professionalization of social work by women social workers. However, in focusing on the refining of technique, social workers distanced themselves from the wider world of policy making. Within Younghusband's own academic department at the LSE, Richard Titmuss was scathing about "the preoccupation with some of the wastelands of technique" and warned of the dangers of specialization by factual content and training in methods.[59] Like another professor of social administration, T. S. Simey, he condemned the "cult of supervision" that was so prominent within the psychodynamic tradition. Titmuss felt this amounted to professionalism without the necessary interest in administration, while Simey felt that it lacked any scientific rigour: "It is easy for them [social workers] to withdraw from contact with social scientists, and critical members of other professions, and to develop the practice and teaching of social work as a 'mystique', carried on in secret, and handed down from generation to generation as a verbal tradition."[60]

In the USA, the practice of social work was consistently linked to the development of a democratic society in that it helped to ensure that each individual realized his maximum potential. Charlotte Towle regarded casework "as a sustaining force within an imperfectly realized democracy".[61] British caseworkers took up this theme. Cherry Morris believed that by its individual approach, casework was "one of the means of reconciling these rival claims of welfare and freedom" in a democratic society.[62] This was a claim on a par with those of early twentieth-century social workers, but it proved impossible to develop in the changed discourse around social provision of the mid-century. Keith Lucas pointed out the tensions between social work principles and practice, in particular that between the commitment to client self-determination and the goal of "adjusting" the client to "reality".[63] To social administrators, it appeared that social work was becoming increasingly inward-looking, suffering from "knowledge out of context", as Titmuss put it.[64] By focusing ever more intently on the internal world of the client, it was in danger of ignoring both wider social problems and administrative realities, which would result in marginalization. Some went further and argued, in line with the now-dominant belief that the causes of poverty were primarily structural and that social provision should be universal, that social workers were actually misinterpreting the whole nature of the client's difficulties.

This was the basis for Baroness Wootton's famous attack on social work published in 1959, the same year that Eileen Younghusband's report for the Home Office recommended a large increase in the number of social workers. In Wootton's view, "the maladjusted [had] taken the place formerly reserved for the poor in the ideology of social work".[65] In her view, economic problems were still being confused with personal failure, but in the name of personality rather than character. Charity had been exchanged for psychology, which had resulted in an increase in courtesy on the part of the social worker towards the client, but at the price of a "fantastically pretentious facade".[66] Wootton mocked the idea of the casework relationship, commenting that the social worker's best hope of realizing it lay in marrying her client, and argued that the notion of a "professional relationship" between worker and client was a chimera. She concluded that in the modern welfare state the place of the social worker was properly to offer practical help in the use of the new services that were provided. A complex welfare system required mediators and co-ordinators. Such an approach offered little to the mentally ill, the abused child or the bereaved. Nevertheless, the hope that the new social work would occupy a central place in the new order was doomed to disappointment. The issues pinpointed by Wootton refused to go away and the largeness of the claims made by the caseworkers, the issue of "social control" versus individual rights, and whether a client's problems were located more in the outer or the inner world continued to be a focus of attack for both the political left and right. The women who took the lead in professionalizing social work in the postwar decades did so on the basis of a preoccupation with relationships and emotions. But to the 1970s left-wing radicals, concerned above all about rights to material provision, psychodynamic social work was irrelevant. To the right-wing radicals of the 1980s, it was an indulgence.

Conclusion

The continuities between the social work of Octavia Hill and Eileen Younghusband were recognized and acknowledged by the latter. Both insisted on working with the individual and the family, although post-war social workers were not comfortable with the extent to which their forebears had often appeared in practice to set out to change the behaviour of poor families. However, in theory, women like Hill had aimed to lead by example rather than by dicta, and their goal of enabling individuals and families to become fully participative citizens would have been perfectly acceptable to their successors. However, whereas early social workers were supported in their endeavours by social theorists and policy makers, their successors were not. Within a welfare system which set out to provide universal benefits, social work remained a residual service, largely confined to the poor and largely perceived as supplementary to the main endeavour. Social work was transformed from a position in which it was conceptualized as constituting the main hope of social transformation while the poor law picked up the "hopeless" cases to one in which the social security system dealt with the "normal unfortunates" and social workers did their best with the rest. Thus, while post-war women social workers were successful in carving out a new-found paid status for their work, their position within the welfare system was marginal.

For so long as women's social work was perceived as central to the work of securing social change, their opinions were likely to be sought. This is not to say that in the early period women social workers dictated policy; far from it. But they were influential, as the position of Hill and Bosanquet on the 1909 Royal Commission indicates. At a time when the value of voluntary work and the principle of charity were broadly accepted, their unpaid status was not an impediment. However, they were not in a position to influence welfare provision when it increasingly became a matter for central government rather than the voluntary sector and local bodies. When women entered paid employment in the post-war welfare state in large numbers, it was chiefly as low-paid service workers, among whom social workers did rather better than most, thanks to the semi-professional status[67] achieved by their post-war leaders. It was not that women were not able to exercise considerable control over the work that they did, but rather that the place that work occupied in the wider scheme of things was highly contingent.[68] The conditions for exerting influence on policy making in the post-war welfare state have been very different from those existing in the early part of the century. There is some evidence to suggest that where social provision has been the most highly institutionalized and the most universally provided – that is in the Scandinavian countries – it has served to enable greater political participation on the part of women, even though the world of paid employment has remained profoundly sexually segregated. In other words, while women did not in the main "make" post-war welfare provision (in any European country), it is possible for them to be the beneficiaries in terms of increased participation in the "woman-friendly" Scandinavian welfare states.[69] In Britain, where Beveridge's plan was not implemented and where welfare provision based on "universal"[70] social insurance did not happen, political participation has also remained low. Indeed, the social policies of the late 1980s and 1990s, which emphasized the importance of introducing market principles into public provision, tended to be accompanied by a species of "macho-management" that further undervalued the caring work performed by women and made their participation in decision-making more difficult still.

Notes

1. T. H. Marshall, *Social policy* (London, 1965).
2. G. Esping Andersen, *The three worlds of welfare capitalism* (Cambridge, 1990).
3. For example G. Becker, *Altruism in the family and selfishness in the market place* (London, 1980).
4. T. Skocpol & G. Ritter, "Gender and the origins of modern social policies in Britain and the United States", *Studies in American Political Development* v, 1991, pp. 36–93.
5. J. Lewis & D. Piachaud, "Women and poverty in the twentieth century", in *Women and poverty in Britain*, C. Glendinning & J. Millar (eds) (Brighton, 1987), pp. 27–45.
6. This is true even of very recent influential analyses, e.g. Esping Andersen, *The three worlds of welfare capitalism*.
7. Although whether it was actually more significant than state provision is a matter of debate; see R. Humphreys, *The poor law and charity. The COS in the provinces, 1870–1890*. (PhD thesis, University of London, 1991).
8. P. Hollis, *Ladies elect women in English local government, 1865–1914* (Oxford, 1987).

9. J. Harris, "Society and the state in twentieth century Britain", in *Social agencies and institutions*, F. M. L. Thompson (ed.), *The Cambridge social history of Britain, 1750–1950* (Cambridge, 1990), vol. 3, p. 67.

10. *Ibid.*

11. *Twenty-Second Annual Report of the Poor Law Board, 1869–70*, C.123, Appendix A, no. 4.

12. S. Webb & B. Webb, *The prevention of destitution* (London, 1912).

13. C. S. Loch, *The future of local charity organisation*. Private and confidential memorandum to members of the COS (London: COS, 1903).

14. C. S. Loch, *A great ideal and its champion. Papers and addresses by the late Sir C. S. Loch* (London, 1923).

15. G. Best, *Temporal pillars* (Cambridge, 1964).

16. B. Bosanquet, "The meaning of social work", *International Journal of Ethics* **11**, 1901, pp. 291–306.

17. B. Bosanquet, "The principles and chief dangers of the administration of charity", in *Philanthropy and social progress. Seven essays*, J. Addams (ed.) (New York, 1893), p. 297.

18. B. Bosanquet, "I. The majority report", *Sociological Review* **2**, 1909, p. 115.

19. *Report of the Royal Commission on Housing of the Working Classes*, C. 4402-I, Vol. II (1885) Minutes of Evidence, Q. 8865.

20. C. E. Maurice, *Life of Octavia Hill* (London, 1913), p. 258.

21. H. Dendy, "The children of working London", in *Aspects of social reform*, B. Bosanquet (ed.) (London, 1895), p. 32.

22. H. Bosanquet, *The family* (London, 1906), p. 96.

23. *Ibid.*, p. 99.

24. *Ibid.*, p. 222.

25. See M. Vicinus, *Independent women. Work and community for single women, 1859–1920* (London: Virago, 1985); Hollis, *Ladies elect*; J. Lewis, *Women and social action in Victorian and Edwardian England* (Aldershot, 1991).

26. A. L. Hodson, *Letters from a settlement* (London, 1909), p. 22.

27. M. Richmond, *The long view. Papers and addresses by Mary E. Richmond*. Selected and edited by Joanna C. Colcord (New York, 1930).

28. B. Webb, *My apprenticeship* (Cambridge, 1926).

29. A. Marshall, "Poor law reform", *The Economic Journal* **2**, 1892, pp. 371–9.

30. B. Bosanquet, "The limitations of the poor law", *The Economic Journal* **2**, 1892, pp. 369–71.

31. Marshall, "Poor law reform".

32. S. Barnett, "Friendly criticism of the Charity Organisation Society", *Charity Organisation Review*, August 1895, pp. 338–44.

33. S. & H. Barnett, *Practicable socialism*, 2nd edn (London, 1894).

34. Fabian Women's Group, *How the National Insurance Bill affects women* (London: FWG, 1911); Women's Industrial Council, "Memo on the National Insurance Bill as it affects Women", TS, BLPES, 1911.

35. Alice Foley recorded here experiences in this capacity in her autobiography, *A Bolton childhood* (Manchester, 1973).

36. V. Markham, "The problem of poverty". Letter to the *Spectator*, 26 August 1911. Markham Papers, Pt. II, 28/55, LSE Archives, BLPES.
37. *Report to the President of the Local Government Board on Guilds of Help in England*, Cd. 5664, 1911; K. Laybourne, *The Guild of Help and the changing face of Edwardian philanthropy* (Lampeter, 1994).
38. For example, M. Richmond, *Friendly visiting among the poor. A handbook for charity workers* (New York, 1899).
39. W. Milledge, "Guilds of Help", *Charity Organisation Review*, July 1906, pp. 46–57.
40. *Report to the President of the Local Government Board on Guilds of Help in England*, Cd. 5664, 1911.
41. N. Masterman, "The Guild of Help movement", *Charity Organisation Review*, June 1906, pp. 139–50.
42. C. R. Attlee, *The social worker* (London, 1920).
43. E. Macadam, *The new philanthropy. A study of the relations between the statutory and voluntary social services* (London, 1934).
44. C. Braithwaite, *The voluntary citizen. An enquiry into the place of philanthropy in the community* (London, 1938), p. 7.
45. R. M. MacIver, *The contribution of sociology to social work* (New York, 1931).
46. E. J. Urwick, *The principle of reciprocity in social life and action*. Second Charles Loch Memorial Lecture (London, 1930).
47. *Ibid.*
48. T. S. Simey, *Principles of social administration* (Oxford, 1937).
49. F. Bruno, "Foreign social work", *Social work year book, 1937* (New York, 1937).
50. W. Beveridge, *Voluntary action. A report on methods of social advance* (London, 1948), p. 320.
51. A. Flexner, "Is social work a profession?", *Proceedings of the National Conference of Charities and Corrections*, 42nd Annual Session, 1915.
52. Richmond, *The long view.*
53. U. Cormack, "Development in casework", in *Voluntary social services. Their place in the modern state*, A. F. C. Bourdillon (ed.) (London, 1945), p. 104.
54. V. E. Robinson, *A changing psychology in social case work* (Chapel Hill, 1930).
55. M. Yelloly, *Social work theory and psychoanalysis* (New York, 1980).
56. E. Younghusband, *Social work in Britain. A supplementary report on the employment and training of social workers* (Edinburgh, 1951).
57. H. H. Perlman (ed.), *Helping. Charlotte Towle on social work and social casework* (Chicago, 1969), p. 196.
58. C. Towle, *Some reflections on social work education* (London, 1956), Foreword.
59. R. M. Titmuss, "Social policy and social work education", TS, Titmuss Papers, Box 300C, BLPES.
60. Simey, *Principles*, p. 113.
61. Perlman, *Helping. Charlotte Towle*, p. 231.
62. C. Morris (ed.), *Social casework in Great Britain*, 2nd edn (London, 1954), p. 11.
63. K. Lucas, "The political theory implicit in social casework theory", *American Political Science Review* **XLVII**, 1953, pp. 1076–91.
64. Titmuss, "Social policy and social work".

65. B.Wootton (assisted by V. G. Seal & R. Chambers), *Social science and social pathology* (London, 1959), p. 269.

66. *Ibid.*, *Social science*, p. 271.

67. Whether feminized occupations such as social work and nursing constitute fully fledged professions has been a perennial source of debate; see A. Etzioni, *The semi-professions and their organization* (New York, 1969).

68. Lewis, *Women and social action.*

69. H. Hernes, *Welfare state and woman power: essays in state feminism* (Oslo, 1987).

70. The notion that the Scandinavian states developed universal insurance provision is controversial, but provision was certainly vastly more inclusive than in Britain.

10

Risk, redistribution and social welfare in Britain from the poor law to Beveridge

Paul Johnson

Introduction

This chapter considers how the nature of social protection in Britain changed between the later Victorian period and the Second World War. It is concerned, therefore, with the functions and outcomes of welfare systems rather than with the policy-making process or with the political pressures that lay behind this process. The contention of the chapter is that a concentration on welfare outcomes produces a less linear and less progressive view of welfare change in this period than is found in most historical accounts.

The dominant theme of nearly all studies of the long-run development of social welfare in Britain since the mid-Victorian period has been the increasing role of the central government in the public provision of welfare resources and services. This historiography developed initially in the 1960s as historians began to search for the administrative origins of the post-war "welfare state" modelled on the war-time plan of William Beveridge. Early twentieth-century legislation – on health and unemployment insurance, pensions, education, school meals, maternity provision – was seen both as a fundamental break with nineteenth-century poor-law traditions and as the precursor of later, more ambitious and more comprehensive public welfare schemes. These were the first steps down the long road to social security, and few doubted that the road led in the right direction. The titles of some of these early histories, as well as their contents, reveal a "Whiggish" view in which the creation of centralized, comprehensive public welfare services appears as part of a generally positive and beneficent process of modernization.[1]

More recent studies have been equally confident of the long-term trend towards increasingly comprehensive central state provision, though they have been less certain that the trend has been either desirable or beneficial for the welfare recipients as evidence has emerged in the 1970s and 1980s that public welfare provision can create as well as solve social problems. The expanding welfare role of central government has been variously interpreted as an example of bourgeois social control, of capitalist domination, and of an illiberal step down the road to serfdom.[2] Although these interpretations and putative explanations of the long run history of welfare provision vary enormously, they continue to focus their attention on the political and administrative causes of welfare-state growth.

This chapter will attempt a different approach by focusing on the economic functions and outputs of welfare systems rather than their administrative forms. In order to study welfare functions it is necessary to have some framework or model that describes in a stylistic way what it is that welfare systems actually do. The first part of the chapter introduces an analytical framework that draws on some simple economic ideas about the incidence of risk in society. The next four sections then survey welfare changes in Britain from the mid-Victorian period to the Second World War from a risk-analysis perspective in order to see how the burden or distribution of risk changed over this period. The final section draws together the strands of the argument by suggesting that a risk-centred analysis of welfare change, rather than a politics-, or ideas-, or administration-centred analysis, produces a generally less progressive and less positive picture of welfare development in the period.

Framework

We must begin with some definitions. These definitions are not contentious – at least not from an economist's perspective – but they need to be clearly established. *Social risk* is defined as the probability-weighted uncertainty that derives from the changing and dynamic world in which people live. A *welfare instrument* is defined as any mechanism that is used to reduce the incidence of social risk. A *welfare system* is simply some combination of welfare instruments. These are, of course, catch-all definitions which are perhaps so general as to be unhelpful in the context of a specific historical study, so some more concrete examples will be given, first in terms of social risk, then in terms of welfare instruments.

Social risk derives from the changing and uncertain world in which individuals live. What counts as risk is to some extent a cultural construction, as is the way in which some risks come to be perceived as social problems.[3] In consequence the perceived incidence of risk will vary not only between individuals, but also between different places, different cultures and over time. All social risks can, however, be thought of schematically as falling into one of four categories relating to health, life-cycle stage, economy and environment, and the strategies adopted to accommodate these risks, whether individual or collective, private or public, form the welfare structures of any society. Across the industrial societies of the later nineteenth century the perception of social risk was similar, as Peter Baldwin has shown, even though there was considerable variation in the national responses to these risks.[4]

Health

The most significant individual risk is related to health. High nineteenth-century mortality rates are the clearest indication that life was chancier in the past than it is today. Although overall mortality rates were strongly influenced by very high levels of infant mortality, adult mortality was also high; fewer than half of all 20-year-olds in Victorian Britain could expect to survive to age 65.[5] Whether the Victorian population was less healthy than the modern population, as well as less long-lived, is a matter of debate. James Riley has suggested that the great increase over the last hundred years in the survival chances of the less fit may have reduced the overall health of the population, but the morbidity data on which this argument rests is far from representative.[6] It is, nevertheless, clear that among small groups of skilled workers the incidence of sickness in any annual period in the later-Victorian period was very high, and the widespread incidence of the normal diseases of childhood, together with the ever-present fear of tuberculosis, makes it seem likely that everyone was touched by recurrent acute illnesses, while many suffered from chronic conditions.[7]

Life-cycle risks

These risks reflect the evolving needs and capacities of family or household units. The extra costs associated with childbirth and childrearing, frequently accompanied by a fall in family income as mothers were forced to relinquish paid employment, was the most widespread familial or life-cycle risk. The cyclical nature of family poverty, and the specific risk of poverty in young families with many dependent children, was highlighted

227

in 1901 with the publication of Seebohm Rowntree's investigation of poverty in York.[8] He found that largeness of family was the second most important cause of primary poverty, after low wages. However, it was not only the young who faced life-cycle risks; declining strength and earning power in old age could combine to create both economic and physical want. Both these life-cycle risks could be amplified by family dissolution through separation or death of a spouse.

Economic risks

Economic risks are endemic to industrial societies in which consumption needs are more stable than is employment income. Fluctuating rates of pay, hours of work and employment opportunities all created substantial economic risks for manual workers which were much more severe than those faced by salaried workers with their more secure employment contracts, or by capital owners with reasonably stable income streams. This economic instability stimulated a wide range of private and public risk-sharing strategies in the period covered by this chapter but, as will be shown below, there was no simple transition from individual to collective responses.

Environmental risks

These include not only storm, flood, tempest and other "acts of God", but also the risks associated with social living, particularly the risks of accident, of fire and of theft. Most of these risks have been viewed as personal rather than social in modern industrial societies, although there is no necessary reason why they should be treated in this way.

These four types of social risk are endemic. Welfare systems are combinations of instruments which reduce the incidence of these risks, either through a reduction in exposure or, more usually, through a diversification of the risk burden.[9] The variety both of potential welfare instruments and of possible combinations of instruments is enormous. Take the case of unemployment. The *exposure* to unemployment may be reduced by policies which increase the employability of individual workers (through education, for instance), or directly reduce the incidence by making work available for the unemployed. The risk burden can be *diversified* through economic strategies which spread the cost of unemployment over time and/or between individuals. A seasonal worker may, for instance, save during periods of full employment in order to accumulate a fund which can pay for living expenses during a period of unemployment – this is an example of individualistic risk-spreading over time. Alternatively, a group of workers may band together (in a trade union, or in an insurance scheme) in order to provide income transfers from those who are employed to those who are unemployed – this is an example of collective risk-spreading between individuals.

However, terms such as "individualist" and "collectivist" that were widely used in late-Victorian and Edwardian discussions of social issues and policies, and which continue to crop up in the historical literature, are imprecise when applied critically to the discussion of strategies to cope with differential risk.[10] From an economic standpoint, *any* strategy that involves risk-pooling is collective, regardless of whether the underlying financial principle is that of reciprocity or redistribution; putting money in a savings account is individualistic, buying an insurance policy *or* paying contributions to the local poor law are both collective.[11] If "individualist" and "collectivist" are unhelpful terms for understanding the way in which welfare instruments are used to respond to social risks, what can be put in their place? There are, I will suggest, four distinct attributes by which welfare instruments can be categorized or ranked:

1. type of risk pool;
2. type of redistribution;
3. nature of entitlement;
4. structure of management.

Let me briefly deal with each of these in turn.

Risk pool

Social risk is endemic, but the probabilities attached to each risk will vary across the population according to both observable and unobservable attributes of individuals. It is variation in these probabilities that are used by insurance companies to set individual or group-specific insurance premiums. Victorian insurance companies and friendly societies were pioneers in the application of occupation-specific mortality data to the setting of life-insurance premiums.

The type of risk pool has an impact on the cost of risk-spreading. If the risk pool is comprehensive, covering an entire population, then the premium will reflect average risk and will impose systematic transfers from low-risk to high-risk individuals. The more specific or restricted the risk pool, the more closely can bad risks be monitored and excluded, and the more limited the degree of systematic transfer. In terms, therefore, of the level of systematic transfer, there is likely to be a significant difference between comprehensive risk pools covering all or almost all of the population, such as the Victorian poor law or the post-1948 national insurance system, and the restricted risk pools of a particular trade union, or even of the 1911 national unemployment insurance scheme.

Type of redistribution

Systematic transfers imply redistribution, but recent analysis of the contemporary welfare state in Britain has shown that systematic transfers do not necessarily imply redistribution between individuals. More than two-thirds of the systematic welfare state transfers in Britain today are found to be intra-personal rather than inter-personal – this means that they serve to shift resources *across* an individual's life-cycle rather than *between* individuals.[12] This novel type of life-cycle analysis has important implications for the study of welfare outcomes. A cross-sectional analysis of the distributional effect of a comprehensive health insurance system, for instance, shows substantial inter-personal transfers from prime-age adults to both the young and the old. A life-cycle analysis shows that the balance between lifetime contribution and lifetime benefit is quite close. Estimates of the level of transfer effected by any welfare instrument will, therefore, depend heavily on the analytical framework adopted by the investigator. In general a multi-risk, multi-incidence welfare system – such as provided by a family or kinship network – will result in intra-personal transfers, whereas a single-risk, single-incidence welfare instrument, such as a workmen's compensation scheme, will result in inter-personal transfers.

Nature of entitlement.

The third important criteria for the categorization of welfare instruments is the nature of the entitlement – by which is meant the legal basis of the relationship between contribution and benefit. Entitlements can be placed on a spectrum from the purely contractual in which benefits are strictly linked to contribution, to the purely solidaristic in which benefits are related to desert within a particular risk pool, however defined. Contractual insurance or welfare instruments tend to emphasize actuarial fairness, solidaristic instruments emphasize a broader conception of social justice. Neighbourhood networks are clearly solidaristic, putting money in a savings bank for a rainy day is obviously contractual, though most welfare instruments can be found at some point on a spectrum between these two extremes. There is no simple relationship between the nature of entitlement and the type of redistribution achieved. The contractual basis of an endowment assurance policy and the solidaristic basis of a family exchange network may both primarily be directed towards intrapersonal transfers across the life-cycle. On the other hand a solidaristic charitable appeal or a contractual disability insurance scheme may both result in transfers that are primarily inter-personal.

Structure of management.

The final criterion is the structure of management. Welfare instruments can be managed publicly or privately, locally or nationally. The public/private distinction is important because it determines the degree of voluntarism associated with the risk-diversification strategy. Public management normally involves compulsion, though compulsion is not necessarily associated with comprehensive coverage – in 1911, for instance, unemployment insurance was made compulsory, but only for a limited range of workers. Nor is compulsion necessarily related to direct public provision; compulsory third-party motor insurance, for instance, was provided through the commercial insurance market. National rather than local management tends to be associated with more formal bureaucracy and with a distribution of benefits according to formal contractual entitlement rather than discretionary judgements about the level of need or desert.

The multi-dimensional character of welfare instruments, summarized in Figure 10.1, means that simple dichotomous characterizations of welfare change in this period from the late nineteenth century – for instance individualist to collectivist – present at best a partial, and often a mislead-

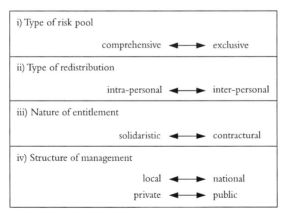

Figure 10.1 Attributes of welfare systems.

ing, picture of the development of welfare outcomes. There is no particular reason for considering the attributes on the right of Figure 10.1 as either more or less "progressive" than those on the left.

The next part of the chapter demonstrates how welfare systems in Britain in the 70 years before the Second World War exhibited a complex mix of attributes that developed along different, and often divergent, paths. This is done by means of a survey of instrumental responses to the four types of social risk – relating to health, life-cycle, economy and environment.

Health

Poor health could impose a double burden on a family, in terms of both medical fees and lost earnings. The risk of poor health was so high, and the cost potentially so burdensome, that most families made some attempt to share risks and costs by joining a medical insurance scheme. This was true throughout the period 1870–1939, and was not altered in a fundamental way by the introduction of contributory national health insurance in 1911. Some of the risks of ill-health were also met by an extensive range of charitable institutions, particularly where treatable disease or injury required hospitalization. This "mixed economy" of medical service provision was fundamentally challenged only during the Second World War by the establishment of the wartime Emergency Medical Service, and by the creation of a universal, tax-financed National Health Service in 1948.[13]

Medical attention did not come cheap in Victorian Britain. Then, as now, prestigious doctors charged prestigious patients fees to match their economic and social status; poor patients were charged more reasonable rates which in the 1870s were between 2s 6d and 5s per visit.[14] With these fees a sustained bout of familial ill-health could be financially crippling. In the mid-1870s a labourer was successfully sued for £12 15s – around a quarter of his annual income – for medical services during a period of fever, charged by the doctor at the rate of 3s per visit plus 1s travel.[15] Where it was the breadwinner who had succumbed to sickness, the collapse of family income could quickly lead, via the pawnshop, to destitution and either charitable or poor-law assistance.[16] Given the exceptionally high cost of individual payment for medical services it is little wonder that strenuous attempts were made by many millions of working-class families to purchase insurance against such calamities.

Health insurance in this period came in many guises and was offered through a multiplicity of institutional forms. The complexity of provision precludes any exact calculation of the extent or cost of coverage, but by piecing together the evidence some rough estimates can be made. At the top of the hierarchy of sickness insurance institutions there were the major friendly societies which provided medical attention and sick-pay for members who were prevented from working by illness, together with funeral benefits and lying-in benefits for members' wives who were in the final stages of pregnancy. Some societies were confined to members of a particular profession, industry or trade, some to a particular locality, but the basic insurance principle of spreading the risk as widely as possible encouraged the growth of national societies with large risk pools, the two largest being the Independent Order of Oddfellows and the Ancient Order of Foresters. In 1901 societies offering a full range of sickness benefits had 4.1 million members in England and Wales, equal to 41 per cent of the male population aged 20 and over. This figure rose to 4.4 million in 1911 and 4.5 million in 1931, by which time the proportion of the adult male population covered had fallen to just under one-third.[17] These friendly society members were almost exclusively males and were mainly clerical and better-paid manual workers.[18] The major constraint on membership was probably cost. Contributions of 6d to 1s per week, depending on age of entry, required an income that was both reasonably high and reasonably stable. In return, sick pay of around 10s per week would typically be offered for the first 13 or 26 weeks, reducing to half pay for the remainder of the year, and sometimes quarter pay thereafter.

These societies combined a mixture of contractual and solidaristic insurance. As already noted, limits were put on the length of time full benefit could be drawn, and by the end of the nineteenth century most societies (but not the temperance friendly societies) required prospective members to undergo a formal medical test in order to limit bad risks (and so the degree of systematic redistribution). In practice, however, the keenness of societies to recruit new members, particularly if connected by family or through work to an existing member, made the contractual rules very flexible.[19] This flexibility, together with the fraternal sentiments that were an important element of the friendly society movement, made the societies much more solidaristic than their formal rules indicate. This was made possible by the local management structure – even in the large national societies the majority of the sickness insurance business was financed and managed on a local (lodge) basis. Generous payments were made to long-standing members because of their fraternal status, even though they had often ceased to qualify for sick pay. This solidaristic approach to sickness insurance which resulted in societies in effect paying disability pensions to some of their older members was, by the end of the nineteenth century, driving many societies towards actuarial insolvency, and was one reason why their opposition to state old-age pensions was so muted.[20] In distributional terms, the expansion of long-term sick-pay was an unanticipated intergenerational transfer which created new inter-personal redistribution liabilities.

But what of the rest of the population, "more than three fourths" according to the Minority Report of the Royal Commission on the Poor Laws, whose sickness was not covered by the provisions of the major friendly societies?[21] At least 300,000 people were eligible for medical services (but *not* sick-pay) provided by medical friendly societies, both registered and informal, though few of these were likely to have been women or children.[22] Yet there were other, private, mechanisms for the purchase of medical insurance which prevented recourse to charity or the poor law. In addition to the registered and unregistered friendly societies, medical attendance insurance was variously available from companies such as the National Medical Aid Co., schemes set up by private individuals, and schemes operated by a doctor or group of doctors themselves.[23] The *Lancet* claimed that in many towns between two-thirds and three-quarters of the population belonged to medical aid organizations of one sort or another,[24] and a long campaign was waged by the medical establishment against such organizations which contracted doctors to treat their members for an average fee in 1905 of 4s 4d (a penny a week).[25] By 1913 it has been estimated that half of Britain's 20,000 general practitioners were engaged in contract practice.[26] The Friendly Societies Medical Alliance recommended that one doctor should not be contracted to serve more than 2,500 patients, although 4,000 patients per doctor were not unknown.[27] Putting these two sets of estimates together suggests medical coverage for at least 25 million people in 1913, and possibly as many as 40 million, or something between 60 and 95 per cent of the population.

This discussion of medical insurance has shown that private provision for ill-health was very extensive well before the introduction in 1911 of the national health insurance scheme, and it continued to be an important part of people's strategies to cope with the cost of illness throughout the inter-war period. Yet contract medical practice did not serve all cases – it was too costly for the very poor, too limited for the very sick. For these cases there was charity or the poor law. Charitable assistance for the sick came in two main forms – provident dispensaries and voluntary hospitals. Provident dispensaries were semi-charitable in that those who were willing to pay a weekly contribution (often a penny per person) received treatment on what was effectively a contract insurance basis, while the very poor were required to pay only a token sum, with the balance supplied by honorary members.

Of greater importance were the voluntary hospitals which, in their outpatients departments, dealt with enormous numbers of people. In 1900 the London voluntary hospitals were said to be treating 1.9 million outpatients annually, rather more than their endowment income could sustain.[28] In 1874 the London hospitals were driven by financial need to establish a Hospital Saturday Fund which collected small weekly sums from workers and gave tickets to contributors which allowed them to nominate deserving cases or escape registration fees.[29] In the inter-war period this arrangement became more formalized in the Hospital Savings Association, which operated rather like a contract insurance scheme; membership in London reached 1.9 million by 1938, by which date total national membership of Hospital Saturday Funds and organized workmen's collections had reached 10.3 million.[30] The voluntary hospitals continued to provide free treatment to outpatients they considered to be necessitous. This concept of charitable desert was initially introduced at University College Hospital in London which in 1872 invited the Charity Organisation Society to vet out-patients in order to determine their ability to pay.[31] The practice was subsequently extended, formalized and generalized through the hospital almoner system.[32]

For those who could not pay and who could not get access to appropriate treatment through the voluntary hospitals (which were concentrated in the larger cities) there were the poor-law medical facilities. These appear to have been a place of last resort, at least in the nineteenth century. Although the Medical Relief Disqualification Removal Act of 1885 gave the (otherwise enfranchised) sick pauper the vote, it did not free poor-law medical care from all stigma. In the 1920s it was still necessary for every patient entering a poor-law infirmary to obtain an admission order signed by the relieving officer, and in London it was claimed that some patients would wait months for a place in a voluntary hospital despite the ready availability of equivalent poor-law facilities.[33] The provision for transfer of the hospital functions of the poor law to the Public Health Committees of local authorities by the 1929 Local Government Act removed the element of formal pauperization in those parts of the country where the transfer took place,[34] but it did not do away with the means test. Local authorities had an obligation to charge for treatment in general hospitals, and were able to make husbands liable for wives, parents for children under 21.[35] Nevertheless, the income they raised through payments was small. In 1934 the income of voluntary hospitals was £14.2 million, of which 41 per cent came from receipts for services rendered, but the public hospitals raised only 7 per cent of their £19.6 million from charges.[36]

Some other medical services were even more mixed in their funding. District nurses were initially established on an entirely charitable basis, and until 1937 neither central nor local government had any general power to organize domiciliary nursing. Nevertheless, from 1892 poor-law guardians were allowed to pay annual subscriptions to district nursing associations, and by 1907 almost 400 associations were being assisted in this way.[37]

In the period from 1870 to 1939 the social risk of ill-health in Britain was met by a complex network of overlapping systems for insuring against the costs of sickness and for providing medical attention. Personal attempts to insure against the costs ranged from solidaristic friendly society membership to the strictly contractual medical aid companies. In addition charitable assistance through voluntary hospitals and means-tested access to poor-law dispensaries and infirmaries provided for those who had no insurance. Private effort was both widespread and financially significant; for instance in a social survey of Bristol conducted in 1937, 62 per cent of working-class households were found to be contributing to a hospital fund.[38] Most of this private effort was organized at a local level and a good deal was self-managed. Where obvious gaps emerged, as with domiciliary nursing, charities and poor-law authorities attempted to plug the gaps in a somewhat *ad hoc* manner.

The introduction of national health insurance in 1911 for full-time manual workers probably did very little immediately to extend access to doctors, although it certainly did give many more men an entitlement to sickness pay. The tripartite contribution – from workers, employers and the government – was redistributive to a degree, but since the system was self-financing this degree of redistribution was confined to the (mainly adult male) workers incorporated in the risk pool.[39] Moreover, the contractual nature of the scheme with its contribution requirements meant that long-term bad risks could be excluded. Workers who were in arrears had their entitlement to benefit reduced or suspended, and the "approved societies" that administered the system could exclude individuals whom they considered to be "bad risks". Excluded workers were required to take out "deposit insurance" with the Post Office, which was simply a form of personal saving. During a period of sickness the individual worker could draw on these savings, but once the stock of assets was exhausted, the poor law beckoned. Despite Lloyd George's insistence that this system be called "deposit insurance"[40] there was no element of insurance in it at all since it contained not even a minimal amount of risk-sharing.

The extent of inter-personal redistribution was, therefore, strictly circumscribed, especially compared to the poor-law or charitable medical services which were more comprehensive, solidaristic and redistributive. The administration of the national health insurance scheme according to strict rules by "approved societies" made it a more contractual and less solidaristic form of insurance than was much friendly society sickness insurance. Although perhaps of considerable significance in terms of administrative innovation, in terms of who got what from whom, when, how often and at what cost, the health provisions of the National Insurance Act of 1911 were of less importance than private insurance. Even by 1938, National Health Insurance covered only 42 per cent of the population.[41]

Life-cycle risks

Life-cycle risks were those identified in Rowntree's poverty cycle as related to birth and infancy, and old age and death. In the 1870s neither life-cycle problem was considered to be the automatic responsibility of any public authority, although poor-law infirmaries and workhouses did provide care for otherwise dependent pregnant women and aged men and women. In practice, however, the number of people receiving residential care was small. David Thomson has shown that even in the peak year of 1901 the proportion of the age group 65–74 in poor-law institutions stood at only 5.82 per cent for men and 2.81 per cent for women.[42] There was, however, much more extensive financial support from poor-law funds for the aged living in their own homes. Charles Booth estimated that in 1891 the proportion of men over 65 in receipt of any poor-law relief was 39.5 per cent in London, 28.5 per cent in other urban and suburban areas, and 25 per cent in rural or semi-rural areas,[43] and Thomson has argued that "over a lifetime, and especially near the end of it, all stood a very good chance of attaining the status of 'pauper'".[44] Striking though these estimates are, their most important conclusion is often overlooked – that for most of the time most aged people *were not* dependent on public support at all. Either they earned sufficient income in the labour market or received sufficient financial support from family, neighbours and friends or from savings to maintain an independent existence. Thomson is certainly right to emphasize both the low rates of co-residence of the elderly with kin and the general acceptance in nineteenth-century Britain of public responsibility for aged dependants by poor-law authorities,[45] but his reliance on poor-law evidence leads him to diminish the role of private provision and self-help.

It should be made clear that this majority of aged persons who lived lives independent of poor-law support did not receive much from charitable sources. In 1909 charities specifically charged with providing pensions and homes for the aged in London received only £342,000, or just over 4 per cent of total charitable income in the metropolis.[46] By the 1940s endowed charities distributed approximately £5 million to old people, including, in 1943, pensions for just over 75,000 elderly people.[47] By this date public pensions were being paid to over 4 million pensioners, at an annual cost of over £100 million.

The introduction of means-tested non-contributory public pensions for people over 70 in 1908 marked an important step in the development of central state welfare services. In terms of the welfare of older people, the pension served initially more to replace poor-law outdoor relief than to provide additional financial support for the previously independent.[48] In terms of finance and administration, however, the pension broke new ground. The removal of the pauper disqualification from pensioners in 1911 relieved over 122,000 aged paupers from reliance on the poor law, thereby transferring from local ratepayers to the national exchequer a financial burden estimated to be in excess of £1.1 million per year.[49] Central exchequer finance and centralized administration (by the Customs and Excise, with payment made through the Post Office) were a fundamental departure from the local basis of poor-law operation. Even so there was a need for local decision-making over individual cases relating to eligibility and the means test, and this local management was supervised by voluntary committees appointed by local councils.[50]

Poor-law pensions had been redistributive from (better-off) ratepayers to (worse-off) paupers and so were, like the rest of poor-law provision, solidaristic in the sense that benefits were related to desert rather than contribution, within a comprehensive risk pool delineated simply by the boundary of the local poor-law authority. The development in larger cities of socially homogeneous poor-law unions did, of course, limit the extent of this cross-class social solidarity. The 1908 non-contributory pension scheme further extended this principle of public solidarity with pensions paid according to a means test and revenue coming from general taxation, but the need to discriminate between the deserving and the ineligible required some local investigative capability. The move to full centralization was accomplished in 1925 with the introduction of contributory national insurance pensions. These pensions required no local management because they were contractual rather than solidaristic – benefit was directly related to prior contribution, and character, income and personal circumstances were immaterial to the award of the pension. The tripartite contribution principle in the National Insurance fund meant that there was some element of inter-personal redistribution in the contributory state pension scheme, but the redistributive intent was much less marked than in either the 1908 pension scheme or in the earlier practice of giving poor law outdoor relief.

Public financial support in old age was gradually transformed from a solidaristic system, in which the risk pool was the whole community and in which contributions were levied on all households with benefits directed to citizens in need, towards a contractual system in which a strictly defined risk pool (contributing manual workers) provided benefits for itself, with redistribution being largely intra-personal (across the life-cycle) and with only a limited amount of interpersonal redistribution determined purely by the actuarial chance of longevity. This drift of public pension provision towards the principles and practice of commercial contractual insurance fits uneasily with simple historical notions that the rise of "collectivism" involved the introduction of more redistributive public welfare systems.[51]

The increasingly contractual approach to public support for the elderly can be contrasted with a consistently solidaristic treatment of infants and children. Public involvement in childbirth and infancy was usually mediated through voluntary or semi-voluntary channels, and was seen as a local rather than a national responsibility. This was true even with such apparently straightforward national legislation as the 1902 Midwives Act, which devolved the funding and administration of midwife training to local public and private bodies. National guidelines, local implementation, and solidaristic funding in which the local community paid for the supply of services which were delivered according to need rather than contractual entitlement was the basis of infant- and child-welfare provision.

The nature of state support for children after 1870 is in some respects the antithesis of public support for the elderly. Whereas outdoor relief and old-age pensions moved from the publicly solidaristic to the publicly con-tractual, education moved in the opposite direction, with schooling first being provided by local school boards in 1870, made compulsory in 1880 and effectively made free from 1891.[52] Responsibility for (and the cost of) education gradually shifted from parents to the local community as finan-cial risks of child-rearing were spread over a risk pool comprising all rate-payers in a school board district. Perhaps these divergent trends reflect a change in underlying social attitudes, with education increasingly being seen as a public good, an investment in future workers, while pensions were viewed more as a public burden.

This discussion of the role of public institutions in infant and child wel-fare must not, of course, be allowed to obscure the fact that the over-whelming responsibility lay in the private sector, with families. Although the state increasingly became involved with the issues of maternity and education, it was content to leave most of the financial, practical and moral responsibilities of childrearing to parents, and intervened only when death, desertion, cruelty or poverty created an obvious child welfare prob-lem. Although the ideological climate was changing before the Second World War, the failure of the family endowment movement to obtain some version of a "family wage" kept the cost of children firmly in the pri-vate sector.[53] Not surprisingly, many, perhaps most, parents attempted to spread and share these costs. Formal insurance provided no opportunities here – children do not represent a short-term, sporadic, actuarial risk – but family, friends and neighbours could all be called on to help in periods of need. The nature, extent and use of kinship and neighbourhood networks in providing regular or periodic child-care services is still an under-researched topic, but existing studies indicate that these networks were vital for many mothers.[54] How far the exchanges between women of goods, money and, above all, time, depended on carefully considered reci-procity rather than more purely charitable sentiments is unknown, but the underlying rules were certainly not those of a formal contract. Commu-nity solidarity meant that it was neighbours in the street, not officers of the state, who were most likely to help if a child was sick or a cupboard was bare.

Economic risks

Cupboards sometimes became bare even in the homes of highly skilled workers who normally experienced regular work. Except for the fortunate few in railway company or government employment, job insecurity and short-time working were an economic scourge from which there was no escape. But if neither prevention nor cure lay within the scope of ordinary workers, protection did. Virtually all households accumulated assets – financial or physical – which they could draw on or pawn in times of economic stringency. By 1900 there were over 10 million savings bank accounts in existence, and an estimated 200 million pledges a year made with pawnbrokers.[55] These personal or familial strategies were far more widespread than formal unemployment insurance provided through trade unions. In 1911 Lloyd George thought that "not a tenth of the working classes have made any provision at all for insurance against unemployment"[56]; according to figures collected by the government, trade union assistance of any sort in times of unemployment was available to no more than 2.3 million workers in 1908.[57]

Even within this relatively small insured group, the value of unemployment insurance varied widely between sectors, from the high levels in printing to the trivial in transport. Effective unemployment insurance was bound to be expensive in the precarious labour market of Victorian and Edwardian Britain, particularly so when conducted by trade unions which were ill-designed to spread risks and minimize costs. Given the trade-related nature of unemployment risks, an optimal risk pool would have been one that included workers from a variety of trades that experienced different cyclical employment patterns; as it was, trade unions compounded risks by uniting workers in a single trade. On the other hand, the solidaristic nature and purpose of trade unions enabled them to operate in a deliberately redistributive manner at times of special need such as during trade disputes and trade depressions. Special levies were imposed on those in work to provide for members temporarily laid-off or locked out, and little attempt was made to run union funds on actuarial principles. Unions operated as "pay-as-you-go" solidaristic insurance clubs, with subscriptions and levies adjusted from year to year to pay for the current level of benefits.

The introduction of a public unemployment insurance system by Part Two of the National Insurance Act of 1911 marked a decisive step towards state centralization but, as with the national health insurance scheme, the move was towards a contractual system. National unemployment insurance was compulsory for the 2.25 million workers in the designated industries of building, shipbuilding, mechanical engineering, ironfounding, sawmilling and vehicles, and tripartite contributions from workers, employers and the government ensured some redistribution from both profits and central government revenue.[58] Levels of contribution and benefit were set by reference to past unemployment experience, the intention being that the scheme would break even over a mix of good and bad years, so that transfers were to be primarily intra- rather than inter-personal. During the First World War unemployment insurance was extended to munitions workers and to virtually all manual workers by stages in 1920, 1927 and 1930. The government in effect directly acknowledged some responsibility for establishing a safety net against the most common of economic risks, although this was done through a system of compulsory contract insurance with principles derived as much as, or more from, the commercial insurance industry as from the trade union experience of fraternal solidarity.

The inter-war practice differed a good deal from the contract insurance principle. With unemployment among the insured population at over 10 per cent for all but one year between 1921 and 1938, and reaching a peak of 23 per cent in 1932, a scheme originally restricted mainly to skilled workers and initiated during a period of high employment was found wanting.[59] For most of the inter-war period the unemployment insurance fund was in deficit, and repeated bailing-out and topping-up by the government made the operation of public unemployment insurance in the 1920s and 1930s much more solidaristic and inter-personally redistributive than had been intended. As a consequence the original goals of broadening the tax base, of encouraging by compulsion a degree of private provision against economic uncertainty, and of separating unemployment benefits from means-tested public doles were all thereby compromised. This should not detract, however, from the very important role national unemployment insurance played after 1911 in creating a degree of protection against economic risks – albeit at a minimal, below-subsistence level – which had never before been available to the majority of the workforce.[60]

Environmental risks

The final type of risk is that which comes from living in a physically hazardous world. The hazards can be entirely impersonal and exogenous – as with storm or flood – or largely personal and endogenous to a particular way of life – as with personal accident. Most of these risks have been viewed as unworthy of public insurance, though they have not been wholly untouched by local and central government action. Private insurance against damage to property by fire was the backbone of the non-life insurance business in the nineteenth century, though it was of little concern to working-class tenants.[61] Insurance against fire damage to personal rather than real property had little to offer manual workers, whose estates on death at the turn of the century were estimated to have an average value of no more than £16.[62] For similar reasons insurance against loss of personal property by theft was restricted to the relatively wealthy. Public action was limited to prevention rather than compensation of loss; in London, for example, public funds were spent on the Metropolitan Police Force from 1829 and the Metropolitan Fire Brigade from 1866.

Accident insurance was also conducted privately, but with an increasing amount of state direction. Personal accident insurance was a product of the growth of railway travel in the 1840s, but for workers, accident insurance resulted from the Employers' Liability Act of 1880 and the Workmen's Compensation Acts of 1897 and 1906. The first of these acts codified the common law liability of employers for injury sustained by a workman as a result of the negligence of his employer, but the 1897 act removed the need to demonstrate employer negligence. Asquith noted that the principle on which the legislation rested was

> that it is to the interest of the community as a matter of public policy, that the workman who sustains an injury in the course of his employment should, as far as money can do it, have the right to be indemnified. It is a new right you are creating for the workman, and a new obligation you are imposing on the employer.[63]

Public authorities created a legal obligation on employers to recompense injured workers, which employers then pooled through commercial insurance companies. This combination of state paternalism and private insurance was, as far as the workforce was concerned, entirely non-participatory, yet it was interpersonally redistributive from employers to workers. It fits neither the solidaristic model of trade union insurance or poor-law provision, nor the contractual model of national insurance or private health insurance, but it was an important and early example of central government action on social welfare issues.[64]

Conclusion

This chapter has consciously taken a narrowly functionalist view of social welfare in Britain between 1870 and 1939, by focusing on welfare outcomes – that is, by looking at how a variety of welfare instruments were used to reduce the incidence of social risk. I have taken this approach not because I believe that ideology, political and economic pressures, social knowledge, the policy-making process, or the aims and ambitions of key individuals are of lesser or no importance in the study of the evolution of social welfare, but because I think this view of welfare outcomes can provide a useful counterbalance to the more common politico-administrative studies. By first identifying the array of social risks faced by people in late nineteenth- and early twentieth-century Britain, and then by chronicling the strategies they adopted to counter these risks, I have tried to show three things.

First, most social risks were met, most of the time, by a complex array of private responses which included both the highly individualistic (private savings) and the highly solidaristic (fraternal insurance in trade unions). The relatively small numbers of people reliant on state support in the late nineteenth century (paupers accounted for about 2.6 per cent of the population in the 1890s) despite the unstable nature of the labour market is itself an indication of the extent of private welfare provision. Of all social groups it was the elderly who were most likely to become dependent on poor-law assistance, yet as pointed out above the majority of the elderly remained independent of public financial support until the introduction of state old-age pensions in 1908. Medical expenses continued to be met primarily by private insurance, with an additional direct supply of medical services from charitable sources, until the beginning of the Second World War. In addition to voluntaristic charity, much financial and other support appears to have been exchanged freely and informally through local kinship or neighbourhood networks. The diversity of these private forms of resistance to or compensation for social risks, and their enduring nature throughout the period 1870 to 1939, must challenge any simple assertions about transition from private to public welfare.

Secondly, the locus of both finance and administration in social welfare did not shift easily or consistently from the locality to the centre. Neighbourhood and kinship networks remained, of necessity, attached to the locality, since they could only be maintained and reinforced by regular and repeated social contact, and most charities continued to be localized in terms of both their donors and their beneficiaries. The formal involvement of the state in the payment of old-age pensions is a clear example of increasing centralization, but public provision of elementary education remained a local financial and administrative responsibility, and the enduring significance of the poor law (and subsequently of public assistance) ensured that the centralizing momentum of the national insurance idea would never completely dominate locally managed, means tested poverty relief payments before the Second World War.

Thirdly, the redistributive intent and performance of any particular welfare structure was not a function of its location on the public/private axis. Public involvement in social welfare ranged from the comprehensive and solidaristic poor law, in which benefit was related to citizenship and need, contribution to ability to pay, to the largely contractual, participatory but exclusive national insurance scheme, to the non-participatory and almost wholly contractual edifice of employers' liability insurance. Private strategies to counter social risks could be completely individualistic (personal savings) or mainly contractual (medical insurance) or partly solidaristic (friendly societies or trade unions) or mainly solidaristic (charitable support for voluntary hospitals or local self-help networks).

Taking these three points together shows that in Britain between 1870 and 1939 there was no simple transition from private to public social welfare provision, nor from "individualism" to "collectivism", nor even from solidaristic to contractual insurance. This study of the way individuals and society responded to social risks cannot, of course, reveal how the majority of working people felt about, or reacted to, the social welfare innovations of the period,[65] nor what the hopes and fears of politicians and policymakers were, nor why policy and practice changed in the manner and at the time it did. But by emphasizing the complex nature of welfare instruments and of the popular use of these instruments in response to social risks I have tried in this chapter to challenge a number of paradigmatic historical accounts of the rise of the British welfare state.

Once the multi-dimensional character of welfare instruments is recognized, the picture of a progressive evolution of welfare provision across the twentieth century becomes blurred. The Victorian poor law, for all its faults, was based on the idea of a comprehensive risk pool, of a solidaristic rather than contractual system of entitlement, and on substantial interpersonal redistribution. The combination of social insurance and social assistance since the Second World War has, in the main, continued to be comprehensive, solidaristic in practice and broadly supportive of interpersonal redistribution. But the Edwardian development of national insurance was a move towards an exclusive risk pool, towards contractual entitlement, and towards a self-financing system of intra-personal redistribution. Viewed from this perspective, the neat lineages of welfare development from the poor law to Beveridge are seen to be an erroneous historical construct.

Notes

1. M. Bruce, *The coming of the welfare state* (London, 1961); B. B. Gilbert, *The evolution of National Insurance in Great Britain: the origins of the welfare state* (London, 1966); D. Fraser, *The evolution of the British welfare state* (London, 1973).

2. K. Williams, *From pauperism to poverty* (London, 1981); J. R. Hay, *The origins of the Liberal welfare reforms 1906–1914* (London, 1975); D. G. Green, *Working-class patients and the medical establishment* (Aldershot, 1985).

3. M. Douglas and A. Wildavsky, *Risk and culture* (Berkeley, 1982); N. Manning, "Constructing social problems" in *Social problems and welfare ideology*, N. Manning (ed.) (Aldershot, 1985), pp. 1–28.

4. P. Baldwin, *The politics of social solidarity* (Cambridge, 1991), pp. 10–21.

5. M. Anderson, "The impact on the family relationships of the elderly of changes since Victorian times in governmental income-maintenance provision", in *Family, bureaucracy and the elderly*, E. Shanas & M. B. Sussman (eds) (Durham, 1977), p. 39.

6. J. Riley, "Working health time: a comparison of preindustrial, industrial and postindustrial experience in life and health", *Explorations in Economic History* **28**, 1991, pp. 169–91; J. Riley, *Sickness, recovery and death* (Iowa, 1989).

7. H. Southall & E. Garrett, "Morbidity and mortality among early nineteenth-century engineering workers", *Social History of Medicine* **4**, 1991, pp. 231–52; F. B. Smith, *The retreat of tuberculosis* (London, 1988).

8. B. S. Rowntree, *Poverty. A study of town life* (London, 1901), ch. 5.

9. An imaginative attempt to analyze welfare state development in terms of collective strategies to cope with risk, though with rather different historical conclusions to this paper, is A. de Swaan, *In care of the state health care, education and welfare in Europe and the USA in the modern era* (Oxford, 1988).

10. These terms were ambiguous even within the parameters of the then contemporary debate; for a discussion see M. Freeden, *The new liberalism* (Oxford, 1978).

11. For a summary of the economic approach to insurance and redistribution, see N. Barr, *The economics of the welfare state* (London, 1987), chs 4 and 5.

12. J. Falkingham & J. Hills (eds), *The dynamic of welfare* (Hemel Hempstead, 1995), pp. 137–49.

13. R. Titmuss, *Problems of social policy* (London, 1950); C. Webster, *Problems of health care: the National Health Service before 1957* (London, 1988).

14. F. B. Smith, *The people's health* (London, 1979), p. 370.

15. *Ibid.*, p. 373.

16. See, for example, the evidence in the following Charity Organisation Society case papers covering the period from the 1870s to 1939, lodged in the Greater London Record Office: Area 1, box 1, case 10409; box 2, case 15194; box 3, case 10788; box 4, case 16735; box 7, case 37/358.

17. P. Johnson, *Saving and spending: the working-class economy in Britain 1870–1939* (Oxford, 1985), p. 57. A slightly higher estimate of 4.75 million members in 1910 was made by W. Beveridge, *Voluntary action* (London, 1948), p. 76.

18. Gilbert, *Evolution*, p. 167; see also Johnson, *Saving*, pp. 57–63.

19. Green, *Working-class patients*, pp. 102–4.

20. B. B. Gilbert, "The decay of nineteenth century provident institutions and the coming of old age pensions in Great Britain", *Economic History Review*, 2nd series, **17**, 1965, pp. 551–63.

21. *Royal Commission on Poor Laws and relief of distress, minority report* ((1909), XXXVII), p. 870.

22. Johnson, *Saving*, p. 56; Green, *Working-class patients*, p. 95.

23. The Lancet, *The battle of the clubs* (London, 1896), pp. 97–104.

24. *Ibid.*, pp. 117, 123, 180.

25. Green, *Working-class patients*, p. 48.

26. F. Honigsbaum, *The division in British medicine* (London, 1979), p. 13.

27. Green, *Working-class patients*, p. 39.

28. Smith, *People's health*, p. 251; K. Waddington, "Bastard benevolence: centralisation, voluntarism and the Sunday Fund, 1873–1898", *London Journal* **19**, 1994, pp. 51–9.

29. G. Rivett, *The development of the London hospital system 1823–1982* (London, 1986), p. 122; B. Abel-Smith, *The hospitals 1800–1948* (London, 1964), pp. 135–6.

30. *Hospitals Yearbook 1940*, pp. 289–300.

31. Smith, *People's health*, p. 278.

32. Hospital Almoners' Association, *The Hospital Almoner* (London, 1935).

33. Abel-Smith, *Hospitals*, pp. 356–8.

34. C. Braithwaite, *The voluntary citizen* (London, 1938), p. 18.

35. Abel-Smith, *Hospitals*, p. 374.

36. Braithwaite, *Voluntary citizen*, pp. 171, 180.

37. *Ibid.*, pp. 268–278.

38. H. Tout, "A statistical note on family allowances", *Economic Journal* **50**, March 1940, pp. 51–9.

39. The degree of redistribution was also confined to the members of each individual "approved society", since they were subject to separate actuarial evaluation. See N. Whiteside, "Private agencies for public purposes: some new perspectives on policy making in health insurance between the wars", *Journal of Social Policy* **12**, 1983, p. 171.

40. W. J. Braithwaite, *Lloyd George's ambulance wagon* (London, 1957), p. 123.

41. Ministry of Health, *National Health Insurance* (London, 1939), pp. 32–4.

42. D. Thomson, "Workhouse to nursing home: residential care of elderly people in England since 1840", *Ageing and Society* **3**, 1983, p. 49.

43. C. Booth, *The aged poor in England and Wales* (London, 1894), p. 14.
44. D. Thomson, *Provision for the elderly in England, 1830–1908*. (PhD thesis, University of Cambridge, 1980), p. 16.
45. D. Thomson, "Welfare of the elderly in the past: a family or community responsibility?" in *Life, death and the elderly*, M. Pelling & R. Smith (eds) (London, 1991), p. 202.
46. Braithwaite, *Voluntary citizen*, p. 104
47. E. W. Cohen, *English social services* (London, 1949). p. 107.
48. P. Johnson, "The employment and retirement of older men in England and Wales, 1881–1981", *Economic History Review* **47**, 1994, p. 122.
49. UK Government, "Statement of persons in receipt of Poor Law relief", Cd. 5612, PP (1911), LXIX, p. 58.
50. P. Thane, "Government and society in England and Wales 1750–1914", in *The Cambridge Social History of Britain 1750-1850*, F. M. L. Thompson (ed.) (Cambridge, 1990), vol. 3, pp. 54–5.
51. Despite his use of risk analysis, de Swaan, *Care*, ch. 6, sees an unproblematic association between collectivism and redistribution.
52. S. J. Curtis, *History of education in Great Britain*, 7th edn (London, 1967), ch. 8.
53. J. Lewis, "Models of equality for women: the case of state support for children in twentieth-century Britain", in *Maternity and gender politics*, G. Bock & P. Thane (eds) (London, 1991).
54. See, for example, E. Ross, *Love and toil* (New York, 1994); J. White, *The worst street in North London* (London, 1986), pp. 71–82.
55. Johnson, *Saving*, pp. 92, 168.
56. *Hansard*, 5th series, vol. XXV, cols 610–11 (4 May 1911).
57. J. Harris, *Unemployment and politics* (Oxford, 1972), p. 298.
58. For details of the unemployment insurance scheme, see O. Clarke, *The law of National Insurance* (London, 1912), pp. lxxvii–xcii.
59. W. Garside, *British unemployment 1919–1939* (Cambridge, 1990), chs 2 and 3.
60. Of workers insured in 1913, 63 per cent were skilled, but only 20 per cent had previously been covered by any sort of private out-of-work insurance. Harris, *Unemployment*, p. 360.
61. B. Supple, *The Royal Exchange Assurance* (Cambridge, 1970), pp. 211–17.
62. L. G. Chiozza *Money, riches and poverty* 3rd edn (London, 1906), p. 51.
63. Quoted in H. E. Raynes, *A history of British insurance* (London, 1964), p. 294.
64. A. Ogus, "Great Britain", in *The evolution of social insurance, 1881–1981*, P. Kohler & H. Zacher (London, 1982), pp. 173–7.
65. For differing views on this see H. Pelling, "The working class and the origins of the welfare state", in *Popular Politics and Society in Late Victorian Britain*, 2nd edn (London, 1979), and P. Thane, "The working class and state welfare in Britain, 1880–1914", *Historical Journal* **27**, 1984, pp. 877–900.

11

Some concluding reflections
Olive Anderson

The transformation of live colloquium into book form is now a natural academic mutation; nevertheless, bets still cannot safely be taken on whether the change will prove a simple translation of speech into print, or something close to metamorphosis. Those who were present at the first Neale Colloquium on 3–4 February 1995 will know that *Charity, self-interest and welfare in the English past* does not exactly replicate those lively proceedings. The Neale Lecture itself can be read here almost exactly as it was delivered by the Director of the Cambridge Group for the History of Population and Social Structure; but there has been some revision of the roster of colloquium papers. Only a few faint traces survive of the many comments and criticisms launched from the floor throughout the day. This is a pity, for although at any colloquium those who attend sometimes offer wider perspectives, shrewder insights, and sounder information than the paper-readers, at this particular colloquium the standard of live discussion was exceptionally high. Some who were there may also regret finding no echo of the continuo improvised from the chair to link the academic arias, recitatives and choruses inspired by the original theme of "Who is my neighbour?". Traditionally, the chair's continuo is replaced at the book stage by the editor's introduction. Martin Daunton's introduction, however, offers neither echoes of his original impromptu link material, nor summaries of the contributions he has gathered together in this volume.

This notable free-standing chapter is an introduction to the colloquium's theme and the issues inherent within it, rather than to its proceedings or its end product. Each chapter is alluded to, but usually in a footnote, as a source of further information on a point raised – although the Neale

Lecture itself supplies a starting point to work against. The original theme, moreover, is expanded into a wider topic still: how past societies (chiefly, but not exclusively, English societies), have coped with welfare risks. The result is more than a simple survey of the welfare past, or even a line up of welfare historians' current shibboleths combined with a historiographical review, for Daunton's definition of the relevant literature and shibboleths emphatically includes recent work in many adjacent fields, above all economics. He leaves cultural approaches and their impact for the most part to Colin Jones's separate fireworks display, "Some recent trends in the history of charity"; but together, these chapters supply a high-flying bird's-eye view of what is presently going on in the welfare history field. Such initial sweep and comprehensiveness may be expected to throw into relief any gaps in what follows – not merely the inevitable gaps in coverage, but gaps in the conceptualization of the subject and in the issues raised; and certainly they prompt many speculations. For example, Daunton's analysis of the welfare mix has four elements – commercial, government (both central and local), community (both voluntary and self-help), and household. How would this work in place of the trinity of charity, self-interest, and welfare?

But what this striking introductory chapter above all brings home is that virtually all advanced societies are currently preoccupied with the topics confronted in this volume, and that the area of welfare has often been in the English past what it is today – an area of concern and conflict, not contentment and consensus. The volume as a whole, indeed, leaves the reader with distinct sensations of *déjà vu,* and supplies continual implicit illustrations of the cyclical nature of prescriptive thinking on welfare provision, and of welfare provision itself. *Pace* Daunton, Jones and Paul Johnson, for some time the temptation has been to succumb, not to evolutionary teleologies or bi-polarities, but to the lure of the cycle. (Welfare historians have long been reporting the inconsistent and erratic nature of the disparate policies and practices they study, and observing that charity, self-interest and publicly funded "welfare" have always co-existed and had complex *raisons d'être.*) This volume seems to strengthen the attraction of David Thomson's contention in 1984 that the alleged "welfare divide" between traditional and modern societies should be replaced by a picture of cyclical oscillations across several centuries around a substantial core of belief and practice. The corollary of this – that every past phase of welfare debate, policy, and practice is actually or potentially relevant to the concerned citizen today – certainly seems plausible enough. Currently, for example, any politician or member of the "caring professions" could surely take a seminar at the drop of a baseball cap on whether the growing burden of supporting aged parents should be the responsibility of the state (through the tax system) or their children (either directly or through the loss of their "inheritance" to pay for residential care) – in other words, on the demographics of welfare policy and practice, precisely the topic at the core of the contributions by Lynn Botelho and Pat Thane, as well as of this Neale Lecture itself.

It would be a great mistake, however, to suppose that its relevance to current welfare problems makes this volume of limited use to students concerned only with their prescribed period of the past. Welfare is often a rather tired section of student syllabuses: Daunton's introduction (with Jones's sequel) should put back some sparkle. There are enough big issues here to provide plenty of fizz. Are English welfare institutions really unique to England, and if so why? (One of the introduction's virtues, incidentally, is that it makes some reference to Scotland, otherwise absent here.) Is it true that risk categories are shaped by demography and economic structure, but state formation settles the outcome? (If so, mid-Victorian budgets, for example, might explain the broad acceptance of tax-funded welfare by later generations of Britons.) Equally crucial, ought cultural explanations to be superseding functional ones in welfare history, as they are in other fields? Some of the novelties strutted here have undeniably been around for quite some time. It is hardly news that there has been too much concentration on the poor law; nor that philanthropy was a social relationship with various meanings; and certainly not that welfare practices were different in different places. But these points are made in a way that implies, not that error has been corrected and there is nothing more to be said, but rather that today's changed starting-points are the best proof that welfare history is not a mature, defined subject, but a sprouting, unpredictable one. The whole volume, indeed, supports the introduction's final proposition that perhaps in matters of welfare "historians and politicians are in a similar plight: a realization that problems need to be solved, and a lack of confidence that a simple answer is to be found".

Those concerned with welfare, present and future as well as past, should certainly not miss Daunton's introduction. What of the other chapters? Is each strictly for its own specialized clientele? Naturally they are a mixed bag, not only in topic or period (and quality), but also in technique, sources, scale, and objectives. Yet they are mixed in such a way that together they provide an instructive demonstration pack of the manifold ways of working and writing about welfare history being practised in England today.

251

Anyone still unfamiliar with the approach of the Cambridge Group for the History of Population and Social Structure, for example, can begin to remedy matters by joining Richard Smith at his starting-point – that demography and familial patterns affect the incidence and nature of welfare, rather than the reverse – and journeying with him through the English way of neighbourliness. To see how different much the same countryside can look with a different tour leader in charge, they can move to Pat Thane's "Old people and their families in the English past", noting at the end a summary of the English way of welfare – "intimacy at a distance" – sure to become a favourite mantra of tutors, examiners, and students. Brian Pullan's outstandingly accessible but deeply expert analysis of charity and poor relief in early modern Italy illustrates the illumination given by explicit or implicit comparison with England's experiences. These three contributions demonstrate different varieties of macro-study; what can be achieved by "generalizable micro-narratives" is well illustrated by two very dissimilar off-shoots from doctoral theses. Lynn Botelho's comparison of two villages in early modern Suffolk not only warrants her quotation of Keith Wrightson's claim that local studies "can make concrete and accessible the abstractions and generalizations of historical interpretation", but demonstrates that they can also invalidate them. As for Keir Waddington's revelations of hospital finance in late Victorian London, today's fundraisers might well recognize there some familiar strategies as well as problems.

Each of the three remaining contributions is of a different ilk. Joanna Innes's lucid analysis of late seventeenth- and eighteenth-century appraisals of the available options for welfare provision is a triumph of solid scholarship and research on a substantial topic. Jane Lewis's chapter (the only one not heard at the colloquium itself) illustrates the current interplay between welfare and gender history, and sees women's influence on the making of social policy as dwindling with the "residualization" of social work – although the argument as presented here is too fuzzily focused to be altogether convincing. Finally, a demonstration of iconoclasm is given by Paul Johnson's "Risk, redistribution and social welfare from the poor law to Beveridge", which borrows from the economists a fresh way of categorizing welfare instruments: according to type of risk pool; whether redistribution is across the individual's life-cycle, or between individuals; and whether the nature of the entitlement is legal and contractual or solidaristic and dependent on a sense of justice. The result is usefully provocative, even if the historical information pressed into service is too often at out-of-date textbook level to carry much weight.

After reading so varied a collection it is difficult to resist some specula-
tion about the likely future of English welfare history. No doubt intergenerational conflict and support will both continue to be as endemic
among historians as we now realize they were among families in the
English past. Retrospectively, this Neale Lecture may perhaps seem a wise
and judicious appendage to a movement of brilliant pioneering research
and bold re-thinking on the verge of acquiring the status of an ageing emi-
nence. It can be fairly safely predicted that Paul Johnson's re-working of
welfare history from 1834 to Beveridge will prompt further experiments
with new vocabularies and re-runs of evidence. Indeed, knocking old historical orthodoxies into striking new shapes with the aid of ideas from
neighbouring disciplines is likely to become a much commoner activity, if
the dose of consciousness-raising administered by Daunton and Jones is
widely swallowed. It is reassuring that Botelho's chapter implies that doctoral theses will go on accumulating the detailed, specific information
about who did what to whom, exactly how, when, and where, that will
make it possible for new *ballons d'essai* to stay afloat. That the history of
ideas on social policy and social action will continue to furnish parallels to
the heart-searching over welfare policies now going on in many developed
countries seems all the more likely in the light of Innes's model analysis.
Certainly the next few years will see women as both givers and recipients
of welfare studied with a depth and many-sidedness hardly foreshadowed
here; while continuing revelations of the behind-the-scenes realities of
benevolent action and fundraising and the complex politics behind central
and local government welfare policies seem equally predictable.

But will there be a flowering of historical studies of the ethical imperatives of welfare at a level abstract enough to ensure that past thinking on
moral desert has something to say to the present? And will the fiscal history
of welfare at last make up the ground it has lost? It is discouraging that in
this volume the treatment of settlement – the chief instrument until quite
recently for controlling public relief expenditure in England – is left to a
few over-general lines in Martin Daunton's introduction; and more dis-
heartening still that the whole issue of entitlement is passed over. Nor does
anything in this volume promise the breaking down of the Chinese walls
separating study of the changing policies, activities and rhetoric of welfare
with regard to the inhabitants of these islands, and colonial populations
and "backward" peoples in perceived need. Yet there have been many
striking *correspondances* and much synchronization between all these; and if
economic, political and diplomatic motives rather than altruistic ones were

often uppermost in aid to colonies and underdeveloped nations, that is simply another similarity with welfare policies and activities at home.

The future of welfare history foreshadowed in this volume is thus not far-fetched: more local research, using anecdotal as well as quantitative evidence; more reconstitution of intellectual debates; a taste for getting behind public faces and public scenes – with gender or cross-disciplinary borrowings as the researcher's favourite fertilizers. Only outside bets seem worth laying on a rush of studies either of welfare's geography of power (along the sub-Foucaultian lines pioneered by Felix Driver, in work not mentioned by any of these contributors), or its religious geography (although there were seemingly some parishes where distinctive religious and welfare practices were linked). On the other hand, visual and literary evidence may well turn out to attract more attention than they have secured here. Altogether, uncertain though the prospects for welfare policy may be in England at present, dissection of the entrails of this volume suggests that for welfare history the omens are good.

Index